THE STORY OF A GENERATION

Life Course Pathways of the Class of '73

By Paul Anisef, Paul Axelrod, Carl E. James, Wolfgang Lehmann, Karen Robson, Erika McDonald, and Erica Fae Thomson

The Story of a Generation, a follow-up to *Opportunity and Uncertainty: Life Course Experiences of the Class of '73* (2000), continues where its predecessor left off. Through surveys and in-depth interviews with a high school class that graduated in 1973, the researchers uncover how these individuals – part of the late baby boomer generation – navigated a rapidly changing world.

Through this process, some patterns emerged: parents' education played a defining role in shaping their children's futures, while technology revolutionized workplaces and homes. Gender roles shifted, with spouses sharing domestic duties, though not yet equally. And as they aged, this generation found themselves at the forefront of redefining retirement, balancing longer lives with evolving financial and social expectations.

Beyond personal stories, *The Story of a Generation* offers a deeper understanding of how broader social forces – economic shifts, cultural changes, and technological advancements – interacted with individual choices. It's more than just a study of one group of Canadians; it's a reflection on how societies transform and how people adapt along the way. For anyone interested in sociology, history, or the human experience, this book provides a rare, intimate look at the passage of time – and the stories we leave behind.

PAUL ANISEF is a professor emeritus of sociology at York University.

PAUL AXELROD is a professor emeritus of education at York University.

CARL E. JAMES is a professor of education and Jean Augustine Chair in Education, Community and Diaspora at York University.

WOLFGANG LEHMANN is a professor of sociology and associate dean of undergraduate students and programs at Western University.

KAREN ROBSON is a professor of sociology and Ontario Research Chair in Academic Achievement and At-Risk Youth at McMaster University.

ERIKA MCDONALD is a PhD graduate in sociology at York University.

ERICA FAE THOMSON is a PhD graduate in sociology at McMaster University.

The Story of a Generation

Life Course Pathways of the Class of '73

PAUL ANISEF, PAUL AXELROD, CARL E. JAMES, WOLFGANG LEHMANN, KAREN ROBSON, ERIKA MCDONALD, AND ERICA FAE THOMSON

UNIVERSITY OF TORONTO PRESS
Toronto Buffalo London

Printed in Canada

ISBN 978-1-4875-7063-7 (cloth)   ISBN 978-1-4875-7066-8 (EPUB)
ISBN 978-1-4875-7064-4 (paper)   ISBN 978-1-4875-7065-1 (PDF)

Library and Archives Canada Cataloguing in Publication

Title: The story of a generation : life course pathways of the class of '73 / Paul Anisef, Paul Axelrod, Carl E. James, Wolfgang Lehmann, Karen Robson, Erika McDonald, and Erica Fae Thomson.

Names: Anisef, Paul, author | Axelrod, Paul, author | James, Carl E., author | Lehmann, Wolfgang, 1965– author | Robson, Karen, author | McDonald, Erika, author. | Thomson, Erica Fae, author.

Description: Follow-up to: Opportunity and Uncertainty: Life Course Experiences of the Class of '73 | Includes bibliographical references and index.

Identifiers: Canadiana (print) 20250303183 | Canadiana (ebook) 20250303205 | ISBN 9781487570644 (paper) | ISBN 9781487570637 (cloth) | ISBN 9781487570651 (PDF) | ISBN 9781487570668 (EPUB)

Subjects: LCSH: High school graduates—Ontario—Longitudinal studies. | LCSH: High school graduates—Employment—Ontario—Longitudinal studies. | LCSH: High school graduates—Ontario—Social conditions—Longitudinal studies. | LCSH: Educational surveys—Ontario. | LCGFT: Longitudinal studies.

Classification: LCC LB1695.8.C3 A55 2025 | DDC 373.12/91209713—dc23

Cover design: Erica Fae Thomson; Kristjan Buckingham
Cover image: geralt-9301/Pixabay.com

We wish to acknowledge the land on which the University of Toronto Press operates. This land is the traditional territory of the Wendat, the Anishnaabeg, the Haudenosaunee, the Métis, and the Mississaugas of the Credit First Nation.

This book has been published with the help of a grant from the Federation for the Humanities and Social Sciences, through the Awards to Scholarly Publications Program, using funds provided by the Social Sciences and Humanities Research Council of Canada.

University of Toronto Press acknowledges the financial support of the Government of Canada, the Canada Council for the Arts, and the Ontario Arts Council, an agency of the Government of Ontario, for its publishing activities.

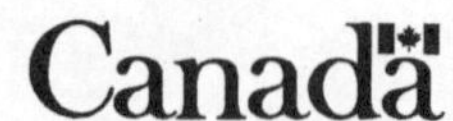

The Story of a Generation:

Life Course Pathways of the Class of '73

PAUL ANISEF, PAUL AXELROD, CARL E. JAMES, WOLFGANG LEHMANN, KAREN ROBSON, ERIKA MCDONALD, AND ERICA FAE THOMSON

Table of Contents

Acknowledgments

We wish to thank David Northrup and York University's Institute for Social Research for preparing and conducting the CATI telephone surveys, Adam Grearson for his technical assistance in locating participants, Etta Anisef for helping to organize and conduct interviews, Firrisaa Jamal Abdulkarim for technical assistance in graphic design, Bob Chodos for his excellent editorial work, Len Husband and the University of Toronto Press for facilitating the publication of this book, and the Social Sciences and Humanities Research Council for its essential financial support. Finally, we thank the members of the Class of '73, many of whom have been involved in this project for some fifty years. The book is a tribute to their enthusiasm and collaboration, and we hope that our work tells their story accurately, sensitively, and engagingly.

Foreword

This book documents the resilience of Paul Anisef and his colleagues, who succeeded in following a sample of high school graduates in Ontario for half a century, from 1973 to 2021. Born in the mid-1950s, this cohort represents the baby boom generation and its social differentiations. The cross-generational perspective exemplifies the interplay of social and economic changes with life histories.

This story of a generation's life course pathways is told as a narrative of transitioning from youth to adulthood and retirement. The book is a remarkable contribution to life course studies because it combines descriptive data analysis with portraits of personal ways of navigating the opportunities and challenges of coming of age in turbulent times.

The authors connect with the international community of life course research with their study. They implement a longitudinal design and "mixed methods" – combining quantitative (questionnaire) and qualitative (face-to-face interviews) data collection techniques. Personal histories were updated via Zoom interviews. Furthermore, the sample's attrition rate over the long duration is presented in tables, documenting the authors' craftsmanship.

Common patterns of transitions from adolescence to the age of retirement are presented as a portrait of generational, social, and cultural change in Canada. In addition, personal histories show the impact of life events and economic circumstances on biographies.

The study covers themes and experiences in education, employment, family life, and life satisfaction in the context of major historical events, like the Great Recession in 2008 and COVID-19 in 2020–2.

Following their book *Opportunity and Uncertainty* (Anisef et al. 2000), this publication presents a strong version of life course research, emphasizing personal expectations, choices, and actions in the contexts of structural determinants and situational conditions. The study shows how growing up and growing old develop from the interaction of personal agency and perceived opportunities. Looking back at their respondents' mobility experiences, the authors demonstrate the importance of education as the driver of the cohort's employment histories and their children's attainment.

The authors highlight that life course decisions are made individually regarding options, community, and family relations. Biographies are constructed about structured economic, gender, and racial inequality.

Anisef and colleagues present a well-crafted narrative, combining survey data analysis with accounts of transition experiences. Like the results of their book *Opportunity and Uncertainty* (2000), this study's message is relevant not only to comparative life course research but also to policymakers in the fields of education, labour market, health, and retirement.

Furthermore, the study shows that social inequality persists in distributing life chances. This finding is comparable to the results of longitudinal research in the United States, England, and Germany.

Walter R. Heinz, University of Bremen, Germany

THE STORY OF A GENERATION

Introduction

In this book, we analyse the perceptions and experiences of a group of late baby boomers who were first contacted in 1973 when they were enrolled in Grade 12 classes in different parts of Ontario. In various publications since that time, we have referred to this cohort as the "Class of '73." More than forty-six years elapsed between that first data collection phase in 1973 and the seventh – and last – phase in 2019–21, when our respondents were in their early or mid-sixties and either retired or approaching retirement (for similar long-term life course studies conducted in the United States, see Mortimer and Staff 2022; Settersten, Elder, and Pearce 2021). Reconnecting with our participants has allowed us to analyse several life-course themes, including their educational and employment experiences, aspects of their family life, their planning for and experience of retirement, and their level of contentment at this stage of their lives.

The participants in our study were typically born in 1955–6, part of the massive wave of post–Second World War youth whose lives were shaped by unique social, political, and economic contexts, which we will track in the pages that follow (Owram 1997; Phillipson et al. 2008). They both consumed and influenced social change, and their life courses signify major developments in the evolution of Canadian society over the past half century (Ranson 2022).

In an earlier book, *Opportunity and Uncertainty* (Anisef et al. 2000), we argued that to understand how social change has affected the transitions made by adolescents as they move into adulthood, we must examine the experiences of previous generations and that life course theory is a powerful vehicle for doing so. In that project, we explained how life course transitions are constructed by individuals within the context of social forces, educational selection, work experiences, and employment options. We demonstrated, too, the importance of time (and its passage), the impact of social structures such as class, gender, region, religion, immigration, and ethnicity on the educational and employment choices made by our participants, and the growing importance of personal agency in influencing their decisions. After analysing quantitative and qualitative data, we concluded,

> The combined effects of social structure and personal agency – of economic challenge and personality – are poignantly illustrated in the life experiences of the Class of '73. Many faced both opportunity and uncertainty in the 1980s and early 1990s. Personal histories, circumstances, priorities, and choices, as well as the vagaries of the economy, gave different shapes to their respective life courses. (Anisef et al. 2000, 113)

In the current study, we have updated personal histories, extended the narrative into retirement years, and tracked significant social and economic changes impacting individual life courses. To reach a broad audience, we utilize descriptive analysis rather than multivariate techniques and present findings through accessible graphs instead of complex tables. Multivariate data analysis, which will interest a specialized audience, will be presented in journal articles. To provide a tangible illustration of the influence of structure and agency (and its combined effects), we present a brief portrait of Jack, one of the interviewees in Phase 7 of our study.

Jack grew up in Toronto, the middle child of a working-class family with a younger and an older brother. His parents immigrated to Canada in 1951 from England, with neither parent having completed a secondary school education. Jack's mother was Austrian, and his father was Ukrainian. Consistent with his working-class roots, Jack was raised in humble circumstances, which he described as follows:

> We were poor because for the [first] five years of my life, we lived in two rooms on the first floor of a three-story house which my parents bought. We rented every single other room in the house out and I remember asking my parents why, and they said, "Well, that's the only way we can afford to live here is if we get renters." So, I think we had three different families living in the house with us.

Despite these circumstances, Jack, like many other children of immigrants, was determined to succeed. He described his parents' consistent efforts to push him to be "somebody." He also credited high school teachers who encouraged him to pursue his education. Jack completed high school and, given his proficiency and achievements in mathematics, decided to pursue civil engineering at university, although his first choice was law.

After obtaining his engineering degree, Jack felt he had the security of that credential to fall back on and subsequently decided to enter law school, working in the summers as an engineer in a structural engineering firm. While articling for law school, Jack started a small company that sold software and obtained a job as a programmer. Subsequently, he established a computer products distributor, which grew from four employees with $4 million in sales to ten people and $16 million in sales. Jack also initiated other companies and acted as a mini-venture capitalist.

In between, Jack took time off and travelled around the world for eighteen months. When he returned from his travels, Jack's younger brother told him that he had obtained a Chartered Financial Analyst (CFA) degree, and Jack decided he would do the same. He secured his CFA in three years, worked as a technology analyst, managed investments for different firms, and decided to retire at the age of forty-seven. However, at the time of our interview in 2021, Jack had founded one company and was in the process of starting another.

This brief portrait demonstrates that while Jack's younger years were shaped by his family's working-class origins and limited resources, he defied the odds by obtaining three professional degrees and becoming a successful entrepreneur. Asked to account for his success, Jack explained,

> Number one was, I would say it was all – most of it was parental influence. It was number one to be somebody, number two, to get out of this – I don't know what the best term for it is, but to get out of this social or this echelon I was in. Like we were in like the lowest. We didn't have a car. We didn't go on vacations. We didn't know anybody . . . So, it was to be somebody, and I guess that's maybe part of being somebody. And I guess the third thing was I figured I was just as smart and just as good and just as ambitious as all those people I'd see on TV or in the newspaper.

This book tracks Jack's story and the stories of many others who came of age in dynamic and often turbulent times and who navigated the life course in diverse and complex ways. Notwithstanding individuals' distinctive routes, we attempt to identify common patterns in one cohort's transition from adolescence to their early sixties. We hope the book and the entire project contribute to a fresh perspective on generational and social change in Canada.

The publication of *Opportunity and Uncertainty: Life Course Experiences of the Class of '73* in 2000 marked a milestone for those of us in the Department of Sociology at York University (that is, Professors Emeriti Paul Anisef, Gottfried Paasche, and Anton H. Turrittin) who joined forces in the fall of 1977 to alter the early study of Grade 12 students into a longitudinal research project. A combination of career path changes, shifts in research interests, and fatigue combined to place the project on an indeterminate hold. Meanwhile, an academic (who ultimately joined our team) remarked on the value of the longitudinal project and the good use he had made of our book in sociology of education courses and recommended that the project be extended.

After weeks of discussion, research team members decided to apply to the Social Sciences and Humanities Research Council (SSHRC) for support to continue the study. We did so for several reasons. First, we were curious about the pathways chosen by members of the Class of '73 since we last surveyed them in 1995. We were motivated by the challenge of finding enough participants to warrant extending the study. Second, we knew there were no longitudinal studies in Canada that had traced the transitions of people from their adolescence to (potential) retirement. If successful, our study would span forty-seven years. We would be able to examine whether the goals people had set in Grade 12 had altered over the years or had remained the same. More generally, we would be able to investigate the factors that influenced the critical life course decisions they made (e.g., education, family, work, retirement) and the paths they had taken.

While the following chapter provides a detailed description of the methodology employed in Phase 7, we note here that the COVID-19 pandemic inspired (and required) us to use Zoom in conducting in-depth interviews with a select group of study participants. Before these interviews, the Institute for Social Research (ISR) at York University conducted detailed telephone surveys with the entire cohort involved in the study.

Organization of the Book

Chapter 1 begins with a review of the life course perspective with a particular emphasis on the dynamic and intersecting components of individuals' life courses, which influence or inform their life trajectories and outcomes. We argue that while individuals act as agents, making personal decisions and choices over which they have some control, they do so in a social and historical context over which, at times, they exercise little or no personal power. As a result, the life course is a product of these dynamic, interacting forces. Also included in this chapter is a detailed discussion of the methodology employed in conducting the seventh phase of this longitudinal study; we describe the process of developing a telephone-administered survey and conducting in-depth interviews.

In Chapter 2 we present portraits of six individuals from the Class of '73, representing a unique cluster insofar as they were all interviewed in earlier phases of the project. These conversations help us flesh out the life course in intimate subjective terms and illustrate emerging themes in the lives of this distinctive generational cohort. We chose these individuals because we believed it would be instructive not only to track their lives since we last communicated with them but also to compare their recent reflections with their views from previous decades.

Chapter 3 focuses on the social, economic, and educational context in which the Class of '73 grew up – the 1960s and early 1970s in Ontario. We note the rise of new social movements, Ontario's broadening diversity because of immigration, the increasing presence of women in the workforce, and migration from rural to urban areas. We highlight the massive expansion of Ontario's educational system and changes in the structure and philosophy of high school education. Finally, we present a preliminary sketch of how all these changes affected the Class of '73.

In Chapter 4, we begin by revisiting the study participants' educational experiences and pathways with an emphasis on how structure and agency affected their chances for academic mobility. Then we discuss the extent to which participants had obtained postsecondary degrees and certificates since 1994. Expanding on the discussion in *Opportunity and Uncertainty*, our treatment offers participants' later-life reflections on their education. It looks at how their own children's educational attainment can be seen as an extension of earlier patterns of educational mobility.

Chapter 5 focuses on how revolutionary changes in technology affected the jobs held by study participants and how they managed to navigate an increasingly multicultural and diverse workplace. The chapter also describes the economic and social context in which occupational life was conducted in the three decades following 1990. It traces the pathways taken by study participants in their effort to reach their ultimate employment destinations and their understanding of the role education played in that process. It illustrates the remarkable changes in the workplace that our participants experienced and how they adapted to those changes. The chapter also explores sources of satisfaction on the job. What rewards did the Class of '73 derive from employment, and what was still required to improve working life? Finally, the chapter examines our participants' experience and perception of equity and discrimination in the workplace.

In Chapter 6, dealing with family life, we examine the life course concerning marriage and partnerships, child-rearing and caregiving, the management of the home, sources of family stress, and the impact of grandchildren on the lives of our study participants. An analysis informs the discussion of the evolution of gender equity, the impact of changes in child-rearing practices in the era in which our participants grew up and became parents, and the effect of these changes on parents' relationships with children. Finally, we explore the degree to which religion, an essential component of socialization within the family and community, mattered in the lives of Class of '73 members.

In Chapter 7, we explain how members of the Class of '73 conceptualize, plan for, and experience retirement, and the influence of demographic factors on the different pathways taken by study participants. An overview of the literature identifies the changing face of retirement in Canada. It reveals that, while earlier generations emphasized the traditional dichotomy between work and retirement, baby boomers appeared to place a higher value on work-life balance in retirement. This suggests that the pathways leading to retirement and the experience of retirement are distinctive for the age group that encompasses the Class of '73.

Chapter 8 focuses our attention on the subjective well-being of study participants, using both survey data and in-depth interviews. Survey items include their self-assessment of stress, personal happiness, physical and mental health, and satisfaction. In addition to describing study participants' well-being, we sought to identify their regrets or unfulfilled opportunities (e.g., regrets about choosing not to enrol in a postsecondary institution, regrets over specific career choices, and regrets around deciding not to have children).

Finally, in our concluding chapter, we review the insights derived from the previous chapters, compare our findings with those of other longitudinal studies of baby boomers, and discuss the wider implications of this research for life course analyses of future generations.

Contribution to Life Course Studies

The Class of '73 project makes a significant contribution to life course studies by offering a comprehensive, longitudinal perspective on individual development within broader societal contexts. This book offers insights derived from tracking Ontario high school graduates over nearly five decades, illuminating the complex interplay between personal trajectories and socio-economic factors. By examining the evolution of key factors such as education, employment, family life, and health over time, the project provides a nuanced understanding of how these elements shape life outcomes. The longitudinal approach employed enables us to identify patterns and influences that may not be readily apparent in cross-sectional studies, thereby offering a more holistic view of human development. By employing mixed methods, including surveys and in-depth interviews, we have been able to create a rich dataset that captures both quantitative trends and qualitative insights into individual experiences.

This approach allows for a deeper exploration of the interplay between structure and agency, revealing how personal choices interact with broader social contexts to shape individual pathways. By combining statistical analyses with narrative accounts, the study offers a comprehensive understanding of life course transitions, aligning with the core principles of life course theory. Furthermore, the Class of '73 project contributes to the field by highlighting the importance of historical time and place in shaping life trajectories. By following a cohort through nearly five decades of social, economic, and technological change, the study offers unique insights into how macro-level shifts influence individual lives and collective experiences.

We hope that this book will advance life course studies in Canada by providing a robust empirical foundation for understanding human development and social change. Its longitudinal design, mixed-methods approach, and focus on the interplay between individual agency and social structures offer valuable insights for policymakers and researchers alike. By addressing methodological challenges and leveraging diverse data collection techniques, the Class of '73 project sets a standard for future longitudinal studies in the field.

1 Tracking the Pathways of the Class of '73

This book explores the world of a cohort of Ontario residents who graduated from Grade 12 in 1973, tracking their life courses over nearly half a century. Most were sixteen or seventeen years old when the study began in the early 1970s, and in their early sixties when the research ended in 2019–21. This study investigates their growth and maturation during a period of extraordinary social, economic, and technological change. It explains how educational, occupational, familial, and retirement pathways have evolved over six decades. It explores the impact of social structure and personal agency on the varied routes that our subjects followed. It is a unique window into the social history of a fascinating and often turbulent time.

This chapter describes our use of life course theory to explore intersecting identities, transitions, and outcomes, and details the methodology employed in the current phase of our research.

Life Course Theory

In telling the story of a generation, it is first important to grasp the meaning of that term. Most references agree that *generation* refers to all people born and living at about the same time, regarded collectively (Owram 1997). It also refers to the average period, generally considered about twenty to thirty years, during which children are born, grow up, become adults, and begin having children. In the social sciences, *generation* is often employed synonymously with *birth cohort* to refer to a group of people born at around the same time or during a certain period (Daly 2020).

As we noted in our previous book, *Opportunity and Uncertainty*, our use of theoretical perspectives shifted during the study from models of status attainment and human capital to life course and transition theory.

European and North American thinking about the dynamic relationship between the individual and society influenced these changes in perspective. These modes of thinking served to sensitize researchers to the interplay between social contexts, socialization, and selection processes across the life course, and to the active part that the individual plays throughout (Heinz 1991, 1995).

As researchers conducting what had become a longitudinal study, we felt then (and continue to believe) that a life course approach is instructive in that it draws attention to time, structure, and personal agency. Specifically, as we indicated in our previous work, life course theory "attempts to explain the dynamic relationship between the individual and social order, allows researchers to examine a cohort's collective experience without reifying it, and remains attuned to individual differences without ignoring social context" (Anisef et al. 2000, 18). Time is defined from the perspective of psychology in terms of personal or individual development, from the perspective of history in terms of social-historical changes of context and their impact on cohorts, and from the perspective of sociology in terms of institutional and social structural changes. The notion of personal agency refers to individuals developing their own life scripts through choices and decisions they make while operating within the opportunities and constraints of history and social circumstances (Elder 1998, 4).

Elder also argues that it is essential to examine the role of historical time and place in that, as time passes, individuals change not only because of human development but also because of exposure to shifting historical contexts. He posits that "the life course of an individual is embedded in and shaped by the historical times and places they experience over their lifetime" (Elder 1978, 1998, 3). Historical context matters immensely in tracking the lives of individuals, groups, cohorts, and generations. As individual agents, people make choices about their futures, but not in a social or historical vacuum. The available options may be limited or multiple, depending on the opportunity structures that society offers up. In a predominantly agrarian society, where survival depends on reproducing the family economy, young people's occupational destinies may be largely predetermined: the farmer's children will be tied to the land throughout their lives. In wartime, youth will choose, or be pressured into, military service, and if they survive, that experience is likely to leave an indelible mark on their post-war pathways.

Another important aspect of life course theory recognizes the tension between constraints imposed by society (social structure) and human agency. The social sciences have witnessed continual debates regarding the extent to which society shapes individuals versus the extent to which individuals can exercise "objective" and autonomous choices in their lives (personal agency) (Green 2010, 20).

Life course theory also seeks to identify the interactions between individuals and the various social institutions they encounter on "life's way." These include family, school, university or college, and the workplace; throughout their life course, individuals move through and between these institutions. As people mature and advance through successive phases of their lives, they interact with evolving institutional and social structures in ways that limit or expand their potential for expression of personal agency and opportunities (Berger and Motte 2007).

As we argue in *Opportunity and Uncertainty* (2000) and maintain in this follow-up study,

> Structure and agency work together to shape the life course and intersect continuously as individuals construct their life "scripts" in the context of conditions that are beyond their control (e.g., the state of the economy) and those that depend on personal choices (e.g., marriage, having children, seeking further education). Thus, individuals do their utmost to express personal agency while recognizing that there is a "system" that may well affect their horizons (Rudd and Evans 1998, 61) . . . Structural factors, both social and organizational, do show evidence of constraining properties, particularly when the earlier phases of individuals' life course pathways are examined. Yet as we move from the adolescent to the adult phases of the life course, we must pay close attention to how individuals, operating within the identities imparted by class, gender, residence, ethno-racial minority status, and organizational structures, construct and negotiate their future biographies. (21–5)

Figure 1.1 illustrates the dynamic, complex, and intersecting components of individuals' life courses. The diagram shows that there is a relationship between the sociodemographic characteristics of individuals (in terms of age, gender, sexuality, ethnicity, race, disability, socio-economic status, etc.), the social and cultural capital constructed and sustained by the schooling and education program in which they participate, and the social and community networks with which they affiliate or to which they belong. All of these are structured by the cultural context and conditions of the society – Canada – in which they live, which ultimately influence or inform their life trajectories and outcomes (or the place at which they eventually arrive). Essentially, life course theory alerts us to the fact that one's life must be examined in relation to the macro-level, meso-level, and micro-level entities through which one has journeyed. And as we explained in *Opportunity and Uncertainty*, while engagements or decisions

Figure 1.1: Components of Individuals' Life Courses

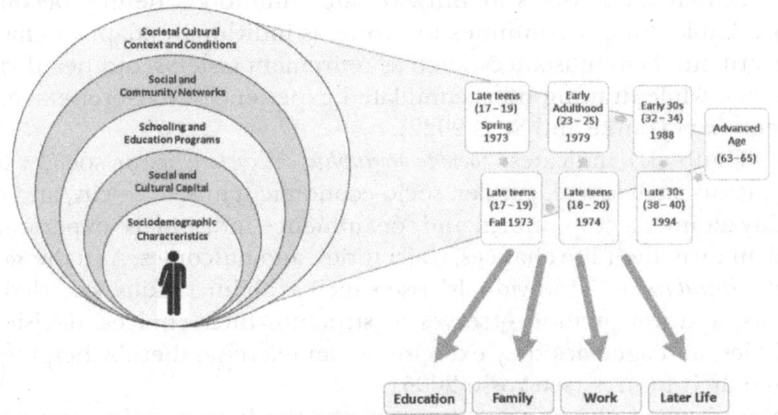

in life might be made individually or through what is referred to as "structured individualization" (identity, familial, school, community, employment, and societal factors), the options one has and the choices one makes all play a role in individual outcomes (Rudd and Evans 1998).

The transition from adolescence to later life involves an interplay between structural factors and individual agency as people navigate their paths from education to employment and, in later life, retirement. While individuals construct personal pathways and make choices, they do so within broader social, economic, and cultural contexts that shape opportunities and constraints. Researchers have used concepts like "structured individualization" to capture this dynamic, recognizing that people often express optimism about their prospects even as large-scale data reveal persistent inequalities based on social background. The life course perspective views transitions as an ongoing process where individual decision-making intersects with structural dimensions beyond one's control, such as economic conditions. While debates continue about the relative influence of agency versus structure, many scholars argue that both elements are deeply interconnected in shaping people's educational, career, and retirement trajectories.

As Jack's story (and the profiles in the following chapter) reveal, identity plays a crucial role in the interplay between structure and agency, serving as both a product and a mediator of these forces. As individuals construct their sense of self, they navigate societal constraints and opportunities, with identity formation being particularly salient during adolescence. This process involves active exploration and negotiation of roles within social structures, while also exercising personal agency in making choices that shape one's identity. In late adulthood, identity becomes more stable. Still, it continues to evolve as individuals adapt to changing structural circumstances, such as retirement systems and healthcare policies, while drawing on accumulated experiences to exercise agency in new ways (Burke and Stets 2022).

As Figure 1.1 indicates, *sociodemographic characteristics* or social identity factors such as age, gender, socio-economic status, ethnicity, and disability all intersect to inform and/or influence individuals' experiences and, in turn, their life chances, trajectories, and outcomes. And the *social and cultural capital* – individuals' assets such as abilities, skills, knowledge, habits, and imagination – serves to structure their choices, decisions, hobbies, and agencies they exercise or can exercise, thereby helping to shape their futures (see Yosso 2005).

Schooling and education programs refer to the Basic (serving as a pathway to the workforce), General (serving as a pathway to college), or Advanced (serving as a pathway to university) program in which individuals were enrolled while in high school. These three program levels and the related courses offered, along with teachers and administrators, influence students' educational, employment, occupational, and career aspirations, plans, and attainments. Other mediating factors include individuals' sociodemographic characteristics; the social, cultural, and economic reputation of the area of residence (rural/urban) in which they live; and the reputation of the high school they attend.

The educational programs that individuals pursue and from which they graduate also contribute to the *social and community networks* they form and the relationships they have with other individuals and groups, and with teachers. As such, individuals are likely to associate mainly with peers within their level of program, which in turn serves to encourage and sustain their post-high school pathways. The social and community networks of individuals have a significant impact on the opportunities and possibilities to which they have access and of which they might take advantage.

All the above factors intersect in complex ways that are structured by the *societal cultural context and conditions* of Canada. These constitute the society's beliefs, norms, traditions, values, beliefs, and meaning-making and ultimately inform all of the other elements or circumstances of individuals' lives (James 2010). Understandably, society's sociocultural conditions change over time, and consequently, so do the individual, familial, community, and institutional components. Therefore, over time, as we returned to our respondents, the information we obtained from them – in terms of their education, family, work, and later lives – has been a cumulative account not only of how they have evolved with respect to familial, community, and institutional settings and conditions but also of how historical and contemporary structures have influenced what we hear from them.

The sociocultural contexts and conditions of the 1970s were significantly different from those of the 2020s. The sample of individuals who participated in the study in 1973 was drawn from an ethnically homogeneous group of high school students who were growing up in a culture in which there tended to be reticence about naming racial and sexual identification. Hence, as society became more ethnically and racially diverse over time, mainly because of immigration, and as the culture changed, individuals would have read their opportunities and possibilities in life to changes in the sociocultural context of society, the stage of their life, and their sense of responsibility and agency. Therefore, when we interviewed participants in 2021, the multiculturalism, employment equity, and gender and sexual diversity discourses and initiatives that had by then become common in public and private organizational ecosystems would likely have helped shape their experiences in their later years.

In *Opportunity and Uncertainty* and in the current project, attention was given to gender differences and how they intersect with urban/rural residency. Other identity characteristics were not as extensively covered, in part because of the relative racial homogeneity of the Ontario student population when we first engaged the cohort of Grade 12 students. In the chapters that follow, we explore the agency, choices, decisions, and accomplishments of respondents. We provide an account of how they fashioned their lives in relation to their education, family, work (or employment and careers), and senior years (or retirement) as mediated by gender, sexuality, dis/ability, place of residence, and other sociodemographic factors, and as they navigated and coped with the formal and informal barriers they faced. It is worth noting that, in some cases, it was the social and/or physical conditions (such as disability) of family members that shaped the life course of individuals in significant ways.

Methodology

Chart 1.1 provides a snapshot review of the various methodologies employed across the seven phases of the Class of '73 project, including sample sizes (n's) in each phase of the longitudinal study. For a detailed review of the research methods employed in Phases 1–6, the reader should consult Appendix 1. In the following section, we provide a detailed explanation of the research methodology employed in Phase 7.

Chart 1.1: An Updated Snapshot of the Class of '73 Project[1]

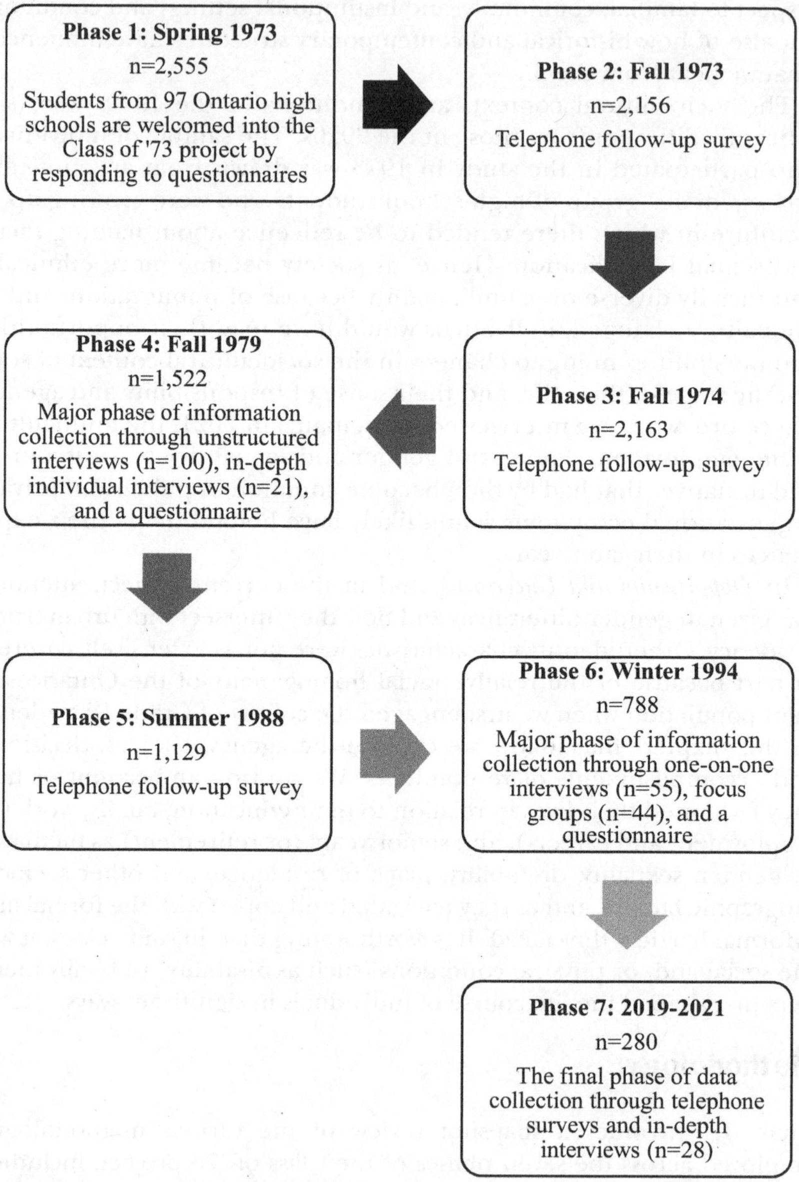

Phase 1: Spring 1973

n=2,555

Students from 97 Ontario high schools are welcomed into the Class of '73 project by responding to questionnaires

Phase 2: Fall 1973

n=2,156

Telephone follow-up survey

Phase 4: Fall 1979

n=1,522

Major phase of information collection through unstructured interviews (n=100), in-depth individual interviews (n=21), and a questionnaire

Phase 3: Fall 1974

n=2,163

Telephone follow-up survey

Phase 5: Summer 1988

n=1,129

Telephone follow-up survey

Phase 6: Winter 1994

n=788

Major phase of information collection through one-on-one interviews (n=55), focus groups (n=44), and a questionnaire

Phase 7: 2019-2021

n=280

The final phase of data collection through telephone surveys and in-depth interviews (n=28)

1 Due to the varying n's throughout the phases of the project, the graphs in this book may have varying n's related to their respective phase or phases.

Preliminary Stages

An application was submitted and accepted by the Social Sciences and Humanities Research Council's Insight Grant program to extend the Class of '73 project in 2018. The starting point for tracing past participants in the Class of '73 project was a twenty-two-year-old file of names, last known addresses, and phone numbers; some respondents supplied information on their parents' contact details as well, though we realized that parents would have been in their eighties and nineties by this point.

In this period, technology had changed dramatically, with many more people relying on email and social media (e.g., Facebook) to communicate. While we were cautiously optimistic at the outset of the Phase 7 project that everyone (including our Class of '73) now leaves a wide internet footprint that could help trace their whereabouts, this proved not to be the case. City or online telephone directories no longer capture populations comprehensively, and without access to sophisticated databases (such as official provincial records), our means of tracing were minimal. Whatever success we had in locating participants can be attributed to two main factors: (a) the efforts of a researcher, Adam Grearson, who employed an eight-step process for examining contacts in the twenty-two-year-old file, and (b) direct calls by the Institute for Social Research (ISR) at York University that were based on the contact information gathered by Grearson.

Grearson took the following steps in attempting to locate the study participants. First, he looked up each name on the online telephone directory Canada 411. If he found the same name and address that were listed in our files, then he could be certain that it was the right person. If he found the same name in the same town on Canada 411, even at a different address, he would assume that it was the same person. However, if he could not find a study participant on Canada 411, he then attempted to trace their parents' contact information using the same two steps. Grearson then checked the address history of the original address and the parents' address, making note of neighbours' information using the website www.whitepages.com and the "reverse address lookup" function. He then turned to the internet and used Google to search the last phone number we had for our subjects to see if there were any hits. He did a Google search of the cohort member's name. If this failed to produce results, he then searched for the name of the subject's spouse or parent. In the final phases of his effort to locate subjects, Grearson checked Facebook to see if they were there, and he also checked obituaries to see if they had passed away.

Development of the Survey

While these efforts to trace and contact participants were underway, the research team developed a survey questionnaire that ISR pretested. After ISR had exhausted all efforts to contact (and interviewed all participants who had been successfully traced and agreed to be interviewed), we managed to secure 280 responses to our questionnaire, or 11 per cent of the original Phase 1 sample of 2,555. A loss of cases is always to be expected when conducting longitudinal studies, and by Phase 6 our sample had been reduced to 31 per cent of the original sample. However, tests of representativeness based on gender, socio-economic status, and geographical location confirmed that our Phase 6 sample was generally like our Phase 1 sample, albeit with some over-representation of respondents from rural areas of the province, some loss of lower socio-economic respondents from Metro Toronto but greater retention of low socio-economic respondents from rural areas of the province. If we compare Phase 7 to Phase 6, the retention rate was higher, at around 35 per cent. This is particularly remarkable given that there was no contact with the cohort members for over twenty years.

In evaluating how our data from Phase 7 compared with our original cohort in terms of representativeness, we found that the sex breakdown was nearly identical across the two time periods. Other metrics that we could identify for sample representativeness were the percentage born outside Canada and whether the respondent lived in a rural or urban location. We found that we had a slightly higher proportion of individuals born in Canada in the latest phase than in the original cohort: 93 versus 90 per cent (Robson et al. 2020). This suggests that there was slightly more attrition among foreign-born cohort members. In terms of location of residence, while attending high school, 32.8 per cent of the cohort were in rural areas in 1973 compared with 40.4 per cent in 2018, indicating greater attrition of our cohort members from smaller cities and towns. Statistical analyses of attrition patterns demonstrated that rural-dwelling cohort members were more likely to have been retained and that members of the lowest socio-economic groups were less likely to have been retained (Robson et al. 2020. For detailed information regarding sample attrition, see Appendix 2).

In terms of education, around 35 per cent of our cohort had a university bachelor's degree or higher; by comparison, 2016 Canadian census data reported that 23 per cent of Ontarians between the ages of fifty-five and sixty-four had degrees (Statistics Canada 2017a).

In 2019, the average retirement age in Canada was 64.3 years, with public-sector workers retiring at a slightly younger average age of 62.6

years, private-sector workers retiring at 64.4 years, and self-employed individuals continuing to work until age sixty-seven (Statistics Canada 2020). At the time of the final interview, the average age of our cohort was approximately sixty-four years. Over half (55 per cent) of our sample reported being completely retired, 15 per cent reported being partially retired, and 30 per cent reported not being retired at all. Of those who worked in the private sector, 41 per cent were completely retired, compared with 46 per cent of those who worked in the public sector and 8 per cent of those who were self-employed. It should be noted, however, that Statistics Canada's definition of *retired* is quite strict, referring to a person who is fifty-five or older, is not in the labour force, and derives at least half of their total income from retirement-like sources (Bowlby 2007).

Conducting In-Depth Interviews

As in previous phases of our longitudinal study, we chose to represent the diversity of life course transitions and trajectories by first profiling study participants who responded to our Phase 7 survey and then identifying those participants we wanted to interview. As we indicated in *Opportunity and Uncertainty*, the exclusive use of a survey approach focuses on analysing aggregate numbers. While survey data are valuable, reliance on them means that we lose sight of individuals and how they develop strategies for making decisions in various domains, including education, employment, family, and retirement. Using surveys and in-depth interviews allows researchers to bridge the macro and micro dimensions characteristic of significant life course transitions, such as school-to-work and work-to-retirement. We found that the complementary use of surveys and in-depth interviews revealed that personality, interests, family matters, and health concerns influenced decisions taken by the Class of '73 and highlighted the reflexive operation of structure and agency in the transition of our cohort from adolescence to adulthood.

While the telephone surveys administered by the Institute for Social Research at York University were conducted in 2019, most of the twenty-nine in-depth interviews occurred in 2021, primarily delayed by the COVID-19 pandemic. We needed to decide how best to conduct interviews during a pandemic. Study participants who completed the telephone survey administered by ISR were asked to supply their email addresses, and 224 study participants complied with this request. Based on our analysis of survey responses, we identified sixty-three participants whom we wished to interview, with the basis of our selection being broad structural (e.g., sex, SES, location of residence) and personal factors (e.g., selecting those self-identifying as LGBTQ2S+, dealing with a disability). Of those identified, twenty-eight agreed to in-depth interviews.

Given that face-to-face contact is an important component of an effective interview and given the continuation of the COVID-19 pandemic, we decided to use Zoom to conduct the interviews. This decision resulted in unforeseen benefits. For one, we could interview participants across Canada and beyond. (Interviews in earlier phases of the project required travelling to participants' homes.) In the end, only a few participants declined Zoom interviews, primarily because of technological challenges. Generally, we found that interviewees were very forthcoming during the interviews, possibly because of their lack of social contact during the pandemic. They seemed willing to talk fully and frankly. Finally, we could probe topics that were not part of the survey, including child-rearing practices, the impact of technological changes on their work activities, and the effect of COVID-19 on their daily lives, all of which deepened our understanding of their life course transitions.

The use of interviews reflects a longstanding and increasingly refined method for recovering the past (Llewellyn, Freund, and Reilly 2015). Oral history captures personal experiences not available through other sources, it provides a diversity of voices, and it allows the researcher to link individual experiences to broader social changes. Interviewees are not necessarily representative of an entire cohort, but they illustrate, poignantly, individual life course pathways. While the subjects' memories may certainly be imperfect, interviews, if used judiciously, can enrich our understanding of the past by humanizing our understanding of historical change. Ethical protocols must be respected, and we have followed Canada's funding agencies' guidelines on "ethical research involving humans" (Janovicek 2015, 73). Interviewees signed consent forms, we have ensured confidentiality, and all names in the text are pseudonyms.

Summary of the Class of '73 Project

To summarize developments from 1973 through 2019: the Class of '73 project began as a short-term study of high school students and their attitudes and behaviour concerning educational plans to provide projection data for postsecondary enrolments to the Ontario Ministry of Colleges and Universities. Over the next four decades, a total of five follow-ups were conducted with the same cohort: in the fall of 1973 (Phase 2), fall of 1974 (Phase 3), fall of 1979 (Phase 4), summer of 1988 (Phase 5), and winter of 1994 (Phase 6), effectively converting the project into a longitudinal study of education, work, and life pathways for a generation that has seen an unprecedented change in the Canadian economy.

Throughout the longitudinal study, significant information collection efforts (such as surveys, individual interviews, and focus groups) were employed in Phases 1, 4, and 6. By 2018, the Class of '73 project had become the first cohort study in Canada to have spanned a long enough period to capture members' entrance into retirement (Robson et al. 2020, 3). However, some considerable amount of time had passed since the last data collection and little or no effort had been made to sustain contact with the Class of '73 participants surveyed in Phase 6. Phase 7, which tracks participants into their early sixties, during or on the verge of retirement, brings a fifty-year longitudinal study to a close.

2 Six Members of the Class of '73

While survey data provide the foundation for this project's analysis, throughout the various phases we have also conducted face-to-face interviews with a select number of participants. Such conversations flesh out the life course in authentic human terms and help us illustrate emerging themes in the lives of a distinctive generational cohort. Individual voices have formed part of previous publications (Anisef et al. 2000), as our participants described their childhoods, educations, family lives, and occupations. In 2020–1, as part of Phase 7 of the Class of '73 project, we interviewed twenty-nine people. This chapter attempts to enrich our analysis by providing a coherent narrative of several individual lives drawn from that group.

The six individuals selected represent a unique cluster in that they were all interviewed face-to-face in earlier phases of the project. For all but one of the subjects, we have transcripts and notes from interviews conducted in 1979, 1994–5, and 2020–1 (one subject, Ella, was interviewed in 1979 and 2020 but not in 1995). We were particularly interested in these participants because we believed it would be instructive not only to track their lives since we last communicated with them but also to compare their recent reflections with their views from previous decades.

For example, in 1979, we asked what they thought of their recent schooling experiences (high school and postsecondary education where relevant), and in 2020, we had them reconsider their views on schooling considering the passage of time. We wondered if they were fulfilled by the choices they had made in their vocations and careers or whether they had regrets. In the most recent interviews, we explored the COVID-19 pandemic's effect on their retirement or retirement plans.

As they report on their opportunities, challenges, joys, and disappointments, the members of this sample group help humanize the study through their individual biographies. These demonstrate in evocative ways the combined, and at times unexpected, impact of structure and agency in their lives, from adolescence to their seventh decades. Through these individual biographies, readers will discover some of the complex ways people navigate the life course. As Elder (1998) explained, the life course model "alerts us to the real world, a world in which lives are lived and where people work out paths of development as best they can. It tells us how lives are socially organized in biological and historical time, and how the resulting social patterns affect the way we think, feel and act" (9).

Ella

The daughter of Japanese Canadian parents, both of whom were born in Canada, Ella grew up in a Toronto suburb. Her mother worked, eventually, as a librarian and her father as a bookkeeper/accountant. The family had a comfortable living standard, and Ella and her brother were well cared for materially. Ella perceived herself, potentially, as a strong high school student, though she considered her actual academic performance average. Ella's parents encouraged her to pursue a university education, but she lacked confidence and a sense of direction, academically and vocationally. Having accelerated in elementary school, she was younger than her classmates and felt like an outsider socially. When first interviewed in 1979, Ella was very critical of her high school education, believing that it failed to prepare her for the demands of university. For example, she did not recall ever having written a substantive essay in high school.

Encouraged by the example of her older brother, who had taken some psychology courses, she majored in psychology, though she had no special interest in the subject. Looking back in 2020, she thought she might have been motivated, at least partially, by a desire to understand herself better. She felt her specialization in this subject had not adequately equipped her for the labour market. Unless she was planning to be a psychologist or a teacher, she deemed her degree "pretty useless." In the late seventies, obtaining a BA was no longer exceptional. Ella claimed that "nobody thinks highly of a BA anymore. Most companies say, 'so what?'"

As a student, Ella worked part-time for a telecommunications company and then full-time while she completed her university courses. She did "boring office work" for which a university degree wasn't required, though she increasingly believed that the company preferred employees with postsecondary degrees, even for lower-level positions. Her job initially involved updating residential information. Her employer offered her a higher position, but she turned it down in favour of travelling for several months with her boyfriend, an experience she loved.

At the time of the 1979 interview, she was still unsure about the future, though a position at the company remained possible. She was perceived as a hard-working, conscientious employee, but she feared settling for a boring job just for the money, though she had no clear idea about what she would do instead. Ideally, "I would like to be independently wealthy and travel forever." Realistically, in five to ten years, "I hope I have a good, steady job that is at least slightly interesting. I can't see myself doing anything special." Marriage was a possibility, and she hoped to be in a rewarding relationship, but she confessed to not liking children very much, despite her studies in child psychology. Ella entered the 1980s in a spirit of vacillation, tending to float with the tide rather than pursuing a direction, more uncertain than unhappy about her current state and prospects.

When we interviewed Ella in 2020, she was retired, single (she never married or had children), and somewhat isolated during the COVID-19 lockdown. Overall, she was pleased by the course her life had taken, and to her surprise, developed new interests after retirement.

Her work had consisted of several secretarial/administrative jobs, including five years at the head office of a large hotel chain, as an assistant to one of the purchasers. She thought this would be a "dream job for life," buying goods for hotels. But she wasn't given enough responsibility, and her boss refused to allow her to help others who had too much to do: "He would rather I just sit there and read a book. And I just couldn't. I had to get out of there."

After working spells at a language training institute and a local library, Ella found a position that proved to be enduring and rewarding. She worked for a municipal police service for twenty-two years, until she retired with a good pension in 2013. She served as the administrative clerk for police dog services, where she had a good deal of autonomy, felt admired by her coworkers and supervisors, and spent time tending to the dogs, which she thoroughly enjoyed.

When first hired by the police service into a clerical position, to her surprise, Ella was encouraged to become an officer, both because she had a university degree and because women were now being sought for the police force. She turned down the invitation – being a police officer was well outside her interests and comfort zone – but she realized that her university degree might have had some value after all. Her educational skills earned her some status, and she employed them, at least to some extent, on the job. When her supervisors prepared reports, "I was appalled at their use of the English language," and they welcomed her editorial assistance. She came to understand that she did a much wider range of office work than others in similar jobs, so she applied for and received an upgrade and salary increase, something she thought should have come earlier. She happily retired in her late fifties, thankful for the security her job had provided.

While she had a few relationships, including a current one that had lasted, on and off, for nine years, she preferred living on her own.

> When you live alone, you are used to doing things the way you want to do them, how you want to do them, what TV shows you want to watch, etc. [Her boyfriend] doesn't take COVID quite as seriously as I do. I don't even want to walk with him that much, because on the sidewalk, we are not six feet apart . . . It's like you have to compromise some stuff, and if you don't want to, well then, so be it.

Ella had become more interested in her Japanese heritage in recent years. She learned more about the cultural and economic struggles her parents and relatives faced during and after the Second World War. Her mother and father talked very little about the past when she was growing up, as they seemed more focused on having their children adapt to dominant Canadian norms, though racist incidents were not unknown in Ella's youth. Ella learned Japanese cooking from her mother, she had begun to learn the Japanese language, and she spent increasing amounts of time (before COVID) at a Japanese cultural centre. She was close to her mother and cared for her until she died in 2019. Her father passed away in 1981.

Ella pursued her interest in travel with some trips abroad, and much to her own amazement, she took up line dancing ("I don't dance"), Spanish music, and exercise classes at the local community centre. She planned to return to these activities once COVID restrictions were lifted.

We asked if she would have done anything differently in her life. Her answer was consistent with her reticent, even self-denigrating tendency: "I probably wouldn't have had the guts to do anything differently." She thought, upon reflection, that she might have gotten more out of university if she had lived in residence, where she could have broadened her social circle. Her nieces were doing so, and "they've just blossomed as people."

Notwithstanding Ella's self-doubts and periodic indecisiveness, she had forged a path that brought her considerable fulfilment. In retirement, she was coming to know and appreciate herself more fully than she had in her youth.

Marco

Marco's parents were Italian immigrants who settled in a suburban community close to Toronto. His father, who worked long hours, ran a successful contracting company, and the family lived comfortably though not lavishly. His mother had been a university-educated midwife in Italy but was unable to practise in Canada because midwifery was not recognized as a legal profession in Ontario until 1991. She spent her time as a homemaker, though Marco periodically sensed her frustration in this role. She would likely have been more fulfilled if she had been able to work in her chosen field.

When we spoke to Marco in 1979, he had completed a Bachelor of Commerce degree and was working as an intern on his way to qualifying as a certified accountant. He considered himself ambitious, practical, and hardworking. However, he found the demands of the workplace, which required wearing a suit and shaving every day, a challenging transition from the informality of his university days.

Marco had strong opinions about the quality of his educational experiences. He thought high school was a "waste of time." There were too many esoteric subjects, and he believed he could have learned what he needed to know in two years, not the required five. University, too, consisted of a lot of "garbage courses." Why, he wondered, did he have to take economic history in his business program? In both high school and university, he tried to avoid courses that required abundant writing; he was more comfortable in the world of numbers.

He had considered two professional pathways, engineering and accountancy, though his parents had encouraged him to think about becoming a lawyer. He never contemplated attending community college after high school. He liked the college's focus on practical learning, but he preferred the status that a university-based professional program offered. In 1994, he looked back with gratitude on his educational and occupational opportunities:

> Our generation had it great. We studied if we wanted to – didn't need to be a genius to get a reasonable mark. Now it's more competitive and more pressure on kids to get higher grades. It's going to be tough for this generation.

By 1994, he had also modified his view about the value and purpose of schooling and higher education. "You gain a little perspective," he said. He had once thought his high school geography and history courses were "useless, and yet I miss them, and I'm glad I took them." He remembered a class on early modern European history clearly – "more than half the business courses I took." When we spoke to Marco in 2020, his outlook on the value of a broad "liberal education" had deepened. He believed that students, even in applied fields of study, would benefit from exposure to the arts and related disciplines:

> I find that the Europeans have a more rounded understanding of the world versus the North American dollars-and-cents mentality, and I think that when you're young, you don't really understand [or] . . . think about that. They don't understand the world type of view and the historical view, whereas I think in Europe they understand that a little bit better.

Indeed, Marco was an avid reader of history. On trips to Europe with his family, he played the role of amateur guide, explaining the historical significance of landmarks, monuments, and events. He found these adventures edifying, and as he approached retirement, he was likely to spend even more time reading and studying history.

In the meantime, he was still working as an accountant, a career now spanning some forty years. After completing his accountancy degree in the early 1980s, he worked for two years with a large firm. (Jobs for accountants were plentiful, he recalled.) He then joined a real estate company for three years as a comptroller. But he was restless and unfulfilled by the large corporate work environment. He was determined to start his firm, which he did with a partner in 1986. It was a significant risk. Using his savings as an investment, he went from earning $50,000 a year to $10,000 as the new company got off the ground. He had to draw on savings for a couple of years, and then the company's fortunes turned. In a booming economy, "we caught the wave of the 1980s – a function more of luck than anything else." By 1994, he had developed a niche practice, specializing in interpreting changing tax regulations, a service that would always be in demand. Still, he was hoping to diversify his practice in the years ahead, though he had very loyal clients whom he never intended to "leave out in the cold."

By 2020, having managed his business alone for many years, Marco was thinking of reducing his workload, and COVID-19 accelerated that process. He anticipated that he would lose a quarter of his practice through the pandemic, which would be the equivalent of a day a week. Fortunately, this was financially manageable. He had planned for retirement – his family had some property and ancillary sources of income: "I'm not a multimillionaire, but I've not done too bad, thankfully."

Family life has been a very high priority for Marco. He married at age twenty-eight, consistent with his (1979) view that young people should not marry too early for fear of incurring financial burdens. He also noted at the time that Italians tended to marry later. He was the father of two children, a son and a daughter. In 1994, he expressed hope that his daughter would become an accountant. Instead, she took up teaching, and in 2020, he was thrilled that she had done so. He admired her for her work: "It's a great profession." She had two children, and Marco loved being a grandfather. Indeed, her family was living at Marco's while their house was being renovated. COVID lockdown regulations and health concerns meant that "cramping" was a periodic concern – one of the children "screams through the night" – but he and his wife appreciated the family's closeness, and they were managing their living conditions well. Marco was certainly more involved in child-rearing than his father had been, owing in part to the life-threatening health challenges his son faced since birth.

He was born with a severe, permanent illness. Excellent medical care and family support helped his son thrive, and in his twenties, he had completed a business degree, was working on his master's, and had a job downtown. His son's condition was life-altering for the family. It was a source of fear, stress, and relief, and it mellowed Marco. His work mattered immensely – he needed to support his family – but he was less driven than he had been in his younger years. In his early sixties, he was reflective about his career choice and his educational experiences. He enjoyed his work as an accountant but wondered whether engineering might have been a more creative route. He so appreciated the strength and duration of his marriage, which was enriched by meaningful communication and alone time with his wife. He also perceived himself as less materialistic than in his youth: "When I was younger . . . I wanted more stuff . . . But you begin to realize that it isn't really that at all. It's maybe playing with your grandkids or helping out a friend . . . There's more to life than a shiny $2 coin."

Willow

Born in southwestern Ontario, Willow moved several times with her family before settling in a small town in the Niagara region. Her father was a "hard-working" brewmaster whose job took him to several cities. After a stint in western Canada, he came back to Ontario, where he experienced a period of unemployment when a conglomerate bought out his company. He finished his career working for a winery. Willow's mother, a homemaker, left the workforce when her children were born. Willow's family lived modestly and struggled at times because of her father's fluctuating employment conditions.

Willow left school before the end of Grade 13. She was "fed up" and eager to get out and work, though she acknowledged in 1979 that she had partied a lot and her grades had suffered. Her parents wanted her to finish high school, but did not pressure her to do so. She recalled in 2020 that she had completed a "pre-test" for university or college. The essay she wrote elicited negative feedback, and she was discouraged by this response: "It kind of took the wind out of my sails." She thought, "I'm not enjoying [school] right now, so I'm going to go and try to work for a while."

There were no jobs in town, so she moved to Toronto and quickly found a secretarial job. She had taken typing and shorthand in school, though no other commercial subjects. She was hired by a law firm and reported in 1979 that while the job offered no real prospects for advancement, she would stay with it for the time being. The firm mostly did legal aid cases, and she worked as a stenographer, typist, and receptionist.

When we spoke to Willow in 1995, she had been working at a large utility company since 1980, beginning in the secretarial pool and then in several successive positions as an administrative assistant to company executives. She had married, and after her first child was born, she took four months off and returned to work part-time, which suited her needs. She filled in for other administrative assistants on leave. She had two more children and continued to work part-time, but the company changed its policy and only employed people on a full-time basis. To remain part-time, she was required to register with an employment agency, endure a significant pay cut, and lose her benefits. She was disillusioned at this turn of events: "I'm at a loss, and I don't know what to do."

A major portion of Willow's salary was spent on childcare, and the income loss made this employment arrangement unaffordable, so she left the job. Fortunately, they owned their home, and her husband, a refrigerator repairman who worked for a gas company and ran his own business, earned enough to support the family. She was out of the workforce until 2000, though "on the bright side, I got to spend more time with my young kids at home." In the 1995 interview, Willow expressed regret at having dropped out of school. She enjoyed working and realized that with more educational credentials, she was likely to have secured more rewarding employment.

In 2000, Willow took on two new positions. One was for a large publishing company, where she continued her secretarial and administrative assistant roles; the other was for a friend who was now running a family business, where she processed payroll, which included some "minor" accounting. As of 2020, she was still working for the publisher, though she planned to retire later in the year.

She lamented some of the corporate changes in recent years. All the "in-house" specialists had gone, as more and more work was contracted out. And the pervasive use of technology had reduced human interaction: "Everything is so impersonal; it's all email. You're hard-pressed to find somebody to talk to and get an answer in five seconds." The COVID pandemic dramatically changed employment practices, and Willow was now working exclusively at home. Just before the pandemic, the company had introduced an open-concept, Google-like workplace system, which she disliked because she didn't have enough privacy. With all these changes, she was ready to retire (her husband retired in 2019). Overall, she had enjoyed her time at the company, particularly because she was able to work part-time for the entire period. However, she was mostly on contract, not permanent part-time, which meant fewer benefits and no pension income. The company "has been good to me, but I won't have anything when I come out of it."

What she did have was a very whole and challenging family life. In 1979, Willow expressed a desire to be married before she turned thirty, once she was financially secure. She believed in getting to know a person well before marrying. She didn't favour living with a partner before marriage, an idea that may have been influenced by her Pentecostal and her husband's Catholic family backgrounds. She was conscious, too, of the high divorce rate, which she believed was worse when couples married too young.

Willow met her husband when she was twenty-two, and they dated for five years before marrying. By 1995, their three children were aged eight and nine (both boys) and three (a girl). Her husband was exceedingly busy, working days and evenings, leaving her with prime responsibility for "meal-making," the household, and childcare. "It can be a bit stressful for me because I have to look after everything," including organizing multiple activities for her children. They did manage to take regular holidays, to Florida in the fall and to Willow's in-laws' cottage on weekends in the summer. They planned to remain living in the city, where she hoped her children would become more aware and "street-smart, and that they would all eventually attend postsecondary education." She hoped, too, that her husband would be able to work less. Coming from modest means, Willow and her husband lived busy, demanding lives and had achieved relative economic security.

But tragedy struck when her eighteen-year-old son was severely injured in an accident at a steel plant in 2005 and became permanently disabled. The subcontractor on the project was fined, and her son received medical and personal support (for life) from the Ontario Workplace Safety and Insurance Board. He lives in the family home, and during the hours when no other support is available, Willow and her husband provide the required care:

> If there's anything that happens with him, or I have to put him back to bed, that kind of thing, or lunch, all his meals . . . everything, I look after for him in that regard. So, we've had a lot of scary moments over the last fifteen years. He's had to have surgeries, and it's not just like somebody regular going into the hospital; it's a whole set of other circumstances – his being in a wheelchair and having to figure out all the extra planning that goes with that. It's been very stressful and worrisome that he's going to have a situation where it's going to be life-threatening.

The family has faced other health challenges. Willow's brother, who lives in a different city, has schizophrenia, and Willow has been his major support. During COVID, she was only able to see him on rare occasions. Her husband has suffered from bouts of anxiety and depression, triggered several years ago by the loss of three close friends and relatives in a short period of time. And Willow herself has been diagnosed with cancer – her father died of the disease – and she was struggling, particularly during COVID, to secure appropriate care and treatment.

Willow and her husband are close to their three children and their extended families. She believes that her second son and daughter were deeply affected by her eldest son's accident. Her second son, who is "very bright," lost his educational focus and left college in his first year. He now works, unhappily, in maintenance for a local school board and still lives with his parents. Once he rediscovers a sense of direction, he hopes to return to school. Willow's daughter, a carpenter, lives in another province. She is returning home with the following plan: "She wants to build a home on wheels so that we can all take a family vacation," something that has not happened since her son was injured.

The COVID pandemic added to family stresses. Willow found food shopping taxing because of lineups, long waits, and the difficulty of social distancing. She was never comfortable ordering things online – she did not like giving out personal information – but her disabled son helped her with this: "He has his own computer . . . and we'll do it together." She struggled with the COVID-induced isolation, but there was one ritual she was not prepared to end: "I won't give up my morning coffee at the coffee shop. That is my best coffee ever." She and her husband enjoyed attending musical theatre and socializing with friends and neighbours. She hoped to return to these activities after COVID.

How did she plan to spend her forthcoming retirement? She had no firm ideas yet. Caring for her son would continue to occupy much of her time, and she was determined to begin organizing her massive collection of family pictures. Her husband was happily engaged in refurbishing the family cottage, which had become his COVID project. He was relieved to have left his job, which he no longer enjoyed by the time he retired.

Looking back at the course her life had taken, Willow had one main regret – that she had not pursued her education. She made the most of the jobs she held and managed to balance work and home life, particularly in the wake of her son's catastrophic accident. In 1979, she spoke about her love of animals and hoped to go into veterinary work. But she would have had to return to school, which was not possible or affordable at the time. In 2020, she again spoke longingly of her interest in animals and in teaching – vocational pathways that, for a variety of reasons, she had not followed. She inclined to look ahead, to grapple resiliently with the world as it was, and to move forward with her life, one day at a time.

Joseph

Joseph grew up in a Toronto suburb in an upper-middle-class family. He appeared headed for advanced education and a traditional professional career, and in some significant ways, this is precisely what he achieved. But the path he followed was not exactly linear. There were surprising twists along the way, and the activities he valued most in life lay outside his job-related endeavours, and in part outside Canada itself.

Joseph's father, an accountant, moved up the ranks of a large insurance company and ultimately was responsible for integrating computerization into the company workplace. His mother was a homemaker, and the family, which Joseph described as "typically WASP of the fifties and sixties," lived very comfortably. Joseph did not recall feeling directly pressured to attend university. Still, the expectation was "internalized . . . It was an assumption I had made for myself" as part of the "natural progression of life." He also recalled in 1994 receiving encouragement from his Grade 8 teachers to pursue the academic stream in high school: "That was good advice. And they were more influential than any of my high school teachers."

High school was an ordeal for Joseph. Somewhat shy, Joseph claimed in 1979 to have disliked school; he was lonely and not highly motivated and felt unprepared for the demands of university. He did well enough to be admitted to a university computer science program and lived at home while pursuing his studies. This was essentially a financial decision encouraged by his parents, who paid his tuition and did not charge him room and board. Had he left the city, the costs would have been far higher.

He did not fare especially well in the science program, and after two years he started working full-time and attending university part-time. From 1976 to 1979, he worked for a large oil company as a computer operator, for which his university training had equipped him. He found computer work interesting, a continuous "puzzle to be solved." He had a brief, disappointing stint at a bank in the audit department in a position that "wasn't as advertised." He returned to university full-time to complete his degree, majoring in economics with a minor in computer science. He said in 1994 that he "appreciated university more" the second time around, and he elaborated on this perception in 2020: "I just wanted to continue to develop my background and create other opportunities for employment . . . to expand my knowledge base and look for other opportunities."

After finishing his degree, Joseph moved to an insurance company where he worked in computer programming and financial modelling; he stayed in that position for more than ten years. He was moving up in the company, but a financial shakeup in the industry led to the layoff of many middle managers, and his prospects appeared unpromising. He chose to move into a relatively new field within the sector: reinsurance, where he spent twenty-one years.

Reinsurance arrangements provide buyers with additional protection against the risk of a first insurance policy. Clients might include underwriting companies with large risk profiles seeking protection against such events as plane crashes or shipping accidents. Joseph's company specialized in providing access to US medical insurance, but the market for his business collapsed after 2012 when the Obama administration introduced the Affordable Care Act.

He took six months off in "semi-retirement," but he was "too young," and it was "too early." He knew he would "go stir crazy" if he sat around the house, so he qualified as a licensed mortgage broker, a position he still held in 2020. He was classified as an independent contractor but had to be affiliated with a brokerage firm to practise: "I operate my own book of business, but it also gives me the freedom to leave the country on a semi-regular basis for extended periods." Working abroad and engaging with young people from around the world was his true passion.

Joseph lived with his parents until he was thirty. He married and bought a home; he and his wife, now a retired teacher, were unable to have children. They adopted a son, "now twenty-five," who, as a child, was diagnosed as being "high-functioning autistic." He was living at home and had a job downtown. For some thirty years, Joseph has built what he considers family-type relationships in a unique way – he and his wife began to host international high school students. He reported in 1994 that two young people from Australia and France had been living with them, and a third, from Argentina, was coming soon. They learned English, adapted to the broader culture, and attended school. In Joseph's words, "They became members of the family."

This work continued over the years, with students spending a year each in Joseph's home. He and his wife visited "our kids" around the world, and at the time of the 2020 interview, he had just had a Zoom call with five of them, "representing four continents and multiple time zones."

Currently, he is involved in a pilot project with an NGO in East Africa caring for political refugees. He had visited the site, met with the politician responsible, and would be submitting a grant application of $200,000 to support the project. If successful, it would require him to spend eight to twelve weeks per year at the site. He was fundraising locally as well.

His commitment to such work stemmed, at least in part, from his religious beliefs. He grew up attending the United Church and was now an active member of the Baptist Church. He noted in 1979 that he was teaching Sunday school, had read sixty-six books on religion, and was taking a Bible study course. His parents were not deeply religious, but he found a sense of purpose and community in the church, which extended into his work with young people overseas.

Joseph expected to continue his volunteer activities and his brokerage work for the foreseeable future. Owing to planned investments, he was relatively secure financially, though because he had no pension his income was susceptible to "gyrations" in the stock market. That could induce anxiety, but he believed he was "better off than 80 per cent of my peers." COVID had put a pause on any travel plans, but he was determined to resume his foreign trips once this became possible. His brokerage business was especially busy during COVID: "I've basically been ten hours a day head down in my office."

Joseph had no major regrets about the course his life had taken, though he acknowledged having spent a lengthy time defining his vocational interests. He wondered if law might have been a better route, but that ship had long sailed: "I have no complaints with the way things turned out."

Lydia

Lydia was born and raised in a small community in north-central Ontario and attended a rural district high school. Her father, who had a Grade 8 education, farmed, and her mother periodically held secretarial positions. Like their neighbours, the family lived very modestly in the predominantly farming community.

Lydia considered herself of average academic ability, but she performed above the norm in school and aspired to extend her education. She preferred math and science courses over those that involved extensive writing – she avoided history, for example – and hoped to work in a technical field. Following a guidance test and a discussion with the guidance counsellor, she discovered the field of radiation technology, an occupation she had not previously heard of but that greatly interested her. She explored available opportunities and moved to Toronto after Grade 13 to enrol in a radiation technology program offered by an accredited private institute. That followed a stressful academic year: secondary school teachers in the region engaged in a lengthy strike while she was in Grade 13.

In 1979, she recalled that of the thirty-seven students in her graduating high school class, about ten attended college, five or six went to university, and most of the others entered the workforce. In 1995, Lydia reported that because there were no longer good opportunities in farming, her four siblings were working in other fields: mining engineer, machinist, mechanic, and office manager. The mining engineer was the only one who attended university.

Had Lydia not found the radiation technology option, she would likely have applied to a university general science program. She had enjoyed living in a small town, with its strong community sense, but she was determined to obtain a postsecondary education and pursue a career independently. While she faced some adjustment issues in the transition to a large city, such as missing home, she adapted quickly. She lived in residence with other out-of-town girls who "were in the same boat. I don't remember feeling uncomfortable or intimidated." She completed the twenty-four-month program and immediately began work in a nearby hospital, where she remained for six years, performing CT scans, angiograms, and related tasks.

In the meantime, Lydia married Samuel, a high school classmate (whom we also interviewed in 2020), who completed an engineering degree and was working in Toronto for a large utility company. The couple enjoyed the city, but they preferred to raise their family in a smaller setting. They moved to a northern Ontario centre for several years, where they both worked and then settled permanently in a mid-sized southwestern Ontario city. By 1995, they had three children, all boys – six, eight, and ten.

Lydia and Samuel loved the community. Their children were involved in numerous activities – speed skating, baseball, Beavers, and the church. "It's great raising kids here," said Lydia in 1995. They travelled with their children to sporting tournaments and had an active social life. She served as registrar for the local football league, and her husband was the president. When asked if she expected the children to attend university, she responded, "I think so. They are all near the top of their class and are in enrichment programs." But if they chose to work in the trades, as her brothers did, she would be fine with that. She felt, too, that a college diploma was more practical than a university degree. She recalled her own parents' guidance on the same issue: "They never said, 'You have to go to university or stay on the farm.' They let us go our way and stood behind us."

When we spoke to Lydia in 2020, she had recently retired, as had her husband. She had spent thirty years on the job at a single location and, over the last decade, had worked as an MRI technologist, which had required additional training through a specialized program in British Columbia. She had worked part-time when her children were younger and again in the last two years before retiring. Her skills and those of her colleagues were in high demand. She recalled only two people being laid off over her three decades on the job.

While postings for qualified staff appeared at regular intervals, incomes had not kept pace with the cost of living, a situation compounded by recent wage freezes in the public sector. Lydia had always worked in a nonunion setting. However, she believed her salary and working conditions matched those of unionized workplaces, as nonunion wages and benefits tended to follow those in unionized settings.

Lydia loved her job, and "couldn't imagine doing anything else. The most rewarding part of it was working with patients and helping them get to a good outcome in their health." Patients undergoing an MRI often worried about claustrophobia, and she successfully helped them relax during the procedure. The hospital could be a stressful environment, not only health-wise but also administratively, as managers had to meet financial targets or introduce new organizational systems. But overall, she found the work experience stimulating and gratifying.

How had her children fared? Now in their thirties, they managed to stay employed during the COVID pandemic. One was a computer programmer; the second, an avid skier, worked in a restaurant in Whistler, BC; and the third had become a civil engineer. Lydia and Samuel were close to their children and their partners – two of their sons lived nearby, though COVID had significantly reduced their visits with one another. They all looked forward to spending summer together at the family cottage.

Once their children had completed schooling and their house was paid off, Lydia and Samuel were able to build up their retirement funds. Samuel, an engineer, had a good pension that he had transferred from one place of work to another. They were financially comfortable and hoped to resume travel once COVID ended (Lydia was a veteran of two hikes on the Camino trail in Spain). Samuel had travelled a great deal in his job, and while he was away, Lydia had independently developed a suitable work and socializing schedule. Spending every day together in retirement, particularly during COVID, proved an "adjustment" for Lydia; Samuel was occasionally at loose ends: "I get up in the morning, and I don't have anything to do for the most part." He and Lydia walked a great deal during COVID – "I've seen more of this town than I've ever seen before" – and he had enrolled in a continuing education series offered by a nearby university. She had recently taken up curling.

Lydia missed working with people, but she had no regrets about retiring, which occurred at the beginning of the COVID outbreak. The demands of hospital work during the pandemic were enormous, and she was relieved to be free of them. Determined, practical, and skilled, Lydia was satisfied with the course of her journey from the family farm of her childhood to an enriching professional, personal, and family life.

James

Bright, restless, and strong-minded, James, a retired tradesman (in 2020), had a complicated start to his working life. He was born in an eastern Ontario village and grew up in a working-class family. His father was a factory labourer who died when James was in Grade 13. His schooling experience was mixed. He finished Grade 12 in the vocational stream and had "breezed through" his courses without doing much homework. Because his grades were high – "over 85 percent" – he was exempted from writing final examinations and each year got out of classes two weeks before most of his classmates. He liked math and technical subjects and considered his machine shop teacher to be the most significant influence in his younger years. Because of his proficiency, James was asked by his teacher to lead some classes in Grade 12. His teacher would "just encourage me a bit to keep going."

He entered Grade 13 but dropped out before completing his courses, just three credits shy of a diploma. The academic classes bored him; he didn't like English, and he felt that the teachers "didn't keep me busy enough to keep me interested in school all day." His parents had encouraged him to go to college, but he lacked the motivation and discipline to do so.

For the next five years, after moving out of his family home, "I kind of knocked around just making ends meet… and having fun." He found it "quite easy" to get unskilled work in the 1970s, and he had several factory jobs, including at the plant where his father had worked. But he found being there without his father too difficult. He realized by 1995 that his father's death had been traumatic for him and likely accounted for his struggles in Grade 13 and beyond. His father had tried to "provide direction," but James had resisted. These were "head-butting years," and "we never got over that" before his father passed away.

Finally determined to improve his qualifications, James completed a four-week community college course in machine shop. He returned to work and was contacted by a local proprietor looking for an apprentice in mould-making – the employer obtained James's name from the college he had attended. James then enrolled in a tool and die maker college program (there was no certified training specifically for mould-making, though the two trades were similar), which included a lengthy on-the-job apprenticeship with the employer's company. Asked why he chose this craft as opposed to other trades such as automotive or electrical work, he responded that he "liked the math" and enjoyed shaping objects from metal: "You can actually make things rather than repair things." He was permitted to count some of his high school credits, which shortened his apprenticeship, and the time normally required to obtain a licence.

James's skills were valued, though over several years, he moved through various jobs because he was not always happy with the pay or the working conditions. By 1995, he had been employed by a major automobile maker for ten years, and he was now making dashboards for cars. He remained with the company for twenty-seven years until he retired. He was now happier with his income, but he was less and less taken with the work itself, and he believed that more interesting mould, tool, and die making was being done outside of Canada. His previous positions in smaller companies also offered greater variety in the work than his current job. Computerization had recently been introduced into the workplace, and he wasn't comfortable with the new technology:

> I have not really made the transition. I like to feel the machines and listen. Computer-controlled machines are basically mentally thought out. You just tell the machine what to do, and if it makes a mistake, it is only the input that is wrong . . . When I handle a machine, I can tell if I'm feeding it too fast by the feel of the machine, rather than hear that it's been fed too fast by the break of the cutter when it's done on the computer . . . I'd rather be right in there.

James had basic training in the new systems but not with large computer programs, and he said, "I don't feel I have the background to delve too deeply." He claimed the company now used graduate engineers with no hands-on experience to supervise the workplace, which created some tensions with the craft workers. James knew that he would never be promoted because he lacked engineering credentials. Still, he earned enough, including overtime shifts, to make the job worth keeping, and looking back in 2021, he felt he had made the right "tradeoff" between job security and creativity.

Meanwhile, his personal life became complicated. When we interviewed him in 1995, he and his wife, parents of two children, had recently separated, and he was living in the house he had grown up in, now owned by his brother. He believed that his wife, who was not employed, lacked ambition, and she complained that he put in too little time caring for the children (He acknowledged working many weekends and over Christmas because they "needed the money"). Financial pressures would now increase because of the need to fund two households. Marriage counselling had proven unsuccessful.

By 2021, James had been in a new relationship for some thirteen years. He and his partner owned their own homes, and each valued their independence. She had a daughter in Europe, and they visited her periodically. His sons were now in their thirties. One, a labourer, lived nearby, and the other worked in a western Canadian steel mill. James had hoped they would become skilled workers – "electricians or carpenters or something like that," but that was apparently a "pipedream." James was a grandfather – his oldest son out west had two boys, but he was not involved in their lives. Apart from occasional visits, "I don't see them very much at all." James believed that this estrangement was linked, at least partly, to his divorce when the boys were teenagers: "We just never patched anything up really from his teen days, and then he wasn't much older than nineteen when he went out west."

Near the end of our recent interview, James spoke openly about other personal challenges. He was a recovering alcoholic, and he had spent time in jail for cultivating cannabis. Heavy drinking, he contended, was part of the local culture, and the problem got worse around the time of his divorce. He managed to keep working and considered himself a "functioning alcoholic." Encouraged by a coworker, James joined Alcoholics Anonymous, and by 2021 he had been sober for some twenty-three years. To his great relief, with peer support, he was able to return to his job.

James retired at age fifty-seven. The Canadian automotive industry was facing difficult times, and when he was offered a buyout, he took it. He was ready to end work, which had become "monotonous." He was given thirty days to accept the proposal, and, perhaps consistent with his sometimes dramatic conduct, he waited until the last minute to accept the company's offer. Had he turned it down, he might well have eventually received a larger payout – "I left about $60,000 on the table," – but he had had enough of plant work. At the time of our interview in 2021, at age sixty-five, he was managing well financially, aided by his income from the Canada Pension Plan and Old Age Security.

In retirement, before COVID, he and his partner travelled annually to Europe and, more recently, took trips around Ontario, visiting museums and other cultural sites. They enjoyed reading and frequented the library. Most notably, James took up the craft of rug hooking. His work was on display at the local art gallery, and he sold several pieces. He came to this activity through someone he met at a tai chi class. His initial response was sceptical. It sounded "too girly to me." But his friend reminded him that as a tool and die maker, he had artistic skills that required "a lot of imagination." Working with repurposed materials – wool suits and jackets, for example – he derived a great deal of satisfaction from this pursuit and considered himself an "artist."

Now content, James regretted some of the turns his occupational and personal lives had taken. He thought it might have been rewarding to attend university, enter a profession, and earn more money. But he realized that his interests were far more vocational than academic, so "I'm happy with the way things turned out. I knew I wanted to work in the trades," an aspiration he most certainly fulfilled.

Conclusion

People have no choice about the time and location of their birth and no control over the families and cultures in which they are raised. As we know from sociological literature, and as this study has confirmed, one's social class origins affect one's future educational and occupational prospects (privilege begets privilege). However, there are many individual exceptions to this pattern, arising from personal choices, unanticipated events, and individual personalities (Heinz 1991).

James was raised in a working-class culture and attended a school that stressed vocational studies. He became a skilled craftsman and worked in this field until he retired. Ella's family was middle class; she was encouraged to attend university and did so. Lacking direction once she graduated, she settled for clerical occupations, though she made the most of them and had no apparent regrets about the route she followed. Joseph had a materially advantaged upbringing, never doubting that he would go to university, but the road to his ultimate entrepreneurial occupation was far from direct.

The economic conditions through which the Class of '73 lived were periodically unsettling, and our subjects were not immune to the impact of these changes. James witnessed transitions in the automotive production industry, including the transfer of manufacturing sites to other countries and the impact of computerization. For the most part, however, our interviewees deliberately worked in fields with reasonably good, sustainable employment opportunities. The health sector continued to expand, and as Lydia noted, radiation technology, her chosen field, almost always required employees. Marco selected accounting over engineering because he believed accounting offered better job prospects. Ella eventually found long-term employment in the public sector, which had expanded in the late twentieth and early twenty-first centuries, and Lydia spent a lengthy period working for a large, stable utility company. And as James discovered, Ontario manufacturers were constantly searching for qualified tradespeople.

All these individuals, whatever their social origins or occupations, were living reasonably comfortable, middle-class lives when we last interviewed them. They were able to do so either because their incomes had grown sufficiently or because they were in dual-income families. The fact that women now worked outside the home in far greater numbers than in the previous generation reflected an opportunity structure that had evolved and diversified. Many occupations still tended to be gender-specific – men were more likely to be tool and die makers, and women dominated clerical and secretarial positions – but higher family incomes were possible. Most significantly, working people at various income levels could eventually afford to purchase homes, especially if they lived, as Lydia and James did, in smaller towns.

Notwithstanding these positive stories, it is important to point out that our subjects were unlikely to have been fully representative of all those in Grade 12 in 1973. Individuals agreeing to participate in surveys and interviews would be less likely to have come from the ranks of the unemployed, the homeless, or the destitute than from the ranks of those whose parents had attained material security and rewarding occupations. Indeed, our study participants were advantaged in at least one significant way. Compared to national averages, our participants had higher rates of home ownership. In our study, 95 per cent owned their home, whereas only 74.6 per cent of the Canadian population over the age of sixty-five owned their homes in 2016 (Statistics Canada 2017c). Notably, our study participants reported an average pre-tax income of approximately $73,400. Many of our respondents had not yet retired and were still earning employment income during the time of data collection. While we do not have precise, comparable data on the incomes of Canadian seniors as a whole, we are fairly certain that our participants were, on average, materially more comfortable than their fellow Canadian seniors (Statistics Canada 2021a).

Exercising agency, all our subjects sought rewarding work, regardless of its pay or prestige. Ella left a clerical job because she couldn't tolerate being insufficiently occupied. James moved from one position to another when the work felt too routine. To obtain greater control over his daily life, Marco became an entrepreneur rather than remaining an employee in a large corporation. Lydia enjoyed being an X-ray technician and later an MRI specialist and served in these positions for some three decades. At the same time, as explored more fully in Chapter 5, everyone was compelled to grapple with the structural changes in the workplace, the introduction of new technology, and the volatility of the economy.

Health challenges could affect all individuals and families, sometimes in life-altering ways. Willow devoted herself to caring for her disabled son from the time he was a teenager. She also tended to her ill brother and then faced her medical trials. Marco's son had lifelong heart problems, and Joseph's son was autistic. Circumstances beyond the parents' control caused these illnesses or disabilities, but they did all they could to sustain and improve their children's lives. James confronted his own demons, including alcoholism, eventually finding stability and security.

COVID-19 shocked the world, leading many governments, including Ontario's, to impose unprecedented restrictions on their residents' mobility. During the "lockdown" period in 2020, when authorities shuttered businesses, closed schools and parks, restricted travel, and enacted social distancing regulations, life changed significantly. Interviewed in late 2020 and early 2021, our interviewees appeared, thus far, to have effectively managed the health impact of the pandemic, but almost everyone struggled with the social isolation the restrictions produced. Living alone, Ella had very little direct contact with others. Lydia and her husband had few external outlets and missed visiting their children. Willow did all her work from home. Joseph was unable to travel but was as busy as ever with his job and volunteer activities. Those with children and grandchildren worried about the disruptive effects of COVID on their lives, and several of our subjects delayed foreign travel plans. They confronted a shared social reality and dealt with its trials in distinctive ways.

As we note in Chapter 7, Canadians were now perceiving and entering retirement in a variety of ways. The legislated end to mandatory retirement in Canada (with some professional and occupational exceptions) meant that employees were better able than in the past to map their retirement pathways. The self-employed had the most autonomy. Joseph, for example, had no plans to stop working. Marco was slowly winding down but remained undecided as to timelines. Willow's retirement was imminent; Lydia was happily retired and relieved not to be working during COVID, an especially demanding time for those in the health sector. James, who found a new creative outlet, was thankful to be out of a job he no longer enjoyed. Social isolation compounded by COVID concerned some of our subjects who were planning or in the early phases of retirement, and some had yet to discover new interests that might engage them once their working lives ended. Attending to the needs of their own parents was an ongoing concern.

Did our subjects' self-images, identities, or values change over time? Somewhat diffident, even indecisive in her youth, Ella appeared more confident in retirement, with a range of new interests and a particular commitment to connecting with her ethnic and cultural roots. Marco evolved from an assured, pragmatic young man to a more serene, questioning individual, profoundly affected by his son's health challenges, and interested in deepening his knowledge of the world through studying history.

After leaving high school early, Willow lacked direction but found work and a family life that proved to be rewarding and fulfilling. Her son's tragic accident permanently altered her world, and she found a way to combine extraordinary caregiving with continuous employment. She always lamented not furthering her education. Resiliently, she faced ongoing health setbacks, personally and within her family. Well-educated, Joseph drifted somewhat occupationally until he settled on a stimulating, busy profession. His deepest rewards, inspired by faith, involved his philanthropic international work. In his sixties, he was fulfilled, industrious, and not ready to retire.

For her whole life, Lydia preferred living in a small town where her hospital work, which she enjoyed, was appreciated, though she had no regrets about retiring. Family life mattered immensely, as did her social and recreational activities. She appeared adaptable and satisfied, though possibly now searching for additional outlets that might enrich her retirement. James's turbulent younger years, personally and occupationally, eventually transitioned to a more stable, gratifying life, including a new vocation that drew upon his artistic talents.

Overall, these individuals, in their mid-sixties, were content, and reflective, cognizant of the uncertainties and challenges of the era, many of which they had confronted directly, and now resolved to enjoy their remaining years with family, friends, and new endeavours.

3 The Social, Economic, and Educational Contexts

The Class of '73 entered young adulthood at a time of historic social changes, some of which were led by youth. Significant changes in society were brought about, in part, by growing economic and employment needs, which prompted rural-to-urban migration and an increase in women entering the workforce. This, in turn, resulted in parents and children having to adjust to the expanded roles and responsibilities of family members. Further, immigration brought an influx of new people to Canada, the majority of whom were racialized individuals from Asia and the Caribbean.

Changing trends in employment and educational opportunities provide greater choice for young people considering their future plans. The post-war growth of the manufacturing and service sectors, the low level of unemployment throughout the 1950s, the stimulus the government was providing to new housing construction, the provision of family allowances, and free university tuition for war veterans all contributed to a climate of optimism for youngsters coming of age in the 1970s. Demographic factors of individual youths, along with changing social, political, economic, and educational trends during the 1960s and 1970s, worked to shape the life trajectories of this group of Ontarians.

To understand the lived experiences, school involvements, educational plans, and social outcomes of members of the Class of '73, we need to pay attention to the social and educational structures that mediate access to opportunities and facilitate the aspirations of individuals as they journey through life.

A Time of Social Change

Social Movements

As elsewhere, there was a proliferation of social movements in Canada in the sixties and seventies:

- Student movements were prominent on many campuses in the 1960s.
- The number of women's groups in British Columbia increased from two in 1969 to over one hundred in 1974.
- The first gay rights organizations were formed in Vancouver and Toronto, and a national association was established in 1975.
- The founding of Greenpeace in Vancouver in 1971 signalled the birth of the modern environmental movement.
- The struggle for racial equality took on new and sometimes more militant forms.
- Addressing the longstanding inequality of Canada's two founding European groups, francophone Quebec sought increased autonomy or even independence.
- Resisting a push towards assimilation, Indigenous people began to assert themselves as a force in Canadian society.

Clément (2009) argues that while "a large percentage of sixties youth remained apolitical or opposed to the radicalism that was so associated with their generation, to accept that most of the youth were not activists, however, is not to vitiate their collective impact on social movements. Many people supported social movements by adhering to the movement's basic principles in ways that affected their everyday lives (and the lives of others)" (7). And as Miriam Smith (2005) writes,

> The social movements of the 1960s were successful in placing new issues on the agenda of both polity and society and reflected a number of important sociological changes in family structure, the decline of both Protestant and Catholic church influence (especially in Quebec), increasing female labour force participation, the expansion of higher education, the increasingly multicultural and multiracial character of Canadian society, and the gradual shift to post-industrial capitalism. (362)

Immigration and Diversity

In and of itself, immigration was not a new phenomenon in Ontario. From early in the twentieth century, immigration from Europe accounted for a considerable portion of Ontario's population increase. Between 1941 and 1951, Canada's net gain from international migration was 154,000; between 1951 and 1961, it was 562,000, with more than 50 per cent of immigrants to Canada settling in Ontario (Rea 1985, 28–30). However, until the 1960s and 1970s, Canada's immigration legislation and policies had restricted the immigration of people from places other than Europe and the United States. For instance, the Chinese Immigration Act regulated the number of Chinese who were allowed to enter the country (Wayland 1997, 46).

In 1962, regulation removed national origin as a criterion of admission, and the points system – based on applicants' age, education, language skills, and economic characteristics – was introduced in 1967. With these changes, it became easy for people born outside Europe and the United States to immigrate to Canada (Boyd and Vickers 2000, 8). By the 1970s, some 60,000 people from countries in Asia and about 85,000 people from the Caribbean immigrated to Canada (Statistics Canada 2016). Most of the new immigrants chose to settle in Ontario (James 2010) where they helped to meet employment needs. And as Boyd and Vickers (2000) write, "During this time, net migration was higher than it had been in almost 50 years, but it accounted for no more than 30 per cent of total population growth between 1951 and 1971. The population effect of the large number of foreign-born arrivals was muted by the magnitude of natural growth caused by the unprecedented birth rates recorded during the baby boom from 1946 to 1965" (7).

When the federal government appointed the Royal Commission on Bilingualism and Biculturalism in 1963, older immigrant groups objected to the idea that Canada had only two cultures. In response, in 1971, the government introduced its Multiculturalism Policy "within a bilingual framework," based on the notion that ethnic group members – other than English and French – could maintain and express their cultures and thereby "preserve and enhance the multicultural heritage of Canadians" (James 2010, 137; see also Haque 2018). This policy would take on greater significance with the growing ethnic and racial diversity of Canada's population.

Women in the Workforce

In its 1970 report, the Royal Commission on the Status of Women documented the conditions faced by men and women and recommended legal and social changes that would foster gender equality (Prentice et al. 1988). There were some advancements for women in several important areas:

• Women constituted 45 per cent of university students in 1976, compared with 38.5 per cent in 1961.

- Women's studies courses were introduced into university curricula.
- Women represented 37 per cent of the labour force by 1971 (Baker 1989, 176).

However, much more needed to change if women were to realize equitable opportunities in society. Both the changes that had taken place and the ones that still needed to happen were reflected in magazine and newspaper articles highlighting the accomplishments of professional women and debating – crudely at times – the merits of feminism (Cornell 1973; *Maclean's* 1975; *Toronto Star* 1973). The prominent presence of the feminist movement in Canadian society at the time served not only to challenge the discriminatory treatment of women in workplaces, in politics, in education, and within the family but also to advocate for progressive social policies with attainable goals, especially in Ontario, Canada's "wealthiest and most economically developed province" (Rea 1985, 14).

Rural-Urban Migration

The farm population of Ontario fell from some 694,700 to 363,600 between 1941 and 1971. Changes in agriculture and animal farming meant that there were fewer jobs in these areas than in the past. However, the rural *nonfarm* population, which had declined during the 1940s, grew steadily in the 1950s and 1960s to reach 995,800 by 1971, or 13 per cent of the total population of the province. At that time, the largest population growth occurred in the regions of Hamilton-Wentworth, Halton, Peel, York, Durham, and Metropolitan Toronto, which had about half the province's population in the 1940s but two-thirds of it by the 1960s (Rea 1985, 27, 30). Further, between 1961 and 2016, Ontario saw its urban population increase from just under five million to 11.6 million. During the same period, rural areas grew as well, but at a much slower pace; from 1.4 million to 1.8 million (Ahmed 2019). Today, just over 73 per cent of all Canadians live in large urban centres (Statistics Canada 2022a).

Expansion of Education

Education as we know it today is central to our lives. Not only do we spend most of our formative young years in it, but we also expect schools, colleges, and universities to fulfil a staggering range of social functions. Beyond teaching essential skills, schools are also key socialization institutions that prepare children to become socially minded, responsible adults. Schools, colleges, and universities are also tasked with preparing young people to assume productive adult roles in an increasingly complex and knowledge-driven economy (Canadian Council on Learning 2006, 2009). Given this central role of education, it is easy to forget that this modern form of mass institution (especially at the postsecondary level) is relatively young. The Class of '73 was at the forefront of many reforms and innovations that have shaped contemporary education in Canada.

Only eight years before our study participants graduated from high school, John Porter (1965) argued in *The Vertical Mosaic*, a key text in Canadian sociology, that an outdated, elitist school system, coupled with the preference of the corporate class for using immigrants as the source of skilled labour rather than training and educating locally, led to entrenched forms of stratification. Expanding access to education was seen as a mechanism by which Canada could become less stratified and more meritocratic and by which equality of opportunity could be achieved (Lehmann 2016).

Erwin and MacLennan (1994) argue that *The Vertical Mosaic* and subsequent policy documents, such as the report of the Royal Commission on Bilingualism and Biculturalism (1967–70), had significant impacts on the expansion and reform of education in Canada in the 1960s and 1970s. Importantly, for the educational experience of the Class of '73, this included the massive expansion of Canada's (and in our case, Ontario's) postsecondary education sector, as many new universities were founded and the community college system was established during that time. By 1975, full-time university enrolment in Ontario had risen to nearly 160,000 from approximately 32,000 only fifteen years earlier, while non-university postsecondary education also increased substantially (Anisef et al. 2000).

Driven by population growth, economic demand, human capital needs, and the promise of social justice and equality of opportunity, between 1961 and 1971, the proportion of Canadians aged fifteen to nineteen attending school full-time had risen from just under 60 per cent to more than 70 per cent (Baker 1989, 8). Indeed, as Donald Fisher (1999) wrote in an article on the place of education in Canadian society,

> As an institutional form, education occupies a unique place in Canadian society. By the late 1960s, education had become a central legitimizing institution in the modern Canadian state. Between 1960 and 1995–1996, the cost of public education increased from $1.7 billion to almost $60 billion. One in fourteen employed Canadians work in education, and 25 percent of the total population is involved with education. Public education is a

major industry involving approximately 16,000 elementary and secondary schools, 200 postsecondary colleges, 75 universities and university colleges, 300,000 teachers, and 60,000 instructors and professors.

In Ontario, the education system expanded significantly in the 1960s and early 1970s, with the number of students attending elementary and secondary school expanding from 1.4 million in 1960 to more than two million in 1970. Full-time university enrolment rose from 32,100 in 1960 to 159,700 in 1975. Over the same period, non-university postsecondary enrolment increased from 16,600 to 59,600 (Axelrod 1982; Rea 1985, 104–5; Statistics Canada 1978). It was during the 1960s that the Ontario government introduced the "Reorganized [Robarts] Plan," which established three streams in Ontario high schools: Arts and Science; Science, Technology and Trades; and Business and Commerce. These programs were offered in five-year or four-year programs of study, and students aspiring to attend university would typically enrol in the five-year Arts and Science stream. The Technology and Business programs, for which the federal government provided substantial funding, were expected to train workers for a growing industrial and service economy. But before long, this system was criticized for failing to equip graduates with usable work skills and for channeling disadvantaged students into non-academic streams, thereby propagating social disparities among young people (Curtis, Livingstone, and Smaller 1992, 87–92; Gidney 1999, 63–6; Rea 1985, 112; Stamp 1982, 205–6).

Further, the 1968 Report of the Royal Commission on the Aims and Objectives of Education in Ontario (the Hall-Dennis Report), promoted a "progressive" educational philosophy that stressed holistic learning, freedom of choice, and a "humane," noncompetitive classroom environment, led to significant changes in both elementary and secondary schooling (Stamp 1982, 217–20).

And in 1969, the Robarts Plan was replaced by a "credit system" that based students' promotion through high school on their successful completion of individual courses rather than on passing an entire grade. Courses were subsequently grouped in four broad areas: communications, social sciences, pure and applied sciences, and arts. Students then had the freedom to select a minimum of three courses from each field, but they needed twenty-seven course credits to earn their Grade 12 diploma. And with the end of Grade 13 provincial departmental examinations in 1968, students needed to earn thirty-three course credits to graduate from Grade 13. Eventually, with less standardized curricula and more flexibility, schools were able to set their own graduation examinations. So too, students could attend publicly funded alternative schools, especially in Metropolitan Toronto, where the teaching was more innovative and less structured.

It was also in the 1960s – specifically 1965 – that the Community College of Applied Arts and Technology system was created to offer extended education and training to high school leavers who were either uninterested in university or not qualified to enter it. The college also served to prepare students for jobs. Based on the school reform of 1968, while students destined for university would have completed courses in arts and sciences at the Advanced level, students enrolled in General-level courses were most likely to enter community college after leaving high school, or to go directly into the workforce like students in the Basic-level stream. Furthermore, with the increasing demands for job skills and academic certification, coupled with the substantial increase in the number of postsecondary institutions – by 1973, there were twenty-two community colleges and fifteen universities operating in Ontario – families recognized that a young person's career prospects depended on the acquisition of some form of postsecondary education.

In fact, for many young people, education was a safeguard against the mounting unemployment rate of the 1970s; despite its flourishing post-war economy, Ontario's unemployment rate rose to 6 per cent in 1975, which at the time was higher than that of three other provinces (Rea 1985, 254). For young people aged fifteen to twenty-four years, the unemployment rate rose steadily during the 1970s, and by 1977 it reached 14.5 per cent, which was more than twice the rate (5.8 per cent) of those over twenty-five (Denton, Robb, and Spencer 1981, 20; Statistics Canada 1978, 51). A decade earlier, the comparable unemployment rates for individuals in these age groups were 6.1 and 2.8 per cent, respectively. Besides, young people with the lowest level of education were the most likely to be unemployed. Specifically, in 1974–7, individuals fifteen to twenty-four years old with only an elementary education faced an average unemployment rate of 23.2 per cent; for secondary school graduates, it was 13.5 per cent; for college certificate or diploma holders, it was 6.3 per cent; and for university graduates, it was 5.4 per cent (Denton, Robb, and Spencer 1981, 20).

The Class of '73: A Preliminary Sketch

Youth moved from secondary education into the labour market in two main ways – either directly from high school or through Grade 13, a university education, and related forms of professional training. Men and women received different kinds of education, especially at postsecondary levels. In 1979, by the time most of the Class of '73 had completed their formal education and had entered the labour force, women's participation in postsecondary education was on par with that of men. As of 1979, men predominated in physical science and mathematics, applied science, business, economics, and commerce majors, while women predominated in the arts, the fine arts, and the humanities. For community college graduates, gender imbalance led to future employment in gender-segregated occupations. Many women surmounted gender obstacles and left rural areas to improve their educational and career opportunities.

In 1974, there were small differences in the proportion of males and females working in skilled and unskilled jobs, but the types of occupations in which they were employed differed sharply by gender. Child-rearing responsibilities may largely explain these gender differences. Women were more often found in occupations and careers with lower earning potential; expected to take primary responsibility for child-rearing, they had to compromise in the workplace. Analysis of this project's survey data through 1995 indicates that the middle class was particularly vulnerable to change and that gender differences favoured greater occupational inheritance among men. While most men and women held high educational and occupational aspirations, there were some notable gender differences both within and among the groups. Women with foreign-born parents were less likely to be unemployed and twice as likely to be self-employed. Participants attached greater importance to marriage in 1995 than in 1979, with women reporting that they were mainly responsible for childcare and child-rearing.

The communities in which members of the Class of '73 grew up and their willingness to relocate helped determine their educational and occupational outcomes. Given the greater likelihood of foreign-born Canadians finding jobs in major cities, respondents with foreign-born parents proved more likely than respondents with Canadian-born parents to reside in urban areas rather than rural areas or small towns. Rural students were significantly less likely than their urban counterparts to enter the Advanced high school stream, but rural women were, early on, highly geographically mobile.

When the Class of '73 was resurveyed in 1979, six years after completing high school, 29 per cent of the participants had completed a university degree, 22 per cent earned a college diploma, 14 per cent had attended some college or university but had not (yet) graduated, and 36 per cent had not formally continued their education beyond high school (Anisef et al. 2000, 61).

University graduates were drawn disproportionately from Metro Toronto, while community college graduates and those with no postsecondary education were more frequently drawn from rural areas and small towns. In 1995, those with city backgrounds were upwardly mobile into managerial and professional ranks, while those with rural origins either were upwardly mobile into skilled occupations (white and blue collar) or remained in the unskilled occupational category. Rural and small-town dwellers earned lower incomes and had less education than urban dwellers. Choosing to leave home in late adolescence shaped personal biographies, with city-dwellers experiencing greater career occupational mobility than rural respondents. Respondents from small towns and rural areas were more likely to report having four or more siblings, and their parents had fewer financial resources to support their children's higher education.

Findings that were reported in Phase 6 of our longitudinal study indicated that the middle class was particularly vulnerable to change, with over 60 per cent moving up or down the ladder of success with respect to intergenerational mobility. At the same time, a minority of respondents from more disadvantaged origins took advantage of economic opportunities and moved into upper socio-economic positions (Anisef et al. 2000, 157). In addition, we also found that region of origin had a substantial effect on career success, independent of socio-economic status. For example, while 77.7 per cent of lower-SES Toronto respondents succeeded in moving up to the middle- and high-SES categories by 1995, only 41.1 per cent of lower-SES small-town and rural respondents made similar transitions. Conversely, upper-SES respondents who spent their high school years in Toronto were less likely to experience downward mobility (35.1 per cent) than were their small-town and rural counterparts (55.9 per cent) (Anisef et al. 2000, 121, 143–4).

In 1973, the children of foreign-born parents began with an SES disadvantage but ended up being better off than their peers with Canadian-born parents. Low-SES respondents were less likely to report that their mothers had encouraged them to continue their education after high school compared to higher-SES respondents. High-SES respondents were twice as dependent on their parents for financial support, and men were more likely to increase their involvement in household finances as their socio-economic status increased.

More members of the Class of '73 pursued postsecondary education – both college and university – than their parents. Figure 3.1 presents the educational attainment of the parents of the Class of 1973 and illustrates that most of them had completed some or all of their secondary schooling. Compared to mothers, fathers were less likely (nearly a 10 per cent difference) to complete their secondary education. While both

Figure 3.1 Mother's and Father's Education (1973)

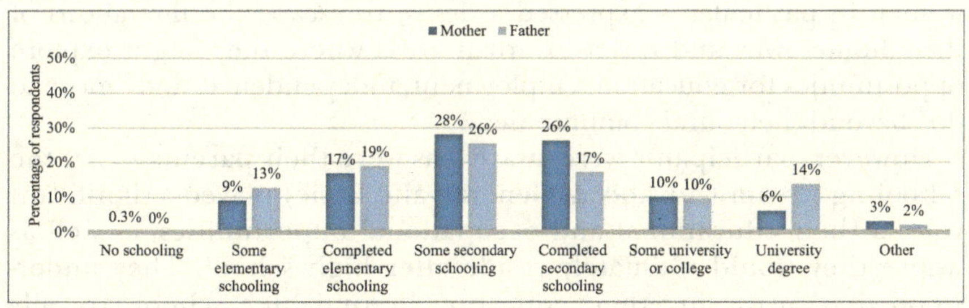

mothers and fathers were somewhat equally likely to have some college or university education, fathers (14 per cent) compared with mothers (6 per cent) were twice as likely to have a university degree.

When parents' levels of education are compared with those of their progeny, changing attitudes relating to the importance of education, high aspirations and support from parents, and the introduction of more technology within the workforce led to more members of the Class of '73 completing high school and entering postsecondary educational institutions. Parents with postsecondary education credentials knew the value of these credentials. They expected their children to follow the same path. Still, parents without postsecondary credentials also often wanted their children to attain the highest level of education possible so that the children might attain the employment and career opportunities that had been beyond their reach.

Education, Employment, and the Decision to Leave Home

A significant proportion of the Class of '73 grew up in small towns where there was a limited range of educational and occupational options compared to those available in larger urban centres. In particular, while 43 per cent of the participating students lived in Metropolitan Toronto or other large metropolitan areas, 24 per cent came from small cities, towns, and bordering urban communities, and a further 33 per cent came from different, mainly rural areas (Anisef, Paasche, and Turrittin 1980, A-10). In most cases, rural areas tended to offer deep family and community ties to the young people raised there. Still, many of the participants – except for those with familial commitments and young women in particular – expressed a desire to escape the limitations of their hometowns and travel to urban areas where they might explore opportunities for education, employment, independence, and "more to do" beyond their rural communities.

However, participants were aware – as were their parents – that the schooling stream (Advanced, General, and Basic) played a significant role in their educational and occupational opportunities, as well as where they would ultimately reside after high school. They understood that furthering their education beyond high school typically required moving or long hours of commuting. And findings indicate that gender differences played a role in program choices and decisions about leaving their communities. Compared to their male counterparts, rural and small-town female students were more likely to graduate from a four-year high school program and remain in their community.

- Talking about what living in her rural community has meant to her, Diane stated,

  I don't want to settle down in Tweed . . . I want to get away . . . where there is more to do. I go bowling just to get out of the house. It's depressing here in wintertime, but it's better in the summer. I don't belong to any groups or organizations. Most of my friends have moved away. Some are coming back, though. I don't have too many friends. There's pressure to get married, but I can't be bothered. I'd rather get more education and save some money. My brothers are educated, and I'd like to be, too.

Diane's reflections – like those of others – and her aspirations to escape the cultural "pressures" and constraints of life in her rural community were seemingly shaped by the emerging attitudes and discourses of women about possibilities that went beyond traditional gendered roles like early marriage. But leaving the protective sheath of their close-knit rural communities and family meant having to weigh the cost of leaving for the unknown, reneging on their caregiving responsibilities within the family, and forgoing the help, mentorship, and connections from which they benefit. Males, on the other hand, did not have the same familial responsibilities that kept them from leaving home and, understandably, neither did they experience the same cultural pressures.

- Penny talked of how family members and friends enabled her to get jobs. And while leaving home had its advantages, she was concerned with not fulfilling her responsibilities and obligations to her parents and younger sibling:

> Most of the help for getting jobs came from relatives, not much came from school. I did most of it myself. Lots of kids go to jobs because their parents worked there. Most of my friends work in stores and factories. There aren't too many jobs around here. I'm thinking of going to New Brunswick. My brother and sister are there, and they say there's work out there. But my mother needs me here; it's a big family. I'd probably get homesick if I went to New Brunswick. I do a lot of stuff around the house. There are five younger brothers and sisters and five older ones. The youngest one is thirteen. Only one is going to school; the rest are working. My sister was skipping school all the time; she didn't like school, so my mother decided she could skip, and now she's got a part-time job.

Penny signalled the train migration that occurs from rural areas, not only to urban areas in Ontario but also, as she indicated for her family members, eastern Canada, New Brunswick. Walter, like other participants, talked of emigrating from Canada to the United States, where he would be able to obtain the job he sought: "I've considered moving to the States or out west. Toronto is one of the big centres in computing, and there are very few of them in Canada. There are many more in the States."

Understandably, changes in schooling and economic trends would help shape the occupations in which young people would eventually work, and their educational plans as they age.

- Rose's first job was in a lumber business her father owned. She recalled that having established his business in 1974, her father "needed a secretary, so I went to work full-time for him." In her follow-up interview (1980), she indicated,

> I've been at home since my first child was born. I'll be home till both go to school. I don't have any plans for the future yet. I'll take a job for a while, so we can build the house we want. I'll get some kind of schooling. I don't want to be in bookkeeping all my life. I'll go back to high school to take science, art, and mathematics. I want to make something of my life. I don't want to just be a housewife.

For members of the class of 1973, and rural and small-town youth in particular, past practices of working with family members were not much of an option. Over time, there was an increased need for people to obtain further education or training, especially to find employment in the area of technology. This meant obtaining relevant job skills and forging new relationships or networks.

Conclusion

The 1960s and early 1970s saw a massive expansion of Canada's education system, particularly at the postsecondary level. New universities were founded, the community college system was established, and enrolment rates increased dramatically. Population growth, economic demands, and a push for greater social mobility and equality of opportunity drove this expansion. Reforms like the introduction of the credit system and more flexible curricula aimed to modernize education, though they also faced criticism.

The Class of '73 came of age during a period of significant social upheaval and activism. Student movements, women's rights groups, environmental organizations, and other social movements challenged existing norms and institutions. These movements reflected and contributed to broader societal changes in family structures, gender roles, and cultural attitudes.

A major demographic shift occurred as many young people moved from rural areas and small towns to larger urban centres in search of educational and employment opportunities. This migration pattern had significant implications for individual trajectories as well as community development. Urban students generally had access to more educational options and experienced greater upward mobility compared to their rural counterparts.

While women's participation in postsecondary education reached parity with men by the late 1970s, significant gender differences persisted in fields of study and career paths. Women faced unique challenges in balancing educational and career aspirations with family responsibilities and societal expectations.

Changes to immigration policies in the 1960s led to increased immigration from non-European countries, contributing to the growing ethnic and racial diversity of Canada's population. This demographic shift prompted policy responses like the Multiculturalism Policy of 1971.

Despite overall post-war prosperity, the 1970s saw rising unemployment rates, particularly among youth. This economic context influenced educational choices, as many saw higher education as a safeguard against unemployment.

In examining the Class of '73, we see a cohort navigating a period of rapid social, cultural, and institutional change. Their experiences reflect broader societal transformations while also highlighting persistent inequalities based on gender, geography, and socio-economic background. This analysis provides valuable insights into the complex interplay between education, social change, and individual trajectories in late twentieth-century Canada.

4 Education and Educational Mobility

Among respondents to the Phase 7 survey in 2019, 24 per cent had attained a bachelor's degree, and about 11 per cent had obtained a professional degree or higher, for a total of 35 per cent of respondents with a university degree. At the other end of the educational attainment spectrum, 25 per cent of study participants had not obtained any education beyond a high school diploma, while 9 per cent attained a technical school diploma or apprenticeship, and 30 per cent completed a community college diploma. It is rather common in longitudinal research that those with higher levels of education and those who are formally more successful are more inclined to respond to renewed calls for participation and share their success with the research team. It is also possible, however, that the Phase 7 survey in 2019 included educational attainment that had not yet been completed and thus not been captured in 1979.

Of the twenty-nine interview participants in Phase 7, this bias towards higher levels of educational attainment is even more strongly evident: seventeen (or 59 per cent) attended university, while five (17 per cent) completed programs at one of Ontario's community colleges, which were still relatively new when the respondents left high school. Only one participant completed an apprenticeship. Six (20 per cent) did not continue to any form of postsecondary education and entered the labour market directly out of high school.

This highlights the importance of understanding the experiences of the Class of '73 from a life course perspective. The changes in higher education, both in the expansion of universities and the creation of community colleges, created opportunities for the members of the Class of '73 that were not available to prior generations. Simultaneously, many structural barriers related to participants' class, gender, or race continued to constrain their agency.

In the context of education, we show in this chapter that family socio-economic status, especially the level of formal education of parents, played a prominent role in the educational pathways of many members of the Class of '73. For example, those from families with more highly educated parents were more likely to continue to university. Gender also played a role, especially in the choices of subjects that women and men in our sample pursued during postsecondary education and, consequently, as outlined in Chapter 5, the careers on which they embarked. This interplay of structural constraints and individual agency has been referred to as *structured individualization* (Rudd and Evans 1998) or *bounded agency* (Evans 2002).

Heinz (1995) explores the idea of the individual within the context of biography and the role of the biographical actor. He emphasizes that individuals can make independent decisions while operating within a framework of possibilities and limitations. They perceive themselves as actively shaping the trajectory of their own lives. In this chapter, we, therefore, discuss the schooling and higher education experiences of the Class of '73, including both survey material from the larger sample and interview data from the twenty-nine participants who spoke to us in 2020–1 retrospectively about their educational experiences. Our emphasis is on understanding how, despite expanded opportunities, educational experiences and pathways were still characterized by bounded forms of agency, especially in terms of participants' social class origins.

Experiencing Education

As Figure 4.1 shows, when looking back and answering the question of whether they were satisfied with their education, participants expressed very high levels of satisfaction. Most respondents in Phase 7 agreed that education improved their communication skills (90 per cent), their reasoning skills (91 per cent), and their career prospects (82 per cent). Similarly, Phase 7 respondents felt very strongly that education made their lives more meaningful (83 per cent).

More specifically, over 90 per cent felt that their education had improved their reasoning and communication skills, and 83 per cent agreed that their education had made life more meaningful. As Figure 4.1 further shows, these findings from Phase 7 reflect a noticeable increase over participants' opinion in the Phase 6 survey, which was carried out in 1995.

Figure 4.1: Education Opinions

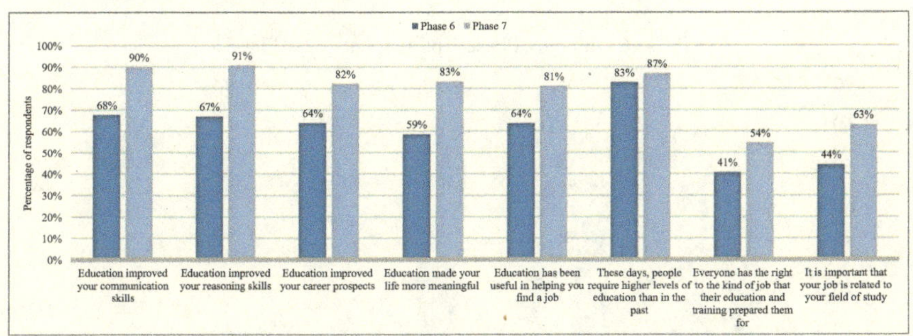

Some of this effect could be attributed to sample attrition, suggesting that those who are more satisfied are likely to remain participants in a longitudinal study with as long a reach as ours. When we analyse these data further, this reflects a genuine reappraisal of the value of education over time. To illustrate, Figure 4.2 only compares participants who responded in both Phase 6 and Phase 7 surveys to gain a more accurate picture of the change in opinions about education. It shows that participants were substantially more likely to be satisfied with their education in 2019 (Phase 7) than they were in 1995 (Phase 6). Conversely, there were fewer participants in 2019 (Phase 7) who still felt unsatisfied with their education, compared to 1995 (Phase 6).

Other survey findings can explain this, at least partially. Many had engaged in further education or skill development between the two surveys. For instance, when looking only at study participants who had completed both Phase 6 and 7 surveys (i.e., accounting for any sample attrition), the percentage of participants who completed a bachelor's degree had increased from 23 per cent to 26 per cent. We saw a similar increase in individuals who completed college diplomas or apprenticeships, from 34 per cent to 39 per cent.

Moreover, as they had entered retirement or were approaching it, participants also reassessed how important their education had been in their success or, conversely, how not completing more education may have constrained them. Our portraits in Chapter 2 provide some illustrations of this argument.

Turning to the interviews conducted with twenty-nine members of the Class of '73 adds nuance to this overall sense of satisfaction and achievement. As we found in the surveys, when reflecting on their education, most interview participants also remembered their high school

Figure 4.2: Education Satisfaction

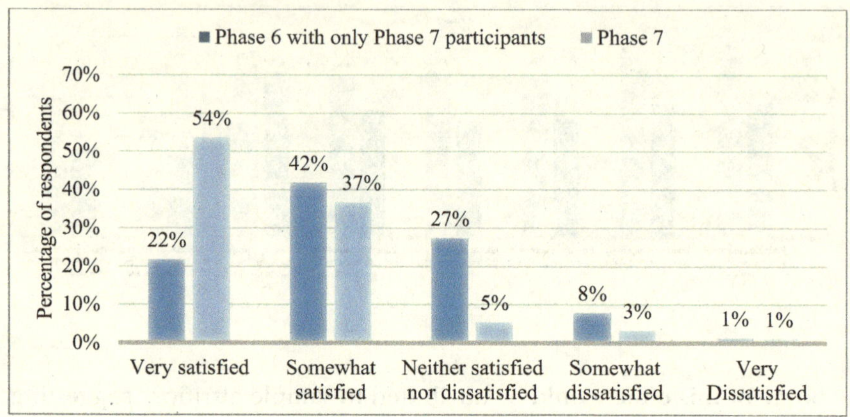

years quite fondly, emphasizing learning (e.g., their favourite courses or teachers), extracurricular involvement (e.g., band, drama, or sports), and friendships.

- As Charlotte explained, "So, I really enjoyed high school. It was a very social event for me, and I liked being at the top of the class and I liked being in all the school shows and the band and everything. So, it was a good experience for me."

Positive high school experiences were more common for participants who came from families in which parents were already highly educated. In other words, in families in which education was more likely to be seen as important, children were more likely to be encouraged to be engaged at school and do well. As parental education is a central dimension of social class, it is therefore worthwhile to have a closer look at differences in educational experiences by social class.

Social Class

Interviewees' high school experiences were strongly related to the educational status of their parents. Those who had parents who were themselves highly educated were much more likely to have experienced high school as a rewarding experience, both academically and socially.

An extensive body of research has shown the relationship between parental education and the schooling experiences and outcomes of their children (Brown 2013; Canadian Education Statistics Council 2010; Finnie, Lascelles, and Sweetman 2005; Goldthorpe 1996; Krahn 2022; Lehmann 2016). Broadly speaking, this literature suggests that school experiences are more positive for those who grew up in families in which high formal education was already present and in which highly educated parents could foster and reinforce a love for learning and schooling (Lareau 2003).

- Violet's experience illustrates this rather well. Like Charlotte, from whom we heard above, Violet was from a family with at least one university-educated parent. She eventually studied at university and followed in her father's footsteps by becoming an accountant. Here is how she describes her high school years:

  Well, if I reflect on high school, I was one of the smart geeky kids. So, I was academically strong. I had a good group of girlfriends. I was not socially popular, but I played in the band, which I really enjoyed. We went on band trips; the band instructor was very fun, and we had band practices on Tuesday night. So, that was one of the extracurriculars that I was involved in pretty well throughout my high school career. And I became a manager in Grades 12 and 13 to help organize the band trips.

- Similarly, Noah spoke about his experience in high school in very positive terms. Noah, who had in his mother a university-educated parent, graduated from university and became a very successful journalist. His comments further illustrate how peer groups tend to reinforce educational dispositions formed in the home:

  I did well at school. I was the president of the athletic council, vice president of the student council, and won lots of awards and so did a lot of my friends. The whole idea of high school being a stressful time, it really wasn't a factor – I don't think for many of the groups of people I associated with anyways.

It is important here to note that none of these participants spoke about the influence of their parents directly, which should not come as a surprise, considering that they were in their mid-sixties when last interviewed and unlikely to remember or reflect on schooling as influenced by parents.

The French sociologist Pierre Bourdieu wrote about attitudes towards education as dispositions that are fundamentally shaped in the family home (Bourdieu 1977 [1972], 1990 [1980]; Bourdieu and Passeron 1990; Bourdieu and Wacquant 1992). Highly educated parents socialize their children to embrace learning to the point at which these feelings about schooling have become so internalized (or embodied, as Bourdieu would call it) that the students themselves no longer recognize the role of parents. Such findings emphasize the socially reproductive relationships between a person's immediate social environment and educational experiences and attainment (Bernstein 1977; Lehmann 2014, 2023; Power et al. 2003; Reay, Crozier, and James 2011).

At the other end of the spectrum, we had only very few participants from lower socio-economic backgrounds whose parents had low levels of formal education and who remembered their schooling years negatively.

- Henry illustrates how difficult times in high school led to disillusionment with schooling, which in turn meant that no postsecondary education was sought. Henry was from a working-class family in which parents had neither been exposed to much education themselves nor could intervene at school on his behalf. He eventually did find refuge in vocational classes and with a few teachers, but these experiences were still buried under an overwhelming sense of school having failed him. Henry, whose family had immigrated to Canada from Eastern Europe, talked about very difficult relationships with teachers and experiences of discrimination in school. His father was a brickyard worker, and his mother worked in a factory (for the role of teachers and the effect of labelling children, see, e.g., Rist 1977). Neither could support Henry with his troubles at school:

High school, in general, was quite an experience for me. To go back a little further, I failed Grade 4 because I had a terrible teacher who beat me and things like that. Then, in Grade 7, they transferred us to another school where things started all right, but then again, I was really a victim of a really nasty history teacher, and it caused me to lose interest. I totally gave up at that time and told my teachers, my (whatever they called them) guidance counsellors at that time, that I had enough, and I wanted out of the system, and I was choosing to enrol into a vocational school.

Engaging in applied rather than academic learning allowed him to graduate from high school and develop skills he could apply in his working life. Moreover, Henry spoke about teachers in vocational courses taking on mentorship roles for students like him who struggled in academic high school programs:

So, that school was a school for failures to give us some chance to excel at something. So I saw these guys and they were going forward, they were learning how to fix cars, they were learning how to, you know, build houses, and

I saw this as an opportunity where I could excel . . . All the [vocational school-teachers] had patience, they had respect, every one of the teachers there I can say were dedicated, not to the system, but to the students . . . I excelled there to the point where I received awards, I got honours awards, you know, and different awards from the board of education and that. I was encouraged by a couple of my teachers to take the opportunity and finish off my education in a normal high school, . . . so that would at least give me some opportunity in life.

Fortunately, such extremely negative experiences were rare in our interview sample. Much more likely, those from less educated family backgrounds remembered and reflected on high school as a social rather than academic experience.

• Robert, who was from a working-class family, recalled,

I graduated in '74 because I didn't have enough credits. And I had to go back to night school and pick up math, of all things. I wasn't a very good student. I didn't really apply myself. And thus, that really kind of sent me on a journey after high school. But I enjoyed high school. I participated in lots of sports and students' council and, you know, dated girls and had a wide circle of friends and participated in dances, clubs, and all that.

Sociodemographic characteristics (here, social class) are never fully deterministic, so it is unsurprising that several interviewees who enjoyed high school did not grow up in families with highly educated parents.

• Caroline, whose parents had not attended university, ended up studying home economics at university in the hope of becoming a teacher. Although she did not fulfil this goal, she had a successful career as a human resource professional. Here she related her high school experience:

I made close friends quite easily, and as I said, after all these years, they're still my friends. I tried to participate in lots of different things. That's one thing an uncle had said to me: try and do different things, don't just stick around with all the same people. High school was completely enjoyable for me. I really loved it.

In addition to her reference above about her uncle's advice, Caroline, later in the interview, spoke about an aunt who was a home economics teacher and who had an influence on her high school and university choices. These suggest the influence of people other than parents with higher levels of formal education.

• Jack told a similar story. A son of poor immigrant parents from eastern and central Europe, Jack nonetheless became a very successful software developer and entrepreneur. He credited his high school teachers with setting him on a pathway to achieve this success:

> I've always been very thankful and appreciative of the fact that my high school teachers had probably one of the biggest impacts on my life . . . They were really my only outlet for an adult that gave advice . . . They had a huge impact on me.

Regardless of their family situation, those who moved on to university generally talked about enjoying high school and having good and supportive relationships with teachers. These types of support, and perhaps mentorship, function as powerful mechanisms to disrupt family circumstances (or structural forces) and introduce possibilities that may otherwise not be considered.

• Samuel, who became a successful engineer, spoke about this as follows:

> You know, I didn't come from a family where mom and dad were both university-educated people. It was just – I mean, my dad was well-read and, you know, above his status as an electrician. But yeah, I knew in Grade 12, I was going back to get Grade 13 so that I could get the marks to go [to university] . . . Like all people in engineering, I was good at math, and it came quite easy to me and quite naturally, and we were set up with good teachers in calculus and algebra and the math and the sciences for the advanced classes.

Finally, note that a successful high school experience did not necessarily mean being placed in an academic stream or aiming for university.

• James and Robert, both from working-class families, spoke about enjoying high school precisely because they were learning in non-academic, applied streams. James eventually entered and completed an apprenticeship and worked in both small and large organizations, using his trade education in machine shops:

> You'd learn a little bit about cars and sheet metal, electricity, drafting, machine shop, and all these different trades. And I thought, well, that sounds like something like I'd like to get into. Because I liked – even at that time, I was kind of working, you know, with my dad a little bit in the car in the driveway, and that kind of stuff, eh, so I thought that would be more for me . . . I believe I was more of a happy high school student . . . I was interested and I paid attention I think in class. And I just – I was just totally interested when the teachers were teaching and just took it on, and it seemed to work out fine.

Unlike James, Robert did not continue in the trades, but he ended up (after several "detours" in the years following high school) in a career that saw him retiring from a management role with the parks and recreation department of a city in Ontario:

Well, my father was a tool and die maker – a machinist. And I – I've always had a liking for the tools and the hands-on and building things and making things. So it was just a natural progression, I think. In public school, we had woodshop and classes like that, that I, that I did well in . . . You know, I think the courses I took in high school, it was like drafting and automotive and machine shop, electricity. They were skills that I apply to this day or that I did later in life and in my career. I can honestly say I utilized a lot of them.

At the other end of the spectrum, a few participants remembered their high school years either negatively or, more often, with a sense of indifference.

• Lucy and Evelyn offer examples of a relatively common type of indifference expressed by interview participants. Both continued to study at one of the only relatively recently established community colleges. Ontario's community colleges were in many ways meant to capture high schoolers such as Lucy and Evelyn, who did not consider themselves academically inclined but had ambitions for the types of middle-class careers that became more common in the second half of the twentieth century. Lucy graduated from college with a qualification as a dental hygienist and went on to have a very successful career in that field. The following excerpt sums up her high school memories:

I was average, you know. I had the cool crowd, not athletic, in the band for a while but no, just average kid and average marks. So no, nothing stands out about high school.

Evelyn went to a community college to study early childhood education but did not find employment in the field after graduation. She spent most of her adult life working as a supermarket cashier but also, later in life, found a second job as an educational assistant, which allowed her to use some of the skills she learned at college. Her reflections about her educational experience, both in high school and college, suggest a certain sense of feeling adrift at school:

I liked the social part of it – my friends. The work was okay. I wasn't much of a student, and I wasn't a real academic person, so sometimes that was a bit of a struggle. But if I had tried harder, I probably could have done better, but you know, it just wasn't my thing. I mean, I passed everything and did fine.

Asked by the interviewer, "Is there any regret on not having tried harder, or are you okay with that?" she replied,

> I'm okay with that, yeah. Yeah, instead of going to community college, I probably could have worked hard and gone to university, but . . .

Socio-economic status or social class is not the only lens through which the stories of educational experience are filtered. In the following sections, we examine gender, race, and sexuality as other important dimensions of education.

Gender

A 1973 study of some 9,000 Grade 12 Ontario students showed that females – especially those from families of lower social status – were more likely to leave school early for work and take up traditionally "female" occupations (Porter, Porter, and Blishen 1982). As Figure 4.3 shows, for most of the Class of 1973 participants, attending university was their plan, but there were notable differences. Males (32 per cent) more than females (25 per cent) aspired to attend a university, while a larger percentage of females (17 per cent) than males (14 per cent) planned on attending community college.

Notably, males (16 per cent) were 10 per cent less likely than their female counterparts (26 per cent) to plan on getting a full-time job

Figure 4.3: Post-High School Plans by Gender, 1973

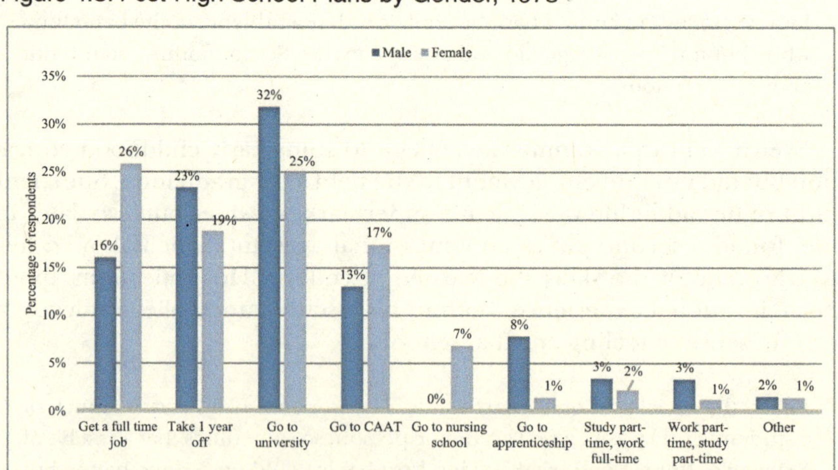

following high school. The gendered aspect of their aspirations is also evident in their other post-high school aspirations. For instance, males were more likely to plan on taking a one-year break between high school and their postsecondary activities, go into apprenticeship, and study and work (and vice versa) part-time. Interestingly, while about 6 per cent of females planned on attending nursing school, no males planned on doing so.

The data signal that the young women of the 1970s perceived greater opportunities and possibilities for themselves in the workforce than previous generations, but typically in "feminine careers" which required only a community college education, like nursing (and even teaching). And they tended to engage in postsecondary education at much higher rates than their mothers. Young women in the Class of '73 were also more likely to be motivated to engage in postsecondary education as a result of the burgeoning feminist movement.

- Drawing on interview data from the early phases of the study, Ada provides an example of being "a product" of the time of feminism and hence being prepared to "fight" against the cultural expectations and stereotypes of women.

I'm a product of the whole feminist thing. It started when I was in high school. Certainly, the women that I know who are ten to fifteen years older than myself seem to be coming to the same point of realization that I'm at. You don't have to remain a homemaker. That's not the sole way of defining ourselves. Of course, then there can be a backlash. The good homemakers and mothers are beginning to feel inferiority complexes, which isn't right. I'd had a lot of old-world ideals from my parents, from their time and background. And you must fight that. I think one of the reasons I embraced the whole women's liberation thing was to rebel against that. I mean, they never really said, "Don't go ahead and prove yourself." It was just that there wasn't much encouragement: "You're the girl, and if you choose not to get on; it's okay because you can get married and have babies and sit at home." It's okay. I think I was just a normal, healthy, red-blooded Canadian girl fighting back to what the parents were saying.

Essentially, the young women and men of 1973 were "coming of age" at a time when constructs of their aspirations required them to grapple with the forces of social change, particularly those about the cultural structure of gendered norms, values, practices, and expectations by which they had to live. Their educational and career paths had been shaped by how well they managed to negotiate the schooling structures, parental coaching and expectations, and accessible social opportunities.

Today, women are outperforming men in nearly all levels of education. Women are less likely to drop out of secondary school, more likely to enrol in and complete university, and more likely to gain advanced graduate and professional degrees (Ferguson 2016). This reflects a remarkable reversal of gendered attainment, which started to take shape during the time the Class of '73 moved through the education system.

Survey data from Phase 7 of the Class of '73 project show that female participants in the study had already gained a slight advantage over men in terms of postsecondary education. As Figure 4.4 shows, 28 per cent of women had gained a bachelor's degree, and 11 per cent had gained an advanced postgraduate degree (that is, a degree in a master's, doctoral, or professional program), compared to 21 per cent and 11 per cent of men, respectively. Men were more likely to have completed postgraduate professional education (e.g., in law or medical schools) and were far more likely to have completed an apprenticeship. It is also worth noting that women had taken advantage of Ontario's new community college system to a much greater extent than men.

The interview data confirm these findings. In the interview sample, we had an equal number of male and female participants who had completed university (eight each) and an equal number who did not continue to any postsecondary education (three each). The subjects the men and women chose to study, however, remained gendered. Women attended university or college to study accounting, library sciences,

Figure 4.4: Educational Attainment by Gender, 2019 (Phase 7)

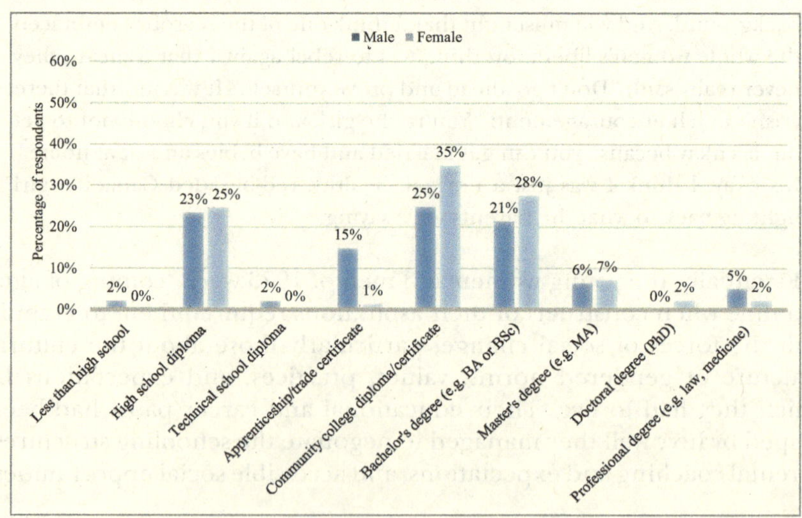

education (including early childhood education), or dental hygiene, whereas the men were in engineering, management, or dentistry.

- Emma, for example, told us the following about her decision to become a teacher:

> Well, my father wanted me to be a nurse. I applied for nursing. "Be a nurse like your aunt. She's doing well." At that time, women didn't do a lot – there wasn't much expectation. I had three brothers, there was more expectation for them, but I'm the one who went further than they did in the end . . . The degrees for that [nursing], you got an RN but you didn't have to go to university, it was a nursing school . . . I got accepted into nursing and then my aunt said, "You don't want to go into nursing because you'll have to do shift work. You won't like that." So that's when I said, "Okay, I'll go into teaching." . . . So she encouraged me to pick something else. And I wanted to do something supportive, helping out. I always was involved with children when I was a high school student, so it was probably secondary. Nursing and then teaching.

Two gendered elements stand out in Emma's story. First, less was expected of her than her brothers, although she had the aptitude and attitude to do well in education. Second, both of her top educational choices were firmly rooted in gendered expectations about caring and nurturing. in the same vein, some women interviewees told us about putting their own education and career on hold or aside and instead following their male partners (usually boyfriends at the time) as they got jobs in different parts of the country.

- Hazel explained, "Okay, after I left high school, I had – I did something I told my daughter not to do. I followed my boyfriend." As the interview continued, Hazel revealed that she had initially started at a university in her hometown, but after at least two moves with her partner, she ended up enrolling in a college program:

> Again, I did something I told my daughter not to do, and I followed my boyfriend [to a new city], and I decided to take a course here at [city's] college. And basically, what I did was I walked up to [city's] college here, and I said, I want to enrol in nursing. And they said that nursing is full. I said, okay, what about lab technology? And they said, oh, we've got room there. And I said, okay, put me down. That is how I entered my lab technology career [laughs]. I had no aspirations of being a lab technologist or anything like that, it was just because my boyfriend was here.

- Similarly, Sophia, although she finished her education degree at university, nonetheless followed her partner (and eventually husband) many times around the country, thus forgoing work as a teacher but happily stumbling into a fulfilling career as a librarian.

Another key difference observed in educational attainment was the gendered uptake of education in what was then a relatively new educational option: Ontario's community colleges. Five of the women participants, compared to only one of the men we interviewed, received diplomas from a community college, for example, as educational assistants, lab technicians, or dental hygienists.

Although the findings described above suggest that the Class of '73 continued to conform to gender norms, there is also a real sense of departure from traditional gendered expectations. This is evident in the high levels of academic achievement of the women we interviewed and the fact that all, regardless of their education, were engaged in a lifetime of employment and had meaningful careers.

In a further departure from traditional norms of gender and sexuality, three of the male participants identified as gay during the interviews. None of the participants identified as lesbian, transgender, or nonbinary.

- Oliver – who grew up rural and poor but was also a small child for his age and, as he revealed later in the interview, gay (but not out) – remembered high school as a difficult and unpleasant time:

High school, I went to [small town] High School for Grade 9 one year, I absolutely hated it. I lived in the country, I was bullied and picked on and – by the people, like the high school, the people, the town kids. I don't know; for some reason, they hated the country kids. And I absolutely hated it . . . To be honest with you, I mean, if they ever had a reunion, I would never go because I was bullied and picked on and stuff like that . . . I was just smaller than the other kids, one thing. They just picked on me, I just – I don't know, for some reason . . . They would call me, like, I'm going to be honest here, faggot, that kind of stuff there. And they just made life miserable for me.

For Oliver, being gay intersected with class and his rural upbringing in a way that made his high school recollections overwhelmingly negative. Like Henry, discussed earlier, he took refuge in applied courses and developed skills he could use in the workplace: "Back then, of course, they had typing courses, they had business machines back then and thank God, I took them because you know, with the computers nowadays and that I can type, like, sixty-five words a minute."

- In contrast, for Theodore, remaining in the closet and being able to pass as straight was a safe way to get through high school, although he also admitted to experiencing tension and perhaps missed romantic opportunities.

High school was fine, it was fun. I did well without really studying. So, it was easy that way. Socially I'm gay, but being gay in the early seventies in a small town was not something that I knew was going to be acceptable. So, there was a little bit of tension, just in the sense that I had to hide these things and be in the closet. But in general, I was never bullied or anything like that . . . I was completely in the closet. And I don't have the feminine characteristics. So it was easy for me, no problem . . . I mean there was inner conflict. Some of the friends I was hanging with were sexy guys and things. And I knew I couldn't make a move, I couldn't risk it, even though there were a few times where I was pretty sure that they were also interested, I was just way too concerned with that getting out, that information.

Race, Ethnicity, and Immigration

Recent events, such as the discovery of unmarked Indigenous children's graves at former residential school sites in Canada or the police killing of George Floyd (and other Black individuals) in the United States, have led to an increased awareness of the legacies of colonialism and other forms of racial oppression. Schools and education systems are responding by updating curricula and pedagogies and aiming to diversify who teaches and assumes positions of leadership. This is especially pertinent in an immigrant nation such as Canada, which sees itself as one of the most successful examples of multiculturalism.

When the Class of '73 project began, Canada had only recently changed immigration rules, introducing a point system that preferred immigrants with high levels of education from their origin countries. This has led to a significant shift in the source countries for immigration and turned Canada into a vastly more multicultural society (Statistics Canada 2022b). Unfortunately, the successes and challenges of racialized immigrants were not yet considered central to educational and employment debates when the first survey of this project was conducted in 1973.

As longitudinal research builds on its original data collection, the issues of race remained largely outside the focus of the study. The fact that the original sample in 1973 was also racially very homogeneous, consisting mostly of white participants, exacerbated this trend. We were therefore unable to conduct any meaningful analysis using the survey data. Although we also had little racial diversity in the interview sample, several participants grew up in immigrant families, which created interestingly diverse educational experiences. This reflects the increasingly large number of immigrants who entered Canada in the 1960s and 1970s to meet employment demands and who settled in Ontario, leading to greater ethnic and racial diversity in the province.

Hence, it follows that those first-generation Canadian students – that is, children of immigrant parents – would be found in Ontario schools, especially in large urban areas such as the Greater Toronto Area, where their parents had settled. As Figure 4.5 illustrates, nearly 30 per cent of the Class of '73 students had at least one parent who was born elsewhere, mostly in Britain and western and eastern Europe; less than 3 per cent were racialized or non-European students. When members of the Class of '73 were first surveyed, very few of them acknowledged a heritage other than Canadian. In fact, they identified primarily as Canadians – a reflection of how their immigrant background informed their experiences and aspirations.

Despite the recent introduction of Canada's multiculturalism policy, participants with immigrant backgrounds in our sample were more likely to speak about integration as the key goal, especially if they were of European descent.

- Emma explained this as follows:

> I don't think there were a lot of immigrants at that time. Like, my parents were Polish, so my mother used to say – I used to say, "Well, where did I – what's my nationality? What's my background?" She says, "You just tell them you're Canadian. Don't say anything else." That's what we were taught when I was a kid. So, I wasn't allowed to speak about anything else.

Figure 4.5: Birthplace of Participants, and Their Parents, 1973

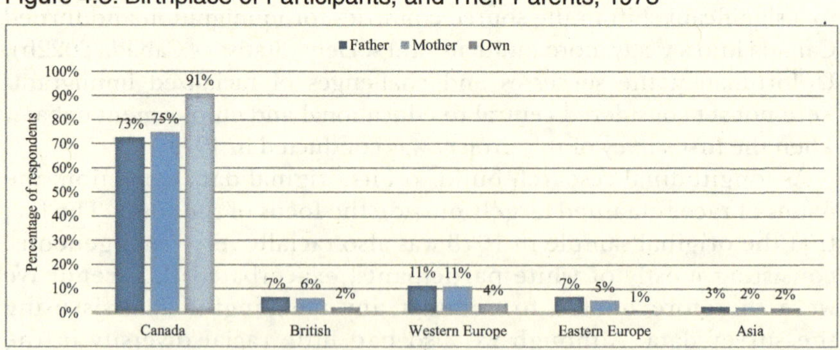

Her school experience is markedly different from those of her children, as she told us later in the interview:

My son grew up in an interracial [community] – in Hamilton, and he had friends over all the time. I was very inclusive to anybody, whatever their background was, into our house. And so, he had that experience. And so, his friends are all mixed races too, which is great.

- Interestingly, Emma's comments about her children's schooling are reminiscent of an interview with Carl that occurred during the early phases of the study. Carl explained in some detail how and why he would distance himself from his immigrant origin, and how he eventually came to accept "having two cultures":

My family is from Portugal. It was a big move . . . it was traumatic. My father came first. I didn't know anyone . . . I was seven or eight years old. I don't want to move again . . . I won't have any discrimination because I'm Portuguese. When I first came, we lived on College Street. All my friends were Italian. I was in a New Canadian class. Everything was different from Portugal, even the math. There weren't any other Portuguese. Once when I was called an immigrant – I hate being called an immigrant – I decided to be English. I spoke only English. I didn't go into soccer, I played football and hockey. Between Grade 4 and 7, I never felt I belonged. From Grade 8 on I felt I belonged. I worked extra hard to belong. I speak English better than I speak Portuguese. Now I'm beginning to appreciate Portuguese. I began to realize what you are doesn't matter. I had wanted to be a Canadian so badly. Now I accept it . . . having two cultures is a plus.

Even as he said, "My parents pushed school; they would say, 'We left Portugal for you,'" Carl told of how he confronted a schooling system in which he faced discrimination, felt alienated, and had to work "extra hard" to feel a sense of belonging, which undoubtedly was an important personal quality or social capital if he were to fulfil his parents' expectations.

Generally, we found that during the earliest phases of the study, students whose immigrant backgrounds were evident because of cultural differences, language, accent, religion, or other identified factors that were used as signals of them having recently immigrated sought to manage their "difference" and the challenge of fitting in by concealing as much about their identity as possible. Some of this was still evident in 2020–1 when we interviewed for Phase 7 of the study.

- Ella was one of the few racialized interview participants in 2020–1. Here she responds to a question about her Japanese Canadian heritage, but also, more specifically, about the Japanese experience during the Second World War, when many Japanese-Canadians were interned:

> My dad almost didn't say anything. We know still very little about what he went through . . . But when the war was over, it was like they had to be as Canadian as possible and not speak any Japanese. So they never taught us anything.

Neither Emma nor Ella, in our Phase 7 interviews, expressed any perceived oppression when talking about their experiences as children in immigrant families. Similarly, for a few interview participants, being an immigrant created motivation to do well at school, especially as a sign of successful integration, but also to validate the sacrifices made by their parents when they left their home countries to make a new life for themselves and their children in Canada.

- Jack, whose parents were immigrants from eastern and central Europe, told us how early poverty and parental hopes combined to make him both a very high-achieving student and a very successful IT entrepreneur in adult life. Many studies have shown that immigrant families have high educational aspirations for their children and that children internalize these expectations (Abada, Hou, and Ram 2009; Krahn and Taylor 2005; Taylor and Krahn 2013), an experience Jack's interview confirmed:

> Well, I think the reason was that my parents were immigrants, and they only had a Grade 4 and Grade 9 education. They always said, "You've got to be somebody." There was no choice because they figured that the only way you could get ahead in life was to have an education.

- In contrast, Henry's schooling experience as an immigrant was one of discrimination and struggle. Immigrating with his parents from a former Eastern Bloc country, Henry had internalized at a young age his parents' mistrust of communism, which he felt put him on a collision course at school:

> In primary school, when I was in Grade 3, because of where we come from, I'm Croatian, and I was raised to think the way my parents thought. And in that community, it was a very tight-knit community, and I learned at a

young age that I didn't like communism, from what I've heard and experienced and seen. So, when I was in Grade 3, I made the mistake of saying that to my teacher because the question was, you know, if you had the ability to change something in the world, what would you change? I made the mistake of saying, "I wish that there would be an end to communism." From that moment on that teacher just had it in for me, you know, whatever opportunity he had, he would belittle me, tell me how stupid I was, in front of the class and that sort of thing . . .

Now, unfortunately for me, I went from Grade 3, I went into Grade 4 and to my surprise I wound up with the same teacher. And he failed me in Grade 4, making me repeat the class again in his class, so that was three years in a row I had this guy. Then he, I went to Grade 5 and again he was my teacher, he did things like beat my head against the blackboard in front of the class, just to break my spirit, I think, you know, it was a very hard time for me.

Henry was eventually transferred to a vocational school, where he found success and more supportive teachers. When talking about the school's student composition, Henry highlighted the intersection of immigrant status and class: "The school consisted of a bunch of immigrant kids and a bunch of Canadian kids that were from, how would I say it, maybe lower class or people with less opportunity."

Although this discussion suggests a homogeneous picture of the Class of '73 and their parents, the comments shared through interviews provide insights into the role that immigrant background and first-generation status played in the schooling, education, plans, and achievements of these students and their parents. Intersectional differences about ethnicity, place of birth and residence, gender, social class, and other identity characteristics notwithstanding, most of these Canadians – both parents and children – believed that through education, they would be able to attain the successes they sought in life. Generally, on this basis, many of these students were strongly encouraged and supported by their parents to pursue education beyond high school. Even as members of the Class of '73 talked about the weight or cost of their immigrant background or mentioned their experiences with xenophobia and discrimination, they were motivated to persevere with their life course choices.

Trajectories of Educational Mobility

A key concern of the Class of '73 project has been to assess the likelihood of social mobility and to understand how our participants' life chances and opportunities were the outcome of individual choices (agency) or social-structural factors outside their control. Education is central to the prospects of mobility. Upward mobility, put simply, means children do better than their parents in terms of education, occupation, or income. Ideally, in a meritocratic society, schools afford all children the same opportunities to be successful and become upwardly mobile. The most talented and hardest-working rise to the top, enter university, and eventually move into high-status, prestigious careers. The emphasis in this meritocratic ideal is on individual agency.

Challenging this meritocratic ideal is a long tradition of sociological research that has identified structural factors that affect school achievement and transitions into postsecondary education (James and Taylor 2023; Lehmann 2016). Social class, and especially its relation to parental education, has remained a stubborn predictor of educational attainment (Chatoor, MacKay, and Hudak 2019; Chetty et al. 2017; Goldthorpe 2003; James and Taylor 2023; Krahn and Barron 2016; Turcotte 2011).

The previous sections have already hinted at the role of class, gender, sexuality, and race in either enabling students or holding them back. In the following sections, we expand this discussion by examining educational mobility for the Class of '73.

The following two figures, drawing on survey data from Phase 7, show the relationships between the survey participants' highest level of education achieved by 2019 and that of their fathers (Figure 4.6) and mothers (Figure 4.7). What both figures show is the strong correlation between

Figure 4.6: Educational Attainment by Father's Education, 2019 (Phase 7)

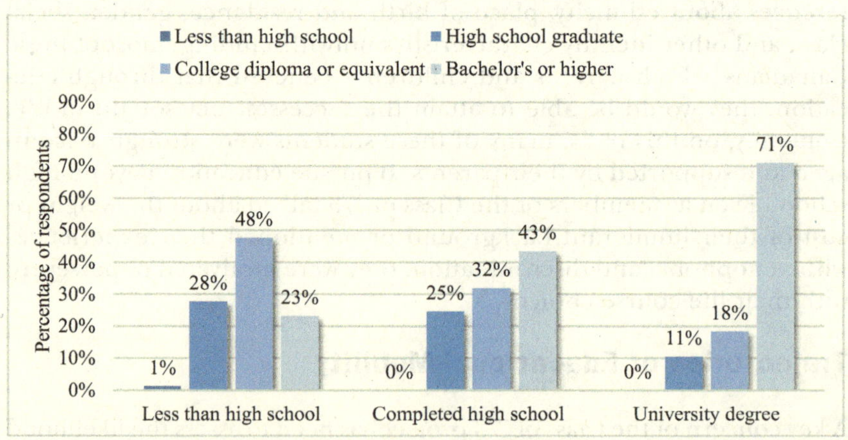

Figure 4.7: Educational Attainment by Mother's Education, 2019 (Phase 7)

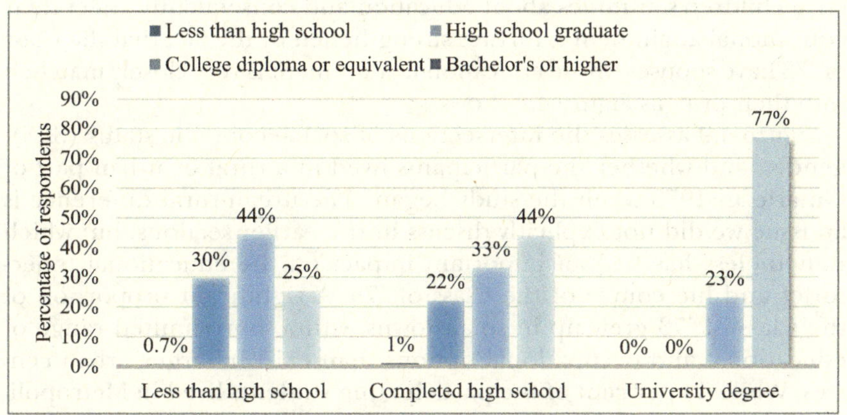

the level of education of participants' parents and their own. The higher the level of education of either fathers or mothers, the higher the attainment of the participants. Having a father or mother with a university degree emerges as a key predictor of participants' university attainment. More concretely, 71 per cent of those participants whose fathers had finished university before them and 77 per cent of those whose mothers had done the same also earned a university degree. Conversely, not continuing to postsecondary education was unlikely for participants with university-educated parents.

Both figures show that downward social mobility is very unlikely in our sample. That is, very few members of the Class of '73 ended up with educational attainment below that of their parents. For those who grew up in families in which parents had low levels of formal education, upward educational mobility, albeit somewhat modest, was the most common trajectory. For instance, those whose fathers or mothers had not completed high school were more likely to achieve a high school or college diploma as their highest level of education (although nearly a quarter of them still obtained a university degree). Those with highly educated parents were most likely to maintain this level of educational advantage.

As we discuss in more detail below, the strong correlation between parental education and the attainment of their children is based on the assumption that parents instil in their children attitudes about the value and importance of education, reflecting what they themselves have achieved (Bourdieu 1990). The tendency of parental education to influence children's attitudes about education and consequently affect their educational attainment is further strengthened by the fact that the Class of '73 have spouses whose educational attainment is very closely matched with their own, as Figure 4.8 shows.

Figure 4.9 assesses the intersections of socio-economic status (SES), gender, and whether the participants lived in a rural or urban part of Ontario in 1973 when the study began. The urban-rural difference is an issue we did not explicitly discuss in the earlier sections, but which nonetheless has had an important impact on the educational trajectories and life course of the Class of '73. A significant proportion of the Class of '73 grew up in small towns with a more limited range of educational and occupational options than exist in larger urban centres. While 43 per cent of the participating students lived in Metropolitan Toronto or other large metropolitan areas, 24 per cent came from small cities, towns, and bordering urban communities, and a further 33 per cent came from other, mainly rural areas (Anisef, Paasche, and Turrittin 1980, A-10).

In most cases, rural areas tended to offer deep family and community ties to the young people raised there. Still, many participants – except for those with familial commitments, and young women in particular – expressed a desire to escape the limitations of their hometowns and travel to urban areas where they might explore opportunities for education, employment, independence, and "more to do" beyond their rural communities. However, participants were aware, as were their parents, that the schooling stream (Advanced, General, and Basic) played

Figure 4.8: Level of Education, Spouses and Participants, 2019 (Phase 7)

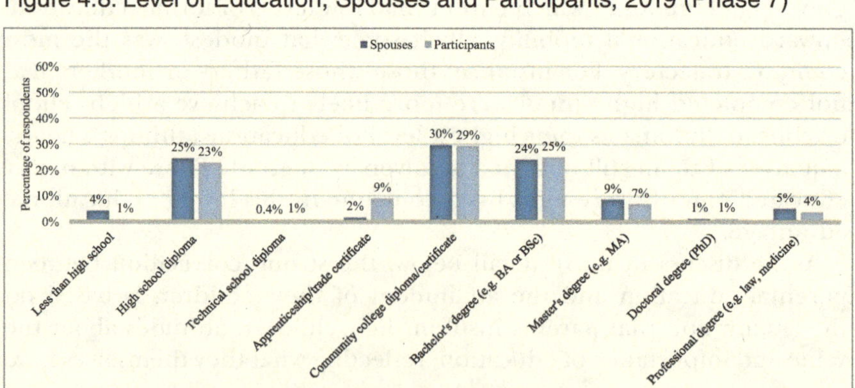

Figure 4.9: Proportion of Group With Bachelor's or Higher by Ses, Gender, and Location, 2019

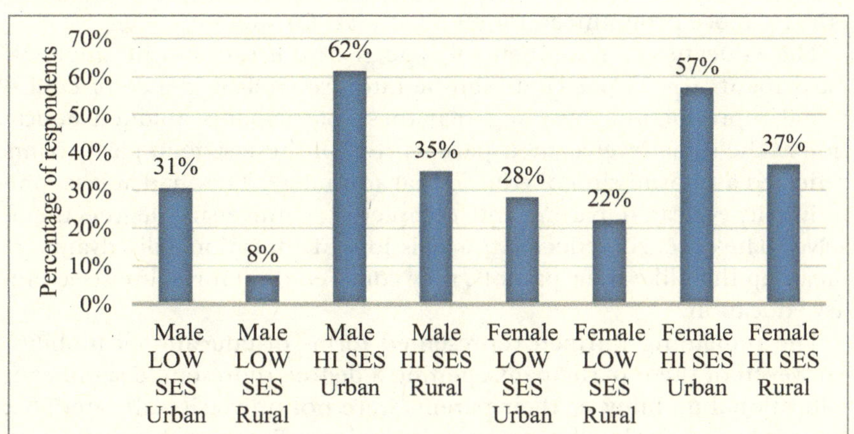

a significant role in the educational and occupational opportunities and where they would ultimately reside after high school. They understood that furthering their education beyond high school typically required moving or long hours of commuting. Findings from interviews in 1973, 1974, and 1980 indicate that gender differences played a role in the program of study and decisions about leaving their communities. Compared to their male counterparts, rural and small-town female students were more likely to graduate from a four-year high school program and remain in their community.

To simplify Figure 4.9, we are constructing SES as a simple dual variable. Those whose family situation in 1973 was considered above average in terms of parental education, occupation, and family income are considered "high SES," and those below are considered "low SES." This generated eight different intersectional identities for women and men who, in 1973, were members of either an above- or below-average SES family and lived either in a rural or urban part of Ontario. Figure 4.9 then looks at the percentage in the intersectional identity group who had, by 2019, completed a bachelor's degree or higher.

This intersectional analysis confirms the findings in Figures 4.6 and 4.7 that SES is a key factor in educational attainment. Those who lived in a high-SES family in 1973 are the most likely to have completed a university education. Moreover, those who lived in a rural region of Ontario in 1973 were far less likely to attain a university degree than those living in urban areas. From an intersectional perspective, Figure 4.9 shows that those who grew up in low-SES families and lived in rural communities were the least likely to complete a university education. However, this effect is more pronounced for men than it is for women.

The educational attainment of sixteen of the twenty-nine interview participants (or 55 per cent) can be interpreted as evidence of educational reproduction, meaning that these participants attained education at the same level as their parents. Ten of these sixteen participants reflected a transmission of educational advantage. They had at least one university-educated parent and completed a university degree themselves. The other six reflected transmissions of educational disadvantage, meaning that, like their parents, they completed no formal postsecondary education.

The remaining thirteen represented forms of educational mobility. For seven of these participants, getting a degree represented significant educational mobility, as their parents were not university-educated. Six participants completed a community college diploma, thus reflecting what may be considered a more modest form of educational mobility. None of the participants experienced downward educational mobility, meaning that none ended up doing worse than their parents in terms of educational attainment.

Reproducing Educational Advantage

Having parents with a degree is such a significant factor in young people's educational attainment, which financial advantages can partially explain. University-educated parents are likely to earn higher incomes and can, therefore, afford the expenses associated with higher education.

- For instance, Olive, who studied economics and commerce, had a university-educated accountant as a father and commented on her parents' influence on her decision to study at university:

  They certainly encouraged it. I'm not sure if they expected it. I have two younger sisters, and my parents basically said, "We'll pay your university tuition; you can pay for your books and spending money." And they said, "It's up to you where you go, but just remember we need to look after your sisters as well."

More importantly, however, growing up in a family in which parents have completed university not only normalizes the idea of higher education but also essentially creates an expectation to attend (Lehmann 2007).

- Theodore, who completed a degree in computing and whose mother was university-educated, explained it as follows: "I think they [parents] expected the three of us, the three children, all to go to university, and we did. My mother, who was born in what, I guess 1926, I think, went to university."

University-educated parents can speak with their children about university as an expected and in fact normal transition following high school (as is evident in Theodore's interview excerpt above). Dinner conversations about going to university, not being presented with any alternatives, and likely being exposed to others with similar backgrounds (either through extended family or family friends and peers from similar backgrounds) will make university appear as an uncontested next step.

- Lucas spoke about the fact that his mother's educational trajectory was held up as an example for him and his siblings to emulate, especially because his father did not follow the same pathway (although he still had a successful career as a bank manager):

Well, my mom had a university degree from McGill, my dad made it very plainly known that when he quit school . . . at age sixteen, that he regretted it. So, mom was the example we were all to follow. And so, we were encouraged all along the way . . . Yeah, the discussion around the supper table was, you know, it was a given.

Parental education appears more important than income when it comes to understanding the formation of dispositions about higher education. As Lucas explained later in the interview, the expectations of attending university were formed even though the family was struggling economically (whereas, as we show below, more affluent parents without postsecondary education were not pushing for university):

There wasn't a lot of money around our home. We had four kids and a German shepherd in a three-bedroom, semidetached, probably . . . 1,400-square-foot home, always a single car up until the seventies. And I know my two sisters, when they went to university, they both required loans, grants, you know, whatever was available, you know, to get to university. So, there weren't expensive vacations, by no means.

- Olive and Sophia (in separate interviews) further explained that the importance of education in their families never really had to be spelled out explicitly, as it was assumed. Olive noted, "Yes, I don't think anything else was ever entertained. It was never spoken about, I don't think, but it was just assumed . . . Because education is very important." Sophia spoke in similar terms:

I don't think – my parents didn't push, but I think I was always considered smart from before I went to grade school. And it was always talked about, going to university and so on. It wasn't that they pushed me, but it was just supposed to be the natural thing that happened with me. So, I never thought I wouldn't . . . I don't ever remember not thinking I was going – wasn't going to university.

Reproducing Educational Disadvantage

Just as having formally educated parents created powerful dispositions for higher education, a working-class background tended to have the opposite effect. Growing up in a family in which neither parent was highly formally educated, higher education was so far outside the lived experiences and social environment of these interviewees' families that attending university or college was never on their radar. Even in situations in which participants' parents had solid lower-middle-class jobs but no formal postsecondary education, there was often no pressure on those participants to consider university.

- Esther (who completed a college program and worked in office administration) explained when asked whether her parents ever encouraged her in that regard:

No. This now really surprises me because my mother was a nurse, and my father had gone to a technical school and was a maintenance technician, but I don't recall being really pushed to go on. I kind of wish now that they had because my daughter went to university, and you know, seeing her experiences, I kind of wish I had done that; but no, they didn't really.

- James (who worked in machining after completing an apprenticeship), for instance, talked about his working-class parents being more concerned with his being safe and employed rather than pursuing higher education:

By the time I started my apprenticeship, my father had passed away. And my mom – you know, she was happy that I was just doing what I was doing and not getting into too much trouble, probably. So, it wasn't really anything that said, "Oh, go do it, or do this or do that." It was all sort of up to me to figure out what I wanted to do, and that's just the way it worked out.

- Willow, who entered work in office administration without any postsecondary education, relayed a nearly identical story:

> No. You know, my parents, my dad, you know, I mean, he probably would have loved for me to do that [go to university], but it wasn't expected. And I think his main focus was that I got a good job, so I think he was happy when I did move to Toronto, and I got the job that I did get.

Moreover, sometimes parents were discussed as having actively encouraged participants to enter careers like theirs rather than considering higher education.

- Robert's father was a machinist who worked in a local factory all his life. Robert, unclear on his post-high school plans, worked there after graduation. This created certain expectations, which he ended up disappointing, although not because he chose to go to university (which he did not):

> Well, there was nobody in our family that ever went to university. My son is the very first to get a university degree. So, I would have liked to have gone to university, but we didn't have anybody in the family to follow . . . Probably the one time I've really seen terrible disappointment in my father is when I told him, "I'm not going to stay in the factory. It's just not where I want to be." And he kind of took it as a little bit of an insult because you know he comes from very humble beginnings, and it served him well – put a roof over our heads, he built a house himself, and so forth and so on. And he felt if it was good enough for him, it should be good enough for me.

For some of our interviewees, aspects of social class intersected with gender-based values: young women were primarily expected to get married and have children rather than a career.

- Hailey, who had no postsecondary education and had recently retired from work as a school custodian, recalled, "I didn't have any encouragement from my father or my mother to go on to a higher education. I think they just expected me to get married and have kids."

It is critical to note here that these findings are not meant to criticize the parents of these interviewees or suggest a form of neglect, but to suggest that the social forces that affect our lives are rooted in dimensions of social class that can be exceptionally powerful in creating dispositions and actual decisions. And for many, these social forces also need to be understood as rooted in a specific era.

- Hannah, who, like her mother, did secretarial work, told us, "My mother worked in an office, and probably her whole life. I kind of followed in her footsteps, as I've been an executive assistant for forty-three years." When the interviewer asked, "Do you recall your mom ever telling you to follow in her footsteps, or would your parents?" she replied, "No, never. Never. I can see that now, but back when I was in high school, there was no influence there, unlike today. So much pressure on children today."

- Rather similarly, Lucy discussed the changing attitudes of her parents over time, reinforcing the notion that the ethos of mobility and life success through higher education was less pervasive when the Class of '73 graduated from high school:

  I will add one more thing. Because when we started, you were asking about my childhood. And my parents didn't finish high school and so there was not a huge emphasis that their kids go to university or college. But I will say that as time went on, my parents were very proud that all seven of their grandchildren went to university or college or both, and they were really believers that times had changed, although they were self-made without education.

Experiencing Mobility

Of the eighteen university-educated interviewees, seven were first-generation students who achieved significant educational mobility by completing a university education, even though their parents often had very low levels of formal education. Just as a social environment can create the conditions for stasis and for dispositions to be reproduced, a social environment can also be a catalyst for change.

- Caroline, who did complete university, explained how her mother's rural upbringing and regrets about her lack of opportunities created conditions and pressures to become upwardly mobile rather than to reproduce her social position:

  On my mom's side, yes. She pushed a lot. She didn't – she grew up in rural Quebec and she felt that I needed a university education to get anywhere, to get a good job. That was her expectation . . . I don't remember feeling any overt pressure, but then again, knowing my mother, you did what my mother said, so . . . My mom just wanted me to have a university degree because she thought that would be the golden ticket, so to speak.

- Similarly, Jack spoke about the fact that his parents' low levels of education and their relative poverty were precisely what created the impetus for mobility:

> Number one was, I would say it was all – most of it was parental influence. It was number one to be somebody, number two, to get out of this – I don't know what the best term for it is, but to get out of this social or this echelon I was in. Like we were in like the lowest. We didn't have a car. We didn't go on vacations. We didn't know anybody. So, it was to get out of that, whatever you want to call that. So it was to be somebody, and I guess that's maybe part of being somebody. And I guess the third thing was I figured I was just as smart and just as good and just as ambitious as all those people I'd see on TV or in the newspaper . . . I don't know if those are three reasons, but my parents were the biggest ones. My mother especially. Like, "Be somebody, don't be like us." That is what they always used to say. Be somebody.

Rather than acting as a force or reproduction, Jack's class position created opportunities for mobility, thus contradicting deterministic models of educational reproduction. This highlights the complicated interplay of structural forces and individual agency that can create and disrupt the reproduction of inequality (Lehmann 2007). In a country like Canada, the structure-agency nexus and the hope for mobility are also intricately tied up with immigration. Jack described his parents as poor immigrants from Ukraine and Austria, for whom coming to Canada meant opportunities for their children, which helps explain their desire for Jack to do better.

- Eric, who had a remarkable journey of both educational and occupational mobility, becoming a dentist, explained this immigrant-mobility connection further:

> My parents are from Germany. Grew up during the war. My dad came to Canada in the early – so maybe '52. Worked north of Thunder Bay at a lumber camp for a bit. I swept streets in Vancouver for a couple of weeks in a mine in Yukon. I applied for a job in Sudbury and got a job there. Went back, proposed to my mother, brought her back, so they – my mother wanted to make sure that there was a future for her kids, so that's why they came to Canada.

The above examples showed evidence of upward social mobility. Downward mobility, however, was absent in the interview data (and rare in the survey data). The Class of '73 graduated from high school at a time when educational opportunities were vastly expanded, in recognition both of Canada's transition to a knowledge economy and of the potential of education to advance social mobility. We, therefore, see their educational trajectories as both confirming and challenging traditional social reproduction patterns, although overall, parental education was still a powerful predictor of both educational experiences and outcomes. These socially reproductive patterns become less pronounced, however, when we look at the educational attainment of the study participants' children.

Multigenerational Mobility: Educational Attainment of Study Participants' Children

Arguably, the conditions for educational mobility have increased since the Class of '73 graduated from high school. In 1973, the community college system in Ontario was only a few years old, and universities were in the early stages of expanding enrolment. In the years since, participation in postsecondary education in Canada has increased to the point that Canada now has the most highly educated population compared to other industrialized nations. Among Canadians aged twenty-five to thirty-four, 63 per cent have a college diploma or university degree, compared to an OECD average of 45 per cent (Zeman and Frenette 2021). We were therefore interested to see whether this was reflected in the educational attainment and potential mobility of the children of the study participants.

In Phase 7 of data collection (2019), the Class of '73 was asked about the educational attainment of their oldest and youngest child (if they had any). Figure 4.10 shows the highest levels of educational achievement for the oldest child of the survey respondents. At 54 per cent, more than half of the participants' oldest children earned a university degree. This includes nearly 20 per cent who completed degrees above the bachelor's level (not shown in Figure 4.10). A further 30 per cent of participants' firstborn children completed college or an equivalent qualification (e.g., an apprenticeship). This means an astonishing 84 per cent of the firstborn children of the Class of '73 survey participants in Phase 7 had completed some form of postsecondary education.

Despite the overall high levels of achievement, we continue to see evidence of the transmission of educational advantage in the attainment of the children of the Class of '73. Recall that earlier, we showed that the educational attainment of the Class of '73 was rather strongly related to that of their parents. More concretely, members of the Class of '73 were significantly more likely to complete university if their fathers or mothers were also university-educated. We still see similar patterns in their children.

Figure 4.10: Children's Educational Attainment by Participant's Education, 2019 (Phase 7)

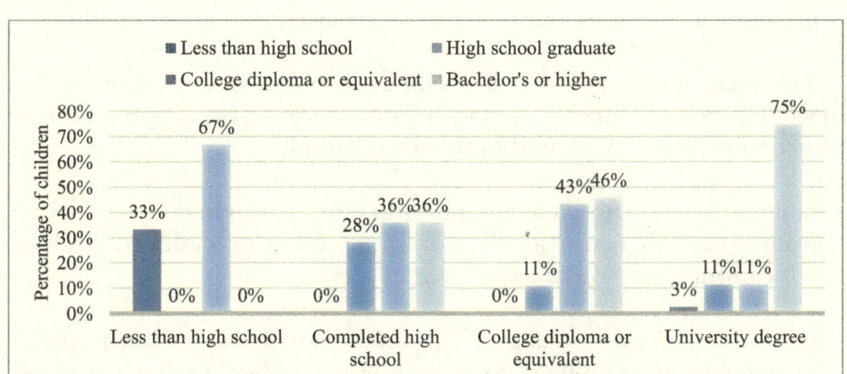

As Figure 4.10 shows, 75 per cent of the oldest children of university-educated members of the Class of '73 also completed university, compared to only 36 per cent of those of the Class of '73 who did not go beyond high school in their own education. These trends are also clear in the group of participants who were interviewed. All interview participants who themselves had a university degree (and who also had children) had at least one child who was at or had completed university. Conversely, families in which none of the children had continued to any form of postsecondary education were those in which study participants also had low levels of formal education. Although one cannot generalize from a small sample, these findings nonetheless lend support to the notion that educational advantages and disadvantages are instead persistently reproduced.

- When asked whether her children's attendance at university was ever in question, Sophia, who embarked on a career as a librarian after finishing university, whose husband was also a university graduate, and whose father, before her also held a university degree, responded as follows,

It [going to university] never was in question. They were all top students. [Son] went into engineering, was an engineer for three years, and decided he didn't like engineering. So now he has a logistics company, and [first daughter] was in theatre and had the best university experience of the three of them because it was fun. And [second daughter], she got a biology degree and knew that that wasn't good enough, so she went back and got an environmental master's, and she works in the same field as my husband. She works for the same company but in a different office.

The relationship between parental and children's education worked in similar ways for interviewees whose educational attainment and experience were at the other end of the distribution.

- James, who did complete an apprenticeship and had recently retired from work with a large automaker, spoke about his children's lack of educational attainment as follows:

I tried when they were young . . . I hoped they would take on a trade, then that would kind of set them up for their lives . . . They just didn't seem to have a – I even tried to talk them into taking electrical which is just basically a handful of screwdrivers and a little bit of math, right? But they didn't like to do math, and they didn't get very good schooling at all.

Although it appears natural that high educational ambitions are passed on in families with highly educated parents, such interpretations betray the complexity of these processes, especially in families in which educational disadvantages were reproduced. Other life events, such as divorce or health problems, often exacerbate these dispositions.

- Henry felt that his divorce from the mother of his children contributed to their lack of educational achievement:

No, they didn't have support . . . Again, for the lack of a better word, they grew up in the ghetto, so my daughter did a lot better than my son because you know, she was a little bit older when my ex-wife and I broke up and maybe I had a little bit more influence on her.

- More tragically still, Willow's oldest son had a serious workplace accident that left him paralysed but also derailed her two younger children:

Unfortunately, the accident happened during the first year of [younger son's] college, and it affected my daughter, who went to high school that first year, and my son, who went to college. So, he kind of bombed out and tried to make another attempt the second year, but he just didn't quite do it, and he hasn't gone back since.

Notwithstanding these examples of educational reproduction, the high percentage of university and college completion is evidence of educational mobility for the children of the Class of '73.

- Although he completed neither university nor college and talked about having never been encouraged by his parents to continue in postsecondary education, Robert had a successful career in the parks and recreation departments in several Ontario cities and towns. Here, he explained how he approached his parenting role differently. His son completed university and an additional college qualification to become a human resources specialist for a manufacturing firm in the automotive sector.
  The interviewer asked him, "You told me earlier that your dad did not push you to go to university. But was that something that you wanted your son to have the opportunity to do? Did you play a role in that?" Robert responded,

  Any parent worth their salt wants to give their children all the opportunities in the world to aspire to whatever they wish to be. And as a parent, I've always felt your job is to introduce them to a wide range of activities, from, you know from piano lessons to gymnastics to Cubs and Girl Guides, or whatever, you know just, you know.

Educational mobility was not always the result of parental encouragement. It was also part of a more pervasive public perception that the children of the Class of '73, unlike their parents, graduated from high school in an era in which career success was no longer possible without postsecondary education.

- Hannah, who did not complete any postsecondary education, worked as a secretary, and had grown up in a family in which her parents were also not highly educated, talked about her daughters' decisions to attend college but also about how college may no longer be sufficient:

  They wanted more, and so they knew that if they wanted to get a job in the oil and gas industry, they needed to have some further education . . . I noticed that most companies want a university degree regardless of what it's in.

Today, postsecondary education has become essential for career and life course success, but the Class of '73 was still part of a generation for whom it may have been possible to move into middle-class careers and lifestyles without extensive higher education. In Chapter 5, we look more closely at their work experiences.

While there are no other longitudinal studies in Canada that track the transitions made by adolescents to their retirement years (mid-sixties), several studies examine the transitions made by high school or university graduates to midlife. Harvey Krahn and his research team in Alberta and Lesley Andres in British Columbia conducted some of these longitudinal studies in western Canada.

Krahn found, similarly to us, that parental education levels had a positive effect on participants' education levels (Krahn 2022). However, the younger generations studied by Krahn and Andres had more educated parents, compared to our participants. For example, Andres et al. (2021) found that 23 per cent of participants had parents with a university degree or greater, and Krahn, Howard, and Galambos (2015) found that 16 percent of participants had at least one parent who completed university, whereas 14 percent of fathers and 6 percent of mothers respectively had a university degree in Phase 1 of our study. In Andres et al.'s (2021) study, 61 percent of participants had obtained a university degree or greater, compared to 39 percent of our Phase 7 participants. This tracks with our study findings that boomers were more likely to obtain higher levels of education than their parents, and by Phase 7, their children were more likely to have obtained a university degree or greater (54 percent) compared to them (36 percent), suggesting an increase in education across generations.

Conclusion

The Class of '73 came of age in a time of significant expansion of educational opportunities in Ontario. University enrolment was expanding, and the newly formed community colleges provided a postsecondary route for those not destined for university. Despite this expansion of opportunities, both survey results and interview data showed that access to educational opportunities remained constrained, especially by factors related to social class. Growing up in families with parents who had high levels of formal education not only positively affected high school experiences but was also shown to make higher education a normal and uncontested pathway. Similarly, those who grew up in working-class families in which parents had low levels of formal education rarely considered higher education as an option.

These relationships, of course, are never fully deterministic. For example, we heard from participants who were children of poor immigrants. Despite their working-class status, being an immigrant was also associated with hopes for opportunity and mobility, which were to be realized through educational attainment. Many members of the Class of '73 were able to move into middle-class career pathways and lifestyles even without high levels of formal education. In the interviews, however, they explained that this was less likely to happen today, which was evident in the high levels of postsecondary attainment of their children.

Overall, the Class of '73 looked back at their education positively. They saw it as valuable for personal development and growth. As the following chapters show, their educational attainment also shaped their working lives, their family relations, and their transitions to retirement in important ways.

5 Working Lives

When we last surveyed and interviewed Class of '73 members – in the mid-1990s – they were in their early forties, well entrenched in their working lives. They had endured significant fluctuations in the economy, including recessions and heightened levels of unemployment in the early 1980s and again in the early 1990s. Given its relative economic strength and diversity, Ontario weathered this turbulence better than other provinces, with an unemployment rate in 1995 of 8.7 per cent, compared to 9.5 per cent for Canada as a whole (Gower 1996). Among Class of '73 members who were working in 1995, 9.8 per cent reported that they had experienced some degree of unemployment between 1978 and 1994, with women twice as likely as men to have been unemployed (Anisef et al. 2000, 104).

Overall, our study participants, particularly those with higher education levels, had progressed in their careers, and the majority (94 per cent) were satisfied or very satisfied with the state of their employment. Individual trajectories, of course, varied significantly. Women continued to "occupy traditionally 'female' occupations, even in light of structural changes in the economy," although their participation in nontraditional occupations had risen from 14 per cent to 20 per cent between 1971 and 1991 (Anisef et al. 2000, 117). Their overall involvement in the labour force was growing and enduring.

Fifty-four per cent of Phase 7 respondents (see Chapter 7 for more details) had retired, and 42 per cent were working full- or part-time (Figure 5.1). Slightly more women than men were working full-time, and almost twice as many women as men were working part-time (Figure 5.2). Men were more likely than women to be self-employed. Of those currently employed, 55 per cent of Phase 7 respondents worked forty or more hours per week. Seventy-six per cent of Phase 7 respondents rated their work or career as being very (48 per cent), or somewhat (28 per cent) important.

Figure 5.1: Work Status

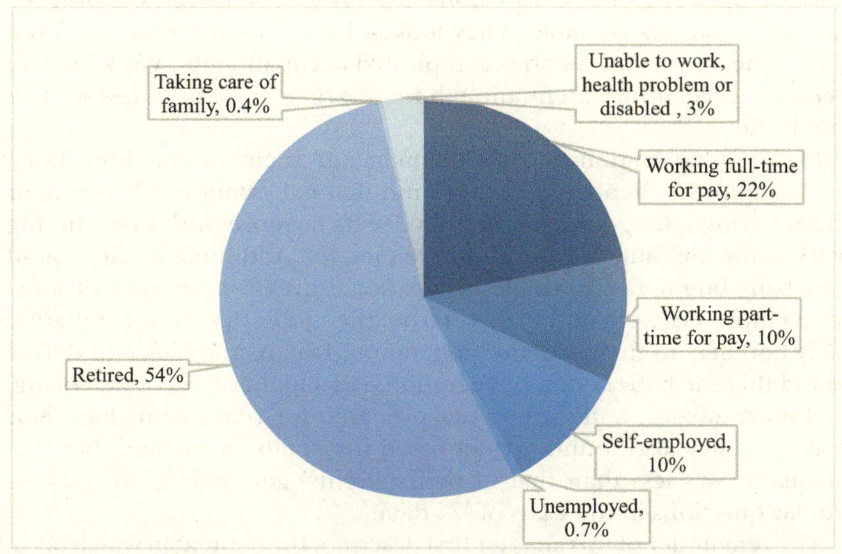

Figure 5.2: Work Status, by Gender

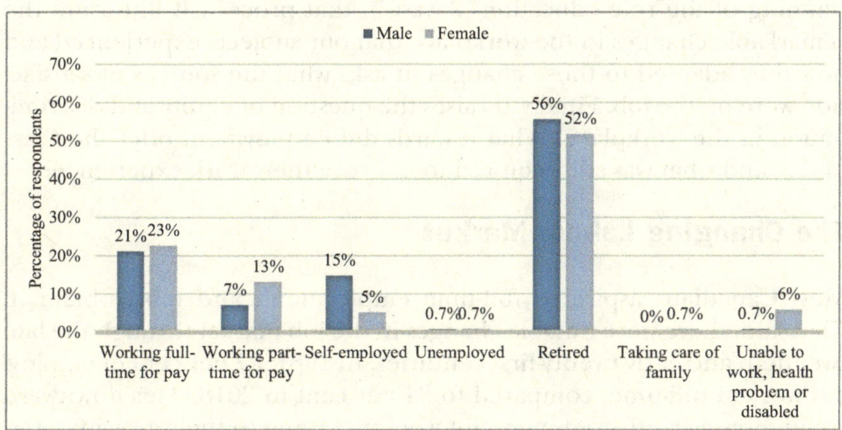

The pace of economic and technological change, if anything, quickened from the 1990s on, as did the volatility of economic life, which featured computerization, robotics, corporate restructuring, a major recession in 2008–9, and a devastating pandemic beginning in early

2020. Notwithstanding these transitions, Class of '73 members journeyed onward, pursuing their occupational interests, or sometimes settling for the best positions available. They looked back with contentment, even with pride, at what they had accomplished occupationally. Work life had been a source of fulfilment, though for a variety of reasons, less so than family life.

In other explorations of baby boomers and their working lives, Bonikowska and Schellenberg (2013) found that baby boomers began their fifties having a long-term job of twelve years or more, with many having worked for the same organization even longer. Additionally, they found that baby boomers had stable occupational lives: 50 per cent of long-term employees were never laid off from their jobs. In a study comparing baby boomers to their parents' generation, Légaré and Cossette (2012) found that the baby boomer generation had a higher level of well-being, had more wealth, and were better prepared for retirement than their parents. They also found gender-based inequality in income, but that inequality was less than that of their parents' generation. We explore similar questions in the Class of '73 data.

The remainder of this chapter first describes the context in which occupational life was conducted in the three decades following 1990. It then traces the pathways that Class of '73 members travelled to reach their ultimate employment destinations and explores our subjects' understanding of the role education played in that process. It illustrates the remarkable changes in the workplace that our subjects experienced and how they adapted to those changes. It asks what the sources of satisfaction were on the job. Finally, it raises the question of equity and discrimination in the workplace. What rewards did employment offer the Class of '73, and what was still required to improve their work experience?

The Changing Labour Market

Most Canadians aspire to full-time employment, and most obtain it. That said, there were notable changes in the job market through the late twentieth and early twenty-first centuries. In 1981, 87 per cent of employees worked full-time, compared to 84 per cent in 2018. This downward trend, however, affected men, not women. Owing to their growing presence in the labour force, women aged twenty-five to fifty-four increased their participation in full-time employment over this period (Morissette 2018, 1).

While women have occupied half the labour force since 1995 – an extraordinary change from earlier decades – the labour market in the early 2000s remained largely segmented by gender. Between 1991 and

2016, women dominated the fields of education, health care, and administration, while men mostly filled occupations in repair, construction, and transportation. Some positions – retail, finance, and accommodation services – showed little variability by gender, and the differences in some fields diminished over time. For example, the gender gap has eroded, though hardly disappeared, in the STEM areas (science, technology, engineering, and mathematics), buoyed by policy initiatives in the public and private sectors designed to achieve greater employment equity (Quinn et al. 2021).

The decline in manufacturing employment over the past several decades represents a significant structural shift in the economy, particularly in Ontario. In 2000, manufacturing jobs accounted for 18 per cent of the province's labour force; in 2019, only 11 per cent. Wage competition from countries with lower labour costs, the introduction of robotics, and the rise of the Canadian dollar all contributed to this shift. The growing service sector (e.g., construction, health care, finance, education, food services, information, recreation, professional and technical services), where many Class of '73 members earned their living, featured prominently in the changing employment landscape. Service-sector jobs accounted for 73 per cent of the Ontario workforce in 2000 and 79 per cent in 2019 (Hirshhorn and Hirshhorn 2015; Moffatt, Couthino, and McNally 2021; Tiessen 2014).

Computerization now affects every facet of the economy, as does "knowledge intensity." Jobs demanding "cognitive analytical tasks" increased, while those requiring "non-routine cognitive analytical tasks" diminished (Frank, Zhe, and Frenette 2021, 1). One survey found that by the end of the 1990s, corporations had undergone major restructuring. They had invested heavily in new technology, and business processes now included "electronic messaging, data accumulation on customers' spending patterns, the centralization of vast amounts of information, supply chain management, and automated manufacturing plants" (Kwan 2000, 17). Corporate competition had intensified, workforces were being reduced, and mergers were increasingly common.

New jobs emerged because of technological change, though not all were secure or full-time. The "gig economy," consisting of independent workers such as digital marketers, Uber drivers, and freelance writers, constituted a growing segment of the Canadian labour force, rising from 5.5 per cent in 2005 to 8.2 per cent in 2016, though the age group occupying these positions was typically younger than the Class of '73 (Jeon, Huju, and Ostrovsky 2019, 1). Workers with high levels of education were more likely to have "high-quality" jobs than those with a high school diploma or less, who tended to lack training and to have jobs with less autonomy and inflexible work schedules (Morissette 2018). Indeed, one study contends that young workers without postsecondary education were still negatively affected by the economic recession of 2008–9 a decade later (Moffatt 2021).

Over the years, culturally dominant groups continued to have better labour market outcomes than new immigrants and racialized workers (Tiessen 2014, 22–3). Regional variations also affected job opportunities in Ontario. Windsor-Sarnia, Stratford-Bruce, and northwestern Ontario saw shrinkage of available jobs between 2000 and 2013, while Kitchener-Waterloo, Barrie, Ottawa, and Toronto experienced significant growth in the labour market (Tiessen 2014, 23).

Veteran workers, including those in the Class of '73, were affected by all these changes in the labour market. However, the impact on them was likely less dramatic than the impact on workers from younger generations, who were attempting to establish careers in a continuously transforming and sometimes quite disrupted employment environment. Veteran workers had more experience, higher positions, some additional training, and greater housing security as they navigated life between the 1990s and 2020. How did they manage this voyage?

Pathways to Employment

Upon completing their formal education, our interviewees found their vocations and careers through a variety of routes. As Figure 5.3 shows, most of them were ultimately employed in the private (44 per cent) and public (37 per cent) sectors, while a minority were self-employed (15 per cent) or in farming (2 per cent). The percentage of Class of '73

Figure 5.3: Sector of Current or Most Recent Job

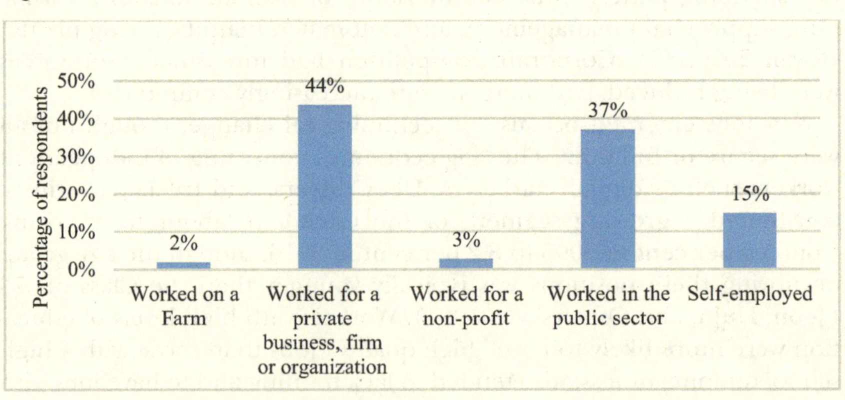

respondents working in the public sector was significantly higher than for Canada as a whole. According to Di Matteo (2015), 26.1 per cent of the workforce was employed in the public sector in 1992 and 24.1 per cent in 2013.

- Upon completing high school, James "bummed around." He thought about attending university, but "I didn't want to put my parents through the expense." He worked in a variety of factory positions before enrolling in a community college, where he completed a tool-and-die trade course. After several jobs with local employers, he spent twenty-seven years at General Motors.
- Henry attended a vocational high school where he concentrated on upholstery and automotive work. He began working in a factory that built "road sweepers, stomp grinders, and brush chippers" – a "decent" job that paid $3.85 an hour, a "good rate in 1973." The company required layoffs three years later, and he voluntarily left so that an older worker could keep his job. His next position, with a company that bought road sweepers, he described as exceedingly "boring." Following several other jobs, which included periods of unemployment, Henry joined a friend who was starting a landscaping business, and he worked successfully in that occupation for nineteen years.

Practical considerations – the rate of pay or the availability of work in their desired fields – shaped the pathways of some of our subjects.

- Esther obtained an early childhood education diploma and worked for a time in a nursery school. But the salary was so low that she couldn't afford to remain, so she undertook office work, which she continued until she retired.
- Charlotte graduated from a university program in theatre arts, but throughout her career she found only part-time and contract work in this field. Over the years, she was employed in a fruit store, as a government clerk, and as a sous chef. Nevertheless, she remained committed to the arts and seized whatever opportunities arose to act and sing. She also taught part-time for nine years at a drama school. She always struggled financially but found ways to practise her trade.

We asked survey participants whether employment required more education than in the past, and whether education improved their skills or was useful in a variety of different areas (Figure 5.4). A large majority

Figure 5.4: Education and Employment

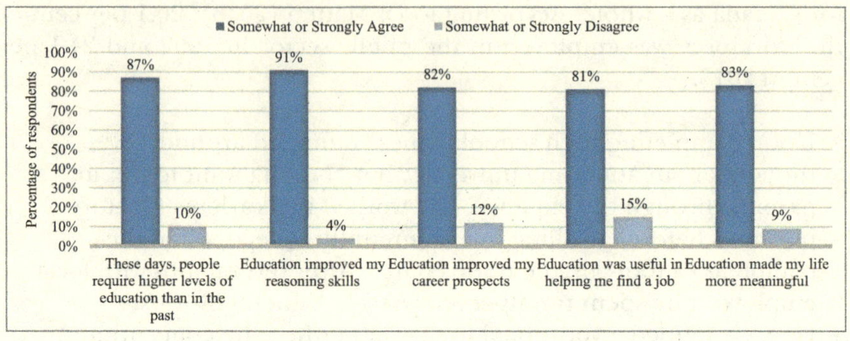

agreed that this was the case, with respect to reasoning skills, career prospects, finding a job, and making life more meaningful. A smaller majority believed that people who worked hard were entitled to a good job, that it was important that jobs be related to one's field of study, and that everyone had the right to the kind of job for which education and training had prepared them (Figure 5.5). There were no significant response differences between men and women with respect to these different areas.

Our subjects appeared to appreciate the broad value of their education, though they were slightly less certain of its instrumentalist function – that is, preparing graduates directly for their ultimate vocations. As we've

Figure 5.5: Education and Employment

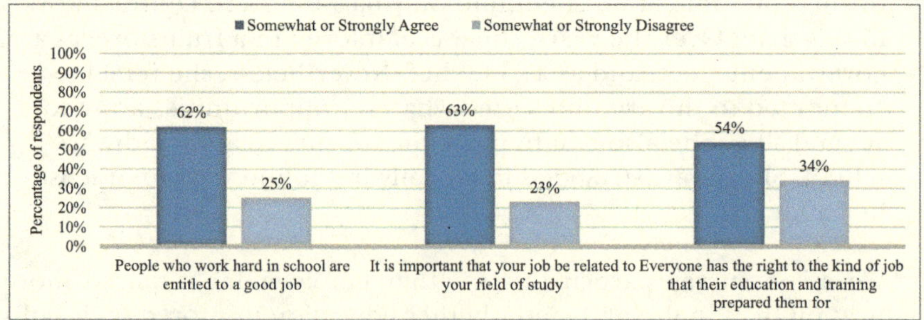

seen, occupational pathways evolve, new interests and priorities emerge, the labour market fluctuates, and individual directions may well diverge. Education was considered essential, though not deterministic, on the road to employment.

The Changing Workplace

As we noted earlier, our subjects entered the working world as it sat on the brink of extraordinary change. Surely, the growing use of technology and the arrival of the digital era played key roles in reshaping the workplace. From the 1980s on, computerization, the rise of the internet, and the growth of "knowledge-intensive and service-oriented sectors" required both employers and employees to adapt to the changing occupational landscape (Pew Research Center 2016, 20). Our interviewees provided instructive examples of the impact these changes had on their working lives, from the front office to the factory floor.

- Eric, a dentist in a midsized Ontario city, witnessed a trend in the delivery of dental services from independent owner-practitioners to the rise of large dental conglomerates, in which the dentist, increasingly, had become an employee (Canadian Dental Association 2022). Corporatization generally brought greater resources to the dental office than individual dentists might have managed, though Eric disliked the model and after working for several years in this structure, he returned to a private practice where he had greater control over his working environment.
  Technological innovations in dentistry have also been extensive. Digitization affected X-raying, record collection, and office management. The use of lasers for treating cavities also spread, though Eric believed it to be oversold. Notwithstanding such changes, which required skill updating for all office staff, Eric contended that the core of dental practice remained "drill, fill, extract."
- Lucy, a dental hygienist, described one of the biggest changes in her work: the introduction of sterilization, gloves, and masking in the wake of the HIV-AIDS epidemic in the 1980s. She also worked in the new corporatized dental environment, in which hygienists were essentially on contract, without benefits, and expected to work quickly to treat as many patients as possible. Such pressures nudged her to retire sooner than she had otherwise planned.

- Marco, a chartered accountant, described the changing standards in his profession – updated about every three to five years – and the new tools designed to increase efficiency and productivity. The introduction of Excel spreadsheets, which eliminated the need to calculate figures manually, proved a key component of the learning curve (Pepe 2011). Marco always enjoyed the personal connections with his clients, but keeping up with the ever-changing demands was a challenge: "I may be showing my age, but I'm getting a little tired of it."
- Violet, also an accountant, played a leading role in her very large firm as an e-learning manager. She oversaw the implementation of educational technology in the tax learning and development area. Near the end of her career, she directed the disbursement and integration of these strategies throughout the company. She found the work rewarding, and she used her prominent position in the organization to mentor other female professionals.
- As a public health lab technologist for the provincial government working in a northern Ontario city, Hazel described the transition from processing patient specimens on site, which she found varied and stimulating, to a new centralized lab system where much of the work was done in Toronto though electronic transfer: "When I got closer to retirement, I was glad to leave because there wasn't much point in having every lab do the same thing when they could centralize certain things. So, we lost a lot of work."
- Over forty years, in her role as a secretary and then an executive assistant, Hannah experienced the profound impact of technological change. She recalls fondly working with an Underwood typewriter ("You could feel each key under your fingers"), which she preferred to the next generation's IBM Selectric typewriter, followed by desktop word processing. How did she acquire these new skills? "On the job," she responded – sometimes aided by short presentations from product salespeople, sometimes on short courses, where she learned how to prepare Excel spreadsheets and PowerPoint presentations and use Microsoft Word.
- Noah described the profound changes that he experienced in the newspaper world. Word processing, of course, replaced typewriters, and digital production replaced the "hot metal press." The "composing room," where traditionally the paper was manually laid out, became defunct, superseded by computer software. Editors (Noah's role) were increasingly involved in that stage of production, adding to their workload.

- Labour-saving technology was one component of change, and economic pressures were another. In recent years, advertising revenue, long the lion's share of newspaper income, has flowed to online platforms such as Google and Facebook, and newspapers have shrunk, laid off staff, or shut down entirely (Chiu 2020). By 2014, when Noah retired, the editorial department had diminished, and "it got difficult to do a good job. I just got tired of it."

- A stationary engineer responsible for the maintenance of refrigerators and related equipment in a food plant, Alexander lived through many organizational and technological transitions over the thirty-five-year period in which he worked for the company. Initially, the plant employed about one hundred workers, with the employer treating them like "family." The company expanded significantly, was bought and sold several times, and faced some difficult financial challenges, arising in part from some questionable business practices. Alexander, who was always represented by a union, adapted to these corporate changes and to the introduction of modern technology. He was proud of the work he had done but was happiest in his early years on the job.

- Lucas noted the profound changes in human resource management since taking on his role as the manager of a large recreational facility. Initially, HR work was "fairly transactional – get [employees] started, get them paid, offer some training on how to supervise, how to manage, work with senior people when a person is underperforming, and coach them through that." That changed to a more "sophisticated mentality, not just in HR, but in the general manager's mind, the chief financial officer's mind, the chief operating officer's mind." They were increasingly required to "understand the culture of the organization, the importance of employee engagement, the importance of having the organization thinking and behaving in consistent ways so that the customer, the ultimate decider on the success of the organization, feels well cared for by that organization."

Continuing Education

As demonstrated by the responses above, workplaces typically require skill adaptation or upgrading to keep pace with new technology and system changes. A 2003 study by Statistics Canada found that one-third of adults in the labour market were engaged in continuing education and training. Two groups – the youngest workers and the most highly educated – partook most frequently in continuing education, whether formal or informal (Peters 2004). Like Hannah, cited above, many employees learned on the job through informal instruction or short "just-in-time" training.

Certain professions had more elaborate upgrading demands, requiring practitioners to complete additional programs and report on their advanced qualifications.

- Olivia worked as an accountant for many years. Still, she had yet to obtain what is now called her Chartered Professional Accountant (CPA) designation, which she knew would open more job opportunities. She returned to school at forty and attended classes part-time for several years until she completed the program. CPAs were required to continue their professional development (PD) by "attending seminars or conferences, or dinner meetings, that kind of thing. They give us a lot of opportunities to get the PD, but they expect that you do it." Dentists, too, must upgrade continuously, which suited Eric: "This is where the nerd thing comes in. I'm always looking for something to make me better . . . This is new; let me try it. Let's see where it goes. I need that."
- After graduating, Lucas worked at a bank but knew that he wanted to advance professionally, possibly in the personnel field. He took night courses offered at the local university and achieved a human resources certification, which he upgraded further through an executive program at a major university business school. He found this training valuable in his position as human resource manager: "I was not doing it for any academic credentials, but rather for advanced training in Human Resources. Along the way I've taken some pretty comprehensive HR training."
- Jack rose from a poor working-class family to a career as a very successful financial analyst, investor, and entrepreneur. Inspired by several high school teachers "who made me feel that I mattered" and who saw his academic potential, he obtained a university degree in civil engineering. He thought, however, that he would like to be a lawyer, so he then completed a law degree. He "hated" his articling position but had enjoyed his summer job working as a supervising engineer on a major construction project. He left law, moved back with his parents, and started a company designing software.
  On the recommendation of his brother, who was already working in the field, Jack acquired a Chartered Financial Analyst degree, which he completed by correspondence over three years. This helped qualify him for work as a technology analyst. He was hired by a company owned by a man who "started the first software company

for Apple computer products in the world." From there, Jack opened a computer products distributor firm, which thrived, and by 1989, "we were doing $20 million in sales, and I sold it to a public company in the US. So that worked out quite well." He travelled for eighteen months, after which, along with a business partner, he worked as a venture capitalist, raising some 40 million dollars over two years, which was invested in about twenty companies. After additional work on Bay Street, Jack retired in 2002 at age forty-seven. He spent his time renovating his house, doing small investments, engaging in volunteer work, travelling, and caring for his parents. Since 2015, he has been involved with a company attempting to market an innovative tennis ball practice machine.

Sources of Work Satisfaction

We asked study participants the following: "Thinking back to when you were in high school and the kinds of hopes you had then, how satisfied are you with the way things have turned out for you now [with respect to your work or career]?" (Figure 5.6).

Fifty-five per cent of our subjects said they were "very satisfied" with how their work or career had turned out for them, significantly lower than the satisfaction they reported deriving from their family lives (see Chapter 6).

Regarding pay, more women (46 per cent) than men (24 per cent) believed that their pay, relative to education, training, and experience – was less than what they deserved; 72 per cent of men felt their pay was about the right amount, compared to 51 per cent of women (Figure 5.7).

Figure 5.6: Satisfaction with Work or Career

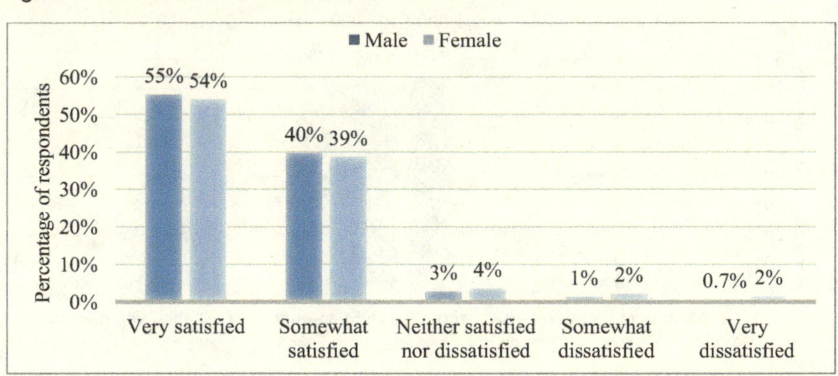

Figure 5.7: Pay, Relative to Education, Training, and Experience

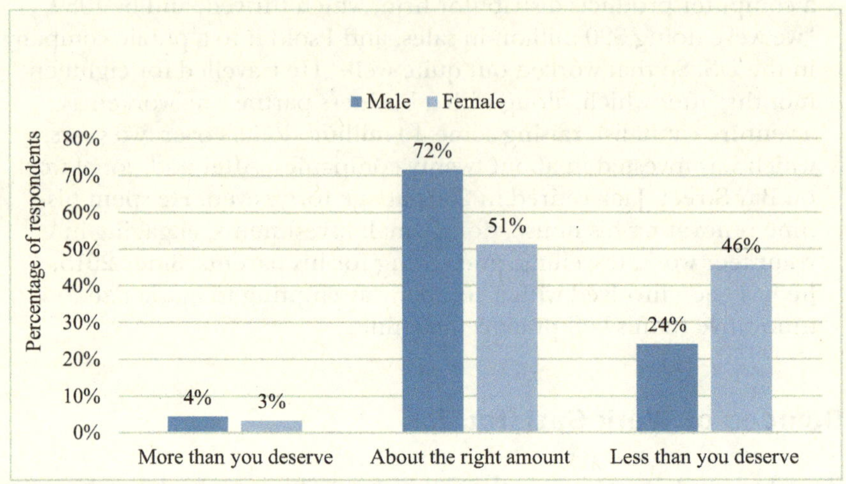

Our survey provided further insight into our subjects' workplace satisfaction by gender and yearly personal incomes (Figures 5.8 and 5.9). Most males at all income levels (more than 70 per cent) believed that their income relative to their education, training, and experience was about the right amount, though a higher percentage of those earning under $50,000 felt underpaid. For women, the patterns were different. At all income levels, and particularly if they earned under $100,000, they felt, far more than men, that they were paid less than they deserved.

Figure 5.8: Pay, Relative to Education, Training, and Experience by Yearly Income, Male

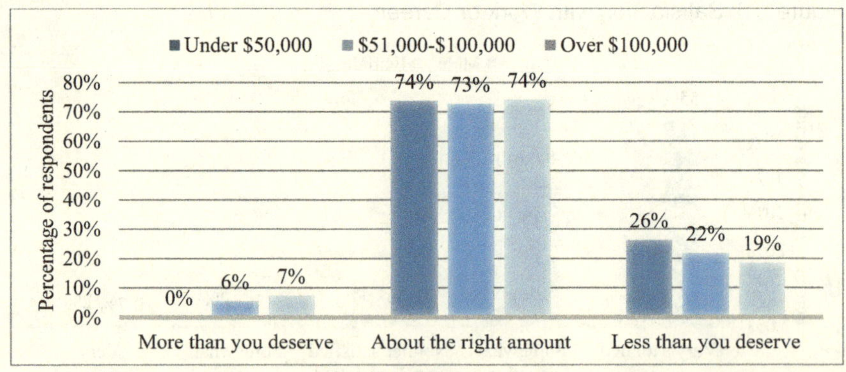

Figure 5.9: Pay, Relative to Education, Training, and Experience by Yearly Income, Female

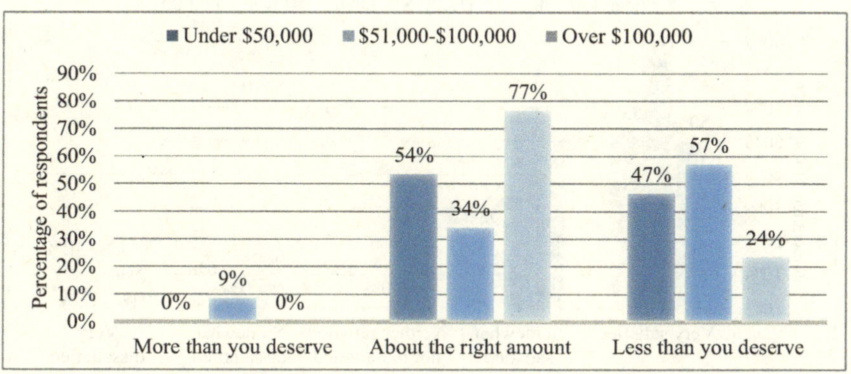

When asked about their satisfaction with their work by yearly income, the patterns were also somewhat different. More than 85 per cent of men earning more than $100,000 were very satisfied, compared to approximately 53 per cent of women. By contrast, 75 per cent of women earning between $51,000 and $100,000 were very satisfied with their work, compared to 56 per cent of men (Figures 5.10 and 5.11).

Figure 5.10: Satisfaction with Work or Career by Yearly Income, Male

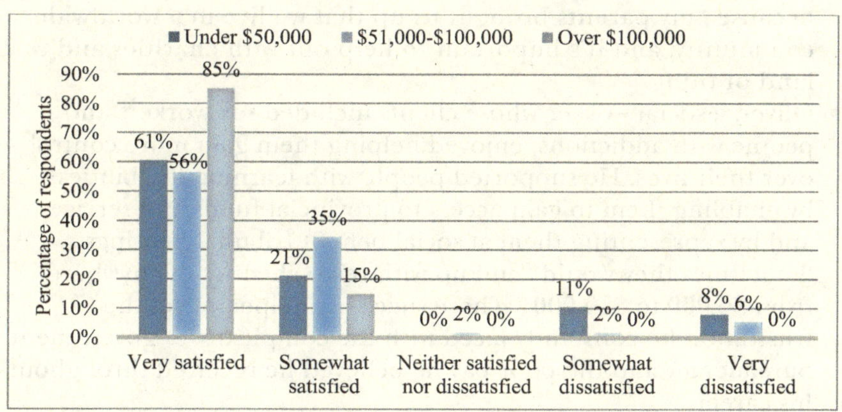

Figure 5.11: Satisfaction with Work or Career by Yearly Income, Female

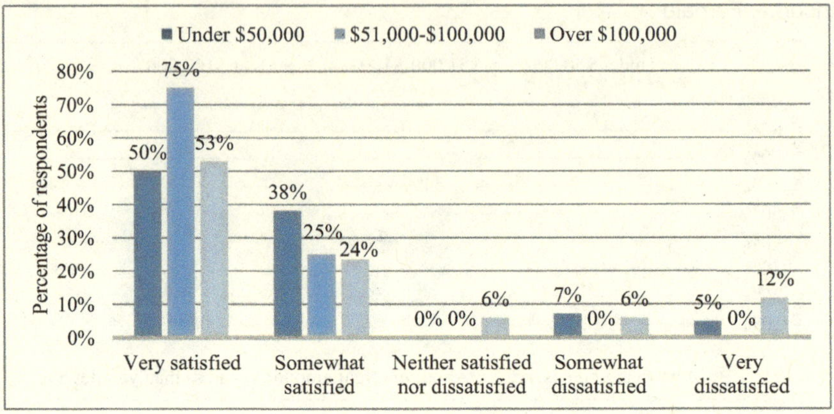

Not surprisingly, responses about sources of work satisfaction in the interviews covered a range of reactions. Several individuals who held occupations with a social mission found their work rewarding and meaningful.

- Olivia worked with a non-profit organization: "I certainly liked the not-for-profit world. I liked the fact that most organizations would have a mission statement; they would have a sort of purpose instead of just money-making. There'd be some idea of trying to better the world." She developed this sense of values because "my parents brought us up that we live in a worldwide community, and it's important to help out with charities and that kind of thing."

- Oliver, a social worker whose clients included sex workers and people with addictions, enjoyed helping them gain more control over their lives. He supported people with learning disabilities by enabling them to gain access to provincial funds and services and by representing them at social benefit tribunal hearings. Sometimes they would "end up with retro cheques of anywhere from $6,000 to $10,000." These successes helped offset the frustration he constantly faced with the complexity of government bureaucracy and the poor pay he believed he received throughout his career.

Opportunities to interact with the public were especially gratifying, both for the social connections they generated and for the special skills that our interviewees offered.

- Evelyn worked part-time in a small-town grocery store, which she enjoyed and planned to continue for as long as possible: "It gives me something to do, and it gets me out of the house. I get to see people."
- Sophia, a librarian, far preferred being "out on the floor" to the "management-administrative tasks" that her job required. When she worked with 180 primary school students, "it was fantastic . . . And making friends at my workplaces, who are still my good friends, was just a wonderful experience. It was very collaborative and just great."

Some jobs that otherwise offered no real prospects for advancement turned out to have some unanticipated perks associated with them.

- Ella worked for many years as a clerk with police animal services, where she spent time with dogs – her "favourite thing" – and got to ride horses in the training area. She felt appreciated over the three decades that she was employed with the police.

Overly routinized and monotonous jobs induced restlessness and the search for new employment opportunities, though the need to earn a paycheque limited some employees' mobility.

- At one point, James, a skilled tradesman, found his work "kind of boring – just doing the same old thing every day. Your group leader would come and give you a sheet of paper, and you do your eight to maybe ten or twelve hours and get it over with and that was kind of it – get out the door. When I was first there, I put a lot of time in, like I was doing a lot of Saturdays and Sundays – pay off the house, get some money, and try to [build] a good security base. It ended up costing me a divorce, [since] I didn't really put enough time into the family."

Not all people valued the social component of work. Some preferred working independently, possibly as entrepreneurs. Where they managed to earn large salaries, or a great return on their investments – as in Jack's case above – their labour was certainly rewarding.

- As an accountant, Marco worked on his own at an office close to home with a very small staff for more than three decades. He avoided rush hour traffic and had flexibility with his schedule: "It's been a fulfilling career."
- Esther, employed by an insurance company, had a fair degree of independence, and appreciated not having someone constantly "looking over my shoulder."

Those engaged in the creative arts relished the opportunity to practise their craft, though as Charlotte (the actor and singer) noted earlier, steady employment in these fields could be hard to sustain.

- Olive, also an actor, similarly worked in a variety of non-theatre jobs and eventually completed a Master of Fine Arts degree. This qualified her for a university position – teaching drama – and she secured a tenured position at a Western Canadian university. She loved the work, which she was able to combine with some "acting gigs" of her own. The teaching program was small, and as the years passed, it faced significant budgetary pressures, particularly considering the decline of the film industry in her province. Olive believed the university was trying to "strangle the department" by failing to replace retiring faculty, a perception that contributed to her own decision to retire.

Class of '73 members brought an array of personalities, ambitions, and educational attainments to their workplaces. As they looked back on their vocations and careers, they identified several elements that contributed to their job satisfaction, no matter their occupations: adequate remuneration, prospects for advancement, the opportunity to serve the public, meaningful social connections, and creative outlets for their interests and skills. In an unsettling era of rapid social and technological change, where opportunities and uncertainties still abounded, work remained profoundly important.

We have noted the much greater participation of women in the workforce compared to previous generations. This pattern was reflected in our questions on the impact of spousal employment in the Phase 7 survey when our subjects were in their early sixties. The employment rates of male (42 per cent) and female spouses (41 per cent) were almost the same. Male spouses were more likely than female spouses to be working more than thirty-one hours per week (80 per cent vs. 56 per cent). Female spouses (27 per cent) were less likely to be self-employed than males (41 per cent), and more likely to work for a private business (44 per cent vs. 39 per cent) or a non-profit organization (8 per cent vs. 0 per cent) than males. Both were equally likely be employed in the public sector (16 per cent male vs. 17 per cent female). Thus, while both spouses followed similar pathways from work to retirement, for those who remained employed, gender distinctions for the type of work they did had not disappeared.

Discrimination and Equity

The Class of '73 came of age in a time when gender inequity, human rights, the treatment of racialized individuals, and the challenges of people with disabilities all drew growing public attention and legislative action. The Charter of Rights and Freedoms, adopted in 1982, embedded antidiscrimination principles in the Canadian constitution and, along with provincial human rights legislation, enhanced legal protections for historically marginalized populations from inequitable treatment in public institutions and the workplace. Religious and racialized Canadians, Indigenous peoples, 2SLGBTQIA+, and people with disabilities now had recourse to unprecedented instruments intended to extend their rights in the pursuit of social justice and equality (Clément 2016; Foot, Yarhi, and McIntosh 2020; Ontario Human Rights Commission 2001).

Legal rights were one thing. Genuine social change in everyday lives, however, was another. To what degree did Class of '73 members experience or witness discriminatory treatment? How did they understand the concept of diversity in their own lives and in the changing Canadian landscape?

Reflecting broader social patterns, all the women we interviewed had ongoing vocations and careers. While many took time off work to be at home with infant children, and while some subsequently worked part-time, they were, overall, a permanent part of the labour force. In some fields, participants experienced relatively full equality of treatment.

- Olivia found that the field of accountancy was no longer male-dominated, including in the top managerial positions. She belonged to a financial executives' group in which half the members were men and half were women. She understood that discrimination could happen, sometimes quietly and sometimes not, "but I was brought up with the golden rule. You treat people the way you want to be treated, and none of us are perfect, but we try to do our best to get along."

- Hailey's experience as a custodian in a rural school was not so positive. Women were being hired in greater numbers as school custodians, but their male fellow workers were not always respectful. In the lunchroom, she would hear comments like, "Did you see the boobs on that girl?" And she lamented, "I got treated worse by teachers . . . I sometimes felt like the dirt on their shoes." A teacher mocked her in front of students for not washing the walls (an "untrue" accusation); when Hailey confronted her, she claimed she was simply making a joke. Another teacher, who began to clean up a child's vomit, was told to stop and let the "janitor" do it.
- Executives like Lucas were responsible for ensuring the implementation of equal pay legislation in an environment where traditional attitudes sometimes prevailed. A night manager was planning to pay an eighteen-year-old female less than a man for the same work because the man was a "breadwinner." Lucas explained, "I had to fight and educate and not just use the law" to confront such "discriminatory" attitudes.

In what ways did Class of '73 members experience or confront racial discrimination?

- Of Japanese heritage, Ella recalled being shunned as a child by two "blond-haired, blue-eyed" girls because their mother thought she was not "good enough" for them. As a teenager, she and her mother were harassed by a group at a shopping mall and told to go back to where they came from. More recently, at the community centre in her neighbourhood, which houses a racially and culturally diverse population, she has been told that she speaks English very well. Her response: "It's the only language I speak." Notwithstanding such episodes, she did have a satisfying career working as an administrator, and, before the outbreak of the COVID pandemic, she had become active in a Japanese community cultural centre.

Most of our interviewees were white and had been exposed to increasing diversity in the population.

- Like others, Violet worked alongside people of colour and believed, overall, that her colleagues were treated fairly. Still, she recognized the possibility of her own "racial bias," notwithstanding her "best intentions." For example, she found the Asian women she worked with in an accountancy firm to be "withdrawn and shy," which might have diminished their prospects for promotion to senior positions, though in more recent years she believed this was changing. In making this observation, she wasn't certain if she was indulging in racial stereotyping.

- Henry worked as a tradesman in an industry that was populated first by significant numbers of European immigrants and then increasingly by workers from South Asia, Africa, and the Caribbean. While people largely got along, there were periodic tensions between these cultural groups on racial grounds, arising from a sense among the Europeans that newcomers threatened their dominance of the trade. As a first-generation immigrant from Croatia with a surname some found difficult to pronounce or spell, as a sign of respect, Henry always made a point of learning how to say people's names correctly.

- Caroline moved to a part of the Greater Toronto Area which by the turn of the twenty-first century had become an extraordinarily diverse community consisting in large measure of Asian, Iranian, Russian, and white European residents. She had the impression that while people intermingled in community centres, grocery stores, and the workplace, their social interaction was minimal – they lived in "cultural silos." She worked in human resources, responsible eventually for "diversity planning" in a communications company. She conducted surveys documenting the cultural makeup of the workforce, which would help inform hiring practices: "The feeling I got from the company was, do it the cheapest, fastest way, with the least amount of effort, so that we meet minimum standards."

- Growing up in a rural Ontario community, Emma recalled tensions – sometimes violent ones – between Protestant and Catholic students who attended different schools: "I was chased around by Protestants because I was a Catholic kid." She became a teacher in an urban school where non-white children were a small minority and treated like an exotic species: "I remember a Black child and all the little kids wanted to touch his hair," behaviour that she repressed in the classroom, though she's sure that it carried on in the schoolyard beyond the teachers' oversight.

- Oliver, a social worker, acknowledged that even as they were able to access public services, refugees encountered intolerance and judgment in both the workplace and the community. There were instances of discrimination, and sometimes, "you would hear derogatory remarks." He was appalled at the treatment such clients received from one case manager, but his supervisors wouldn't do anything about it.

- By contrast, Lydia worked closely and rewardingly with people from different backgrounds in a hospital during the Syrian refugee crisis and witnessed her community providing extraordinary support for refugee families.
- Joseph questioned equity-driven programs. Notwithstanding his own work with young African people, he felt that "as we've become more inclusive, we've become so politically correct that some of the traditional religions and ethnicities are discriminated against in favour of the newcomers."
- Eric, a dentist, also questioned the social focus on race and identity: "The way I practise, it's all about the patient. It doesn't matter where they come from or whether they are poor or rich." He resolved to treat everyone in the same way.

Several respondents lived in Ontario communities that bordered on Indigenous reserves, and there appeared to be a cultural gulf between white and Indigenous communities.

- Lucy, for example, witnessed "stereotyping and racism." She worked in a dental office and found that some of her non-Indigenous patients resented the "free" dental care available to members of the local reserve. If a truck were stolen, people would say, "It's probably on the reserve."
- Hazel lived in a northern Ontario city and noted considerable interaction between the Indigenous and non-Indigenous communities. Her daughter began identifying as Indigenous once she learned that her grandfather was Indigenous. Hazel supported her daughter in her ongoing quest to (re)define her cultural identity.
- In her youth, Olive worked on a northern Ontario reserve teaching canoeing. She later became a university teacher in western Canada, where the number of Indigenous students had increased in recent years. The university's programmatic initiatives designed to address Indigenous cultural and educational interests had achieved mixed results. The city itself remained notably divided, residentially, by race.

While acknowledging that social attitudes towards same-sex relationships had become more civil and accepting than in the past, several of our interviewees talked openly about challenges they encountered as gay men as they navigated through life.

- Theodore joined a gay association at university, and because of the "hate" that his activities elicited fell into a deep depression, for which he was hospitalized. His father expressed regret that his son had come out as gay. "I wish you hadn't told me," he said, though he became more supportive of his son in later years. As he entered retirement, Theodore was living with his partner, generally in good health, though continuing to experience periodic bouts of depression.

- Jack, who forged a very successful business career, encountered incidents of intolerance that left their mark. One manager made a homophobic joke and "looked at me to see if it affected me." A lesbian colleague avoided him, later confiding her worry that if she associated with him, her sexual orientation would be discovered, and she would be fired. "This was in 2002," Jack noted, wistfully. Although the environment had changed, illustrated by public sponsorship of gay pride parades, Jack's uncertainty about how he would be perceived and treated as a gay man meant that he remained cautious – he was never open about his sexual orientation while he worked on Bay Street.

- Oliver was not "openly gay." He did not deny his sexual orientation, but "I don't talk about it." When he was younger, he was "bullied and beaten up" and called a "fairy and faggot." In his early working years, he believed that he was denied certain jobs because he was gay. During the 1980s and early 1990s, during the AIDS epidemic, "it was very difficult because people were saying, 'It's the wrath of God. They're killing off the homosexuals.'" He never told his mother that he was gay, though he wished he had. "I was too afraid of it," having observed the ostracization of gay friends from their families. He appreciated the growing acceptance of gays and lesbians in society, but as recently as three years ago, a gay colleague who identified as "queer" was accused by two coworkers – unjustly in Oliver's view – of professional misconduct. He was deeply troubled by this case.

One final example of social marginalization:

- One of the members of a gun club Hazel belonged to was transgender and asked people to call her by her new chosen feminine name, which her own family refused to do. Other members of the club appeared to avoid referring to her by name at all. She participated in this community activity without being fully accepted.

The Class of '73 lived through an era of significant social change. Conventional values were being questioned; campaigns for greater social justice and equity were ascendant; human rights legislation required institutions to modify their hiring and administrative practices. The transitions these initiatives engendered were sometimes challenging and not always smooth. Undoubtedly, like the larger community to which they belonged, members of the Class of '73 responded in a variety of ways to these changes – ranging from enthusiasm to questioning to resistance. Their story is still being written.

Conclusion

How do our findings on labour force participation compare to those of other longitudinal studies in Canada? Krahn (2022) and Andres (2015) found, as we did, significant differences by gender in the labour market. We learned that in 1995, Class of '73 women were more likely than men to be unemployed, and Andres reported that between 1988 and 2010, British Columbian women worked fewer full-time years than men. In their study of 983 Grade 12 students from six high schools in a large city in western Canada, Krahn and research associates found that fewer women than men participated in the labour force and that earnings also varied by gender, with males earning more than females. Nevertheless, gender had no significant effect on occupational status and career satisfaction (Krahn, Howard, and Galambos 2015). Andres et al. (2021) found that although gender equality had been achieved in first university-degree attainment, women earned only 66.7 per cent of men's earnings. This underscores our finding that while most males felt they earned incomes appropriate to their level of education, women at all levels felt underpaid.

No matter the sector or profession, workplace change was continuous through the late twentieth and early twenty-first centuries. Corporate restructuring, new management practices, and revolutionary technology touched the lives of employers and employees alike. Males and females all felt the impact of these changes, though in a variety of ways, the labour market, regarding both occupation and income, continued to be segmented by gender. Notably, and unlike past generations, spouses were typically both employed.

Like other Canadians, our participants responded in varied ways, both in the community and the workplace, to initiatives taken to address the population's growing cultural and racial diversity. Opportunities and rewards were accompanied by hurdles and anxieties in our subjects' working lives. Overall, their ships reached their destinations, though often through turbulent waters. This may well explain why Class of '73 members expressed having obtained greater satisfaction from their families than from their working lives.

6 Family Matters: Children, Marriage, Caregiving, and Home Life

Members of the Class of '73 forged ahead with their educational, occupational, and personal lives through the 1980s and beyond. In an era of continuing social change and deep economic uncertainty, they sought security and success for themselves and their children. Family life formed the locus of their most meaningful personal relationships.

In this chapter, we track their life course with respect to the following issues: marriage and partnerships, child-rearing and caregiving, household management, sources of family stress, and the impact of grandchildren. Finally, we examine the degree to which religion mattered in the lives of Class of '73 members. Traditionally an important component of socialization within the family and community (Cornwall and Thomas 1990; Hwang et al. 2022; Pearce 2015), religious values and practices were changing in Canada through the late twentieth and early twenty-first century. To what degree was this true in the lives of our cohort members? Did religion still matter? If so, how did that manifest?

Family, Children, and Marriage

Most Class of '73 members – 80 per cent – were married or living with a partner when we re-interviewed them, and 90 per cent of respondents had at least one child (Figure 6.1). Another 2.1 per cent were widowed, and 7 per cent were divorced or separated. This latter figure appears to track with the country as a whole, with the divorce rate for Canadians who married in 1980 (when Class of '73 members were about twenty-five years old) sitting at 8.2 per cent (Statistics Canada 2015). The median length of marriage for married respondents approached thirty-nine years.

In some important ways, these late Canadian baby boomers seemed increasingly resolved to make their own choices rather than follow

Figure 6.1: Marital Status

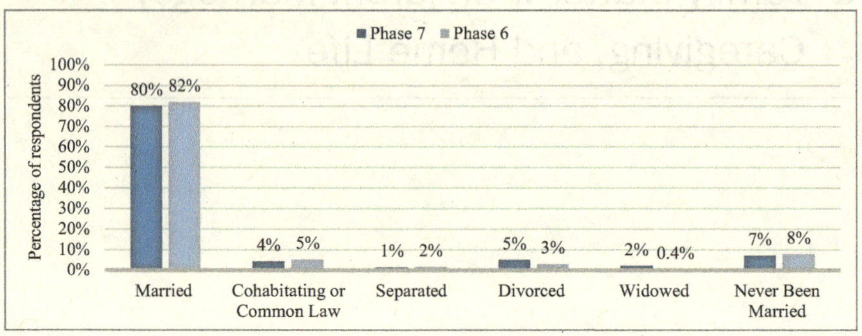

behavioural traditions in the ways they organized their occupational and family lives. For example, unmarried couples were cohabiting far more often than in the previous generation. Married couples constituted nearly 92 per cent of census families in 1961 and only 67 per cent in 2011, reflecting the substantial rise in common-law living arrangements over this period (Statistics Canada 2012, 1). As Balakrishnan, Lapierre-Adamczyk, and Kroki observed in 1993, "The commitment to early and universal marriage as the most desired life course is no longer true. Women delay marriage to a later age, and it appears that the proportion who may never get married is on the increase" (238).

The number of same-sex partnerships was also climbing. According to Statistics Canada, they comprised 0.5 per cent of all Canadian couples in 2001, a figure that rose to just under 1 per cent in 2016. Same-sex marriage became legal in Ontario in 2003 and across Canada in 2005. In 2006, 16.5 per cent of same-sex couples were married (Eichler, Pedersen, and McIntosh 2021). Among members of the Class of '73 surveyed in 2019, only one person out of 272 surveyed reported being in a same-sex partnership.

Married or not, couples were now delaying having children as they first sought to maximize their human capital – that is, education and employment prospects (Campbell 2016; Mitchell 2010; Twenge 2023). As women both entered and stayed in the workforce in far larger numbers than in the past, women typically had their first child later in life than in previous generations. The average number of children per Canadian family declined from 2.7 in 1961 to 1.9 in 2011 (Statistics Canada 2012, 4). Our most recent survey of the Class of '73 found a mean of 2.3 children per family, somewhat higher than the Canadian average (Figure 6.2).

• One interviewee, Sophia, was married for seven years before she had her first child: "I just wasn't ready." Did she delay parenthood because she and her husband wanted to be more financially secure, or did they want to do other things with their lives? "Probably both," she replied. Although they had anticipated having more money by the time her first son was born, she and her husband had enjoyed their child-free lifestyle: "It was fun just being the two of us." But the parenting years that followed were also very rewarding.

Notwithstanding the fact that both parents in the early 2000s were commonly employed outside the home, they also spent more time involved in child-rearing compared to parents a decade earlier (Human Resources Development Canada 2003). What's more, among European Union countries, only Poland, Austria, and Belgium surpassed Canada with respect to the proportion of employed mothers who had young children. The Class of '73 was part of a generation managing and reconciling, in unprecedented numbers, the demands of employment and parenting. Our Phase 6 data revealed that 85 per cent of women with children living in the household were employed.

How did they accomplish this? According to Bianchi, Robinson, and Milkie (2006), working parents were now including children in adult activities, multitasking, and readjusting housework routines. Women

Figure 6.2: Number of Children

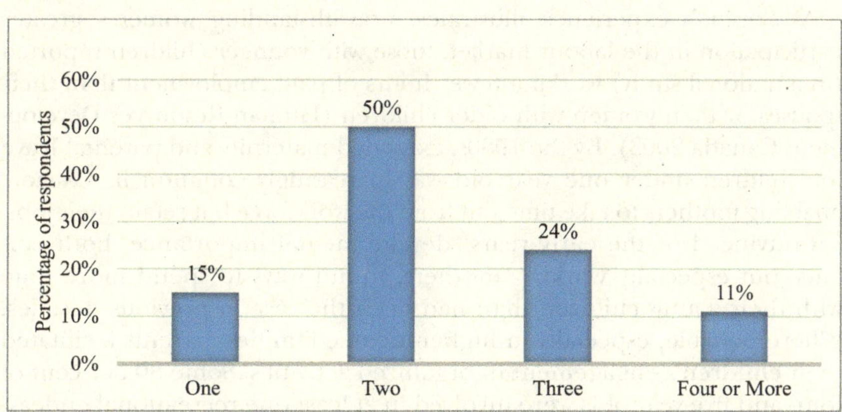

were doing slightly less housework and men slightly more, though women still retained principal responsibility for domestic tasks.

- Hannah, the mother of two daughters, delayed having her second child until her first was in school because she "couldn't afford to have two children in daycare at the same time." Even though her husband was at home with one of the children when he was unemployed, she considered herself primarily responsible for rearing the children. She put in "a full day at work and a full day at home . . . I got paid for one [job] and not the other."
- Sophia described the cooperative arrangement she forged with other mothers to better manage her time: "I got to know some ladies and joined a babysitting co-op. There were about twenty-one of us, and we would exchange hours. You watch my kids for four hours, I'll watch your kids for four hours, so I did that a lot too. Just a short time, like if you were going shopping or whatever, we did that. And it was also a social thing, and at Christmas, we gave each other gifts, and we got together with the kids – it was kind of nice to get to know people too." A librarian whose shifts included some evening and weekend hours; she organized her work schedule around her child's caregiving needs:

  I worked a couple of evenings a week, so I'd be home in the morning with him, and my husband would have him in the evening. Because I had that time, I signed him up for all the regular things like kinder gym, swim, and art for toddlers. This was a disaster – because he couldn't sit still – but I tried to do all the things that I would have done had I been home.

As Sophia's experience illustrates, notwithstanding women's greater participation in the labour market, those with younger children reported (in a national study) working fewer hours of paid employment than their spouses or than women with older children (Human Resources Development Canada 2003). By the 1980s, extended maternity and parental leave for children under one year old was increasingly common in Canada, enabling mothers to take time out from the workforce but retain their jobs.

Convinced of the early years' developmental importance, both parents, but especially working mothers, found ways to spend more time with their young children than had been the case in previous decades. Where possible, especially in higher-income families, parents facilitated their children's engagement in organized activities. Some 80 per cent of four- and five-year-olds were involved in at least one recreational endeavour such as sports or arts (Human Resources Development Canada

2003). Parents assisted children with schoolwork (Mandell and Sweet 2005), organized playdates with other families, and, in general, regulated their children's lives in ways that appeared more expansive than in earlier generations. Similar patterns were found in the United States and elsewhere (Bianchi, Robinson, and Milkie 2006).

How did Class of '73 parenting styles compare to what they had experienced as children and youth? While practices certainly varied, our interviews detected some common patterns reflected in research elsewhere. Trifan, Stattin, and Tilton-Weaver (2014) found a decline in "authoritarian" parenting among baby boomers (see also J. Campbell and Gilmore 2007 and Twenge 2023).

- Noah's reflections on parenting resembled those of other Class of '73 members:

  My parents were hands-off: as long as you didn't hurt yourself . . . you could do pretty much what you want. I think that was common back then. We were a lot more involved in [our children's] lives – I don't think to a damaging point. But my father, other than coming to watch me play sports, and going for walks in the woods, we didn't do an awful lot together.

- Marco didn't "really remember" his father too much because he was out the door at five in the morning, working pricing jobs and trying to get ahead in the evening. And so, there was less involvement by my dad in our lives than, let's say, myself in my children's lives."
- Sophia's parents both worked outside the home: "So, they did their own thing, and I did mine, and if I wasn't too late getting home at night, they were fine. They kind of gave me a long lead." During her own parenting years, "some of my friends were really helicopter moms and dads. They were all over their kids, whereas I kind of let [my kids] go, especially when they went off to university. I still found some of my friends were on their kids when they'd come back for the summer, and I just didn't do that."
- Hailey was admittedly "strict" with her children:

  I wouldn't let them get away with nonsense, speaking to me in a rude way or something. And I never would have done that to my parents . . . I probably would have got a cuff across the behind. I never hit my children, but I would say my mom, especially, had a big influence on how I raised them.

- Like Willow, whose parents induced a "fear factor" among her children, Caroline had a "very controlling mother" and a "subservient" father who said, "Just listen to what your mom says." Her own parenting style was very different: "I totally did not control my kids . . . I would direct them and advise and love them and listen to them, and my goal was to be the mother my mother was not."

- Evelyn recalled, "I think now more than then, there's more talking and explaining things to kids. Whereas when I was younger, it was, 'Do it because I told you to. And if I feel like telling you why, I will; if not, just do it anyway.'"
- Robert did not expect his father to be a dominant presence in his childhood years: "His priority was to put food on the table and a roof over our heads and all that stuff. So, even though he was a great father, he was a different father than me."
- By contrast, in raising her own children, Lucy was very much influenced by her parents' child-rearing values. She worked weekends on her father's construction site, and the family always had meals together. She and her siblings acquired a "strong work ethic" and learned to "pay the bills, have fun but don't overspend, moderation . . . That's the way we raised our kids too." They drove their children to all their activities, supported them in their educational pursuits, and tried to teach them responsibility.
- James, who grew up on a farm, began working at an early age. At five or six, he used to carry the toolbox for his grandfather on his rounds as a carpenter. By age twelve, he was cutting grass and shoveling snow, "putting money in my pocket. I pretty much worked all along." When his own children were young, he didn't push them, though he tried, without success, to get them picking apples for pay at age twelve. Provincial labour regulations largely prevented such practices.

In the more recent era, the parenting years were extended, as children permanently exited the home later than their generational predecessors. Extended schooling and employment challenges (including the erosion of traditional occupational sectors in North America and the high cost of housing) kept young people in the family home, dependent on parents, for longer periods; frequently, after leaving, they returned home in the face of financial uncertainties.

As Beaujot and Kerr (2007) note, adolescence and young adulthood have become delayed, prolonged, and less linear than in the past (see also B.A. Mitchell and Gee 1996). Recent alterations in the timing of these intertwined and interdependent life cycle events suggest that the transition to maturity has become increasingly protracted, extending well into the third decade of life. These trends were borne out in our most recent survey of the Class of '73, where 26 per cent of the families

Figure 6.3: Do You Have a Child Living at Home?

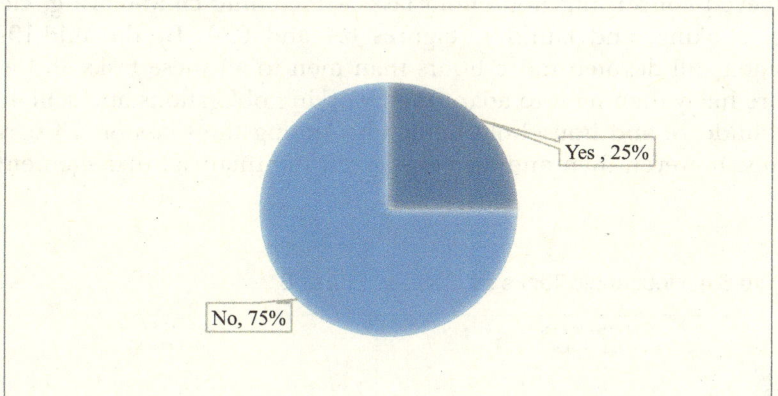

had at least one child still living at home, and the average age of children residing with study participants was twenty-eight (Figure 6.3). The children of 42 per cent of study participants left home and then returned to live with their parents.

- Willow's thirty-five-year-old son, a maintenance worker for the local school board, had been working on a "floating" basis and continued to look for other positions, possibly in computer technology, in which he was interested: "It's expensive for kids to move out these days, so he's with us here still." Her twenty-nine-year-old daughter was planning to return home from British Columbia to pursue carpentry training.
- Caroline's twenty-seven-year-old daughter and twenty-one-year-old son were living at home, both involved in apprenticeship programs, and both affected by disruptions in the labour market caused by COVID-19. There was a certain amount of "tenseness," arising in part from the need to stay home during the pandemic and by competition for the use of a single bathroom. Still, they got along with one another and were adjusting to these challenging circumstances.

Household Tasks

As we reported in *Opportunity and Uncertainty*, the feminist movement in the late twentieth century enhanced women's opportunities outside the home. It encouraged men to take on greater household responsibilities than in the past. However, something short of gender equity has been achieved concerning household tasks – including child-rearing, cleaning, cooking, and laundry (Figures 6.4 and 6.5). By the mid-1990s, women still devoted more hours than men to all these tasks and were more likely than men to adapt their working obligations and schedules to childcare and household demands. Among the Class of '73 participants, however, men and women shared the financial management of

Figure 6.4: Household Tasks by Gender, Phase 6

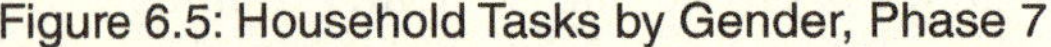

Figure 6.5: Household Tasks by Gender, Phase 7

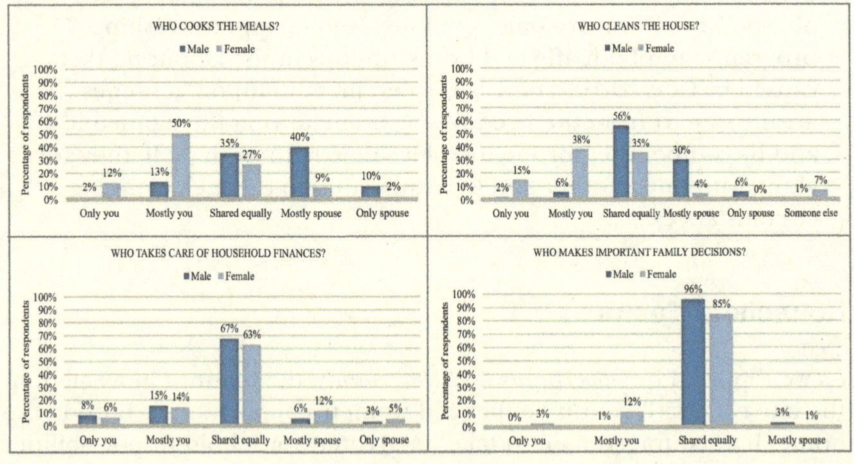

the home equally – this even though women in the labour force, overall, earned less than men.

As noted above, while fathers continued the trend of contributing more time to housework, by the late 1990s women still carried more of the household workload. According to the Canadian General Social Survey, between 1986 and 1998, for mothers, "housework, including cooking time, remained about the same, but fathers increased their housework by 50 percent, or four hours a week. Men in 1998 did 60 percent of women's housework compared to 38 percent in 1986" (cited in Bianchi, Robinson, and Milkie 2006, 197).

When our survey participants, now in their early sixties, were asked to report on responsibility for household duties, these historical patterns appeared not to have changed (Figure 6.5). In male-female relationships, while men played some role in carrying out domestic tasks, women continued to do the lion's share of cooking, cleaning, grocery shopping, and laundry. For their part, men did most of the household maintenance. Managing money was the one task perceived to be relatively equitable, with 68 per cent of men and 63 per cent of women agreeing that this task was shared equally.

With respect to family decisions, while 96 per cent of men believed that these were shared equally, only 85 per cent of women perceived this to be the case. Overall, participants regarded the division of labour in the home as either very fair (60.6 per cent) or somewhat fair (34 per cent). Only 6 per cent saw the division as somewhat unfair or very unfair. However, significantly more female respondents (11 per cent) than male respondents (0.8 per cent) found that household task-sharing was somewhat unfair or very unfair.

- According to Caroline, the sharing of household tasks was

> typical – my husband does the typical male things, and I do the typical female things . . . He's finishing our basement. I do the cleaning and the dishes. In terms of finances, he has the expertise, but "you better keep me informed." That's my philosophy. In terms of big expenses, like when we bought this house, it was a joint decision.

Thus, while household tasks, to a considerable degree, were still determined by traditional gender roles, the allocation of spousal responsibilities had evolved by the early twenty-first century. The high participation rate of women in the labour force, the deep involvement of parents in the regulation of their children's activities, and the continuing impact of the movement for gender equity have led to some renegotiation of household obligations.

Family Stresses

In the wake of the liberalization of divorce laws in 1968, the Canadian family structure was potentially less fixed and less uniform by the time the Class of '73 had moved into adulthood. Almost one-quarter of children growing up in the 1990s experienced "parental separation" before they were six years old. In the 1960s, the comparable figure was 8.4 per cent (Human Resources Development Canada 2003). Single parenthood reached 15.7 per cent of all families with children by 2000 – demonstrating a further outgrowth of these social changes (Human Resources Development Canada 2003; Statistics Canada 2012).

Mother-led single families were more likely to struggle economically than dual-parent families, and low-income parents faced more difficulties and strains than their more affluent counterparts. Indigenous children were at especially high risk since 60 per cent of them were living in poverty (Human Resources Development Canada 2003).

- Hazel's husband died when their daughter was eighteen months old, and she raised her child (now in her forties) as a single, working mother. It was "difficult," she acknowledged, but she drew upon the support of her own mother, who lived close by. The family – grandparents, mother, daughter – remained deeply bonded to the present day.

In their study drawn from time-diary evidence, Bianchi, Robinson, and Milkie (2006) concluded that working mothers were able to devote as much time as they did to their children by reducing job hours and household chores when child-rearing demands were especially high. Supporting this observation, Mandell and Sweet (2005) found that parents' involvement in children's homework was actually higher in families where mothers were employed. Such demands led to feelings of "always being rushed" and the need to "juggl[e] more than one thing at a time" (Bianchi, Robinson, and Milkie 2006, 168). Fathers contributed more to child-rearing than in the past without lowering their work hours by cutting back on leisure time or time alone. Both parents nevertheless lamented their inability to spend more time with their children.

- Lyle offers an example of family "juggling." He worked twelve-hour shifts three or four days a week as a stationary engineer at a food plant, while his wife worked in accounting, frequently with late hours. When he was home, Lyle cared for his two children and prepared meals for them. His wife managed the children's needs on other days.

For all its bountiful rewards, family life for the cohort that included the Class of '73 could be a source of disquiet and apprehension, particularly concerning child-rearing. Historian Peter Stearns, who tracked the history of anxiety within American families, identified numerous worries that preoccupied baby-boom parents. Despite material advantages enjoyed by those in the middle class, Stearns noted that many feared for their children's fate in what they perceived as turbulent times.

These parents were determined to create ideal environments in which their children would mature, thrive, and prosper. From the 1980s on, however, their confidence was often undermined by a catalogue of potential ills – some real, some imagined, and all sensationalized by the media, including the emerging social media. These included growing crime, child abduction, Hallowe'en poisonings, drug consumption, bullying, and sexual abuse, leaving the impression that the streets were unsafe and custodial vigilance was required. Children, according to Stearns, were perceived as vulnerable, and parents sought to protect them by doing everything from driving them to and from activities to purchasing childproof medication bottles.

Their children's success in schooling and their prospects for high-status postsecondary education also consumed parents, especially those in the middle classes, as did the impact of the high incidence of separation and divorce on their children's sense of self-esteem and mental health. How-to books on effective child-rearing strategies flew off the shelves as parents looked to experts for counselling and advice (Fass 2016; Stearns 2003; Twenge 2023).

Similar trends were evident in Canada. A 2002 *Maclean's* magazine article cited surveys documenting parental stress, including one by Health Canada regarding health and education workers: "Nearly 59 percent reported high levels of overload compared to 47 percent a decade earlier, with women much more likely than men to say they were dealing with more than they could handle." As one researcher noted, "It's quite different from a generation ago . . . when kids were more often left to do things on their own" (Doyle Driedger 2004; see also Mandell and Sweet 2005).

Parental stress and anxiety were compounded by the challenge of caring for physically or mentally ailing children.

- Marco's son, born with a damaged heart, required a heart transplant at thirteen. Managing his care taxed the family's emotional resources, though with support he completed a university degree, secured a job, and was working on a master's degree.

- Willow's son, now in his early thirties, was injured in a factory before he turned twenty and has been living as a paraplegic in the family home ever since. Although she worked when she was able, managing her son's care became a priority. Over the years, Willow assumed primary responsibility for his care, and there "have been a lot of scary moments over the last fifteen years. It's been very stressful and worrisome that he's going to have a situation where it's going to be life-threatening."

- Caroline's twenty-seven-year-old daughter had longstanding mental health issues, which were worsened by the isolation imposed by the COVID-19 pandemic: "She can't see her friends, and making friends was always difficult for her. My heart aches for her sometimes. But she will be fine. She's a very strong woman in terms of knowing what she wants out of life."

- Alexander's daughter was born with a medical condition that caused a limp. An excellent student, she eventually became a teacher, obtained her master's degree, and then worked as a curriculum development officer.

Successful Relationships

We asked participants about the secret to a successful marriage.

- "Low expectations," responded Violet with a smile. She identified three factors that sustained her marriage. She and her husband had their own careers, and he strongly supported her in hers; they had their own interests – he was an adventurous hiker, and she travelled periodically with female friends; they were bound to their children: "We just love getting together with the kids, and you know, we have a cottage as well, and that's a fantastic family thing if you can afford it. I know not everybody can."

- Lydia similarly reported that because her husband travelled a lot for his work, "we looked after ourselves." She was busy with her three children and her work as an X-ray technologist. With the changed pace of life and increased time she and her husband spend together, retirement has been "an adjustment."

- Lucy had been married for forty-one years: "It's a lot of work and a lot of compromise. You've really got to communicate. Many people focus on their kids, and they forget about each other. And I think it's important to make time for each other" – wisdom she has attempted to pass on to her children. She and her husband babysit their grandchildren once a week so that her daughter and husband can have a night out: "It's when you get rid of everything else and can just relax, and you realize you really do have fun together."

- After a "shocking" and bitter divorce, Henry remarried and had been with his wife for more than thirty years: "I get along great with my spouse. I love fishing and the outdoors. She loves the couch and the TV." They make decisions together, but "I'm still quite independent . . . she doesn't deter me from any of my dreams."

Being Single

Of course, not all members of the Class of '73 were married or in common-law relationships or had children. Twelve per cent of those surveyed in 2019 were living alone.

- Ella was proposed to "a couple of times" – once when she was twenty-one, which she thought was too young. She subsequently had a boyfriend, who was nine years younger, for almost a decade. She told him that "nothing's going to come out of this," and nothing did. Increasingly involved with the care of her aging mother, she found herself "too busy" to date and thinks she may have been "commitment-phobic." She claims not to have liked small children but developed a very close and enduring relationship with her two nieces. As a retiree, she was content, still caring for her mother and very involved in the local community centre, though COVID-19 had left her feeling unusually isolated.
- Charlotte met her first partner at the age of sixteen and broke up with him when she was thirty-two. She had hoped they would have children and was crushed when he married someone else and became a father. One of his two children died at the age of sixteen, and Charlotte's bitterness dissolved, turning into deep empathy for her former partner and his wife. Still, she regretted not having become a mother.
- Olivia, who dated over the years – "never anything really serious" – has always been single, not necessarily out of choice: "I think it was just how things sort of worked out."

Caregiving through the Life Course

Caregiving responsibilities for our study participants do not generally end when their children mature and leave the family nest. Indeed, family caregiving may extend well into retirement and continue in various ways (Fast et al. 2020). Along with taking care of spouses, retirees may also care for parents, siblings, adult children, grandchildren, and even great-grandchildren as life expectancies increase (Rosenthal and Gladstone 1993). Caretaking responsibilities may also extend to friends, colleagues, or neighbours, depending on relationships in an individual's life (Penning and Wu 2015).

Additionally, as we noted earlier, economic conditions and issues around housing affordability may make it difficult for children to adopt an independent lifestyle by moving out of their parents' homes. Increased longevity and low birth rates also mean that there are fewer younger family members to help care for older members (Fast et al. 2020; Fingerman and Dolman-MacNab 2013; Statstics Canada 2017d). Therefore, baby boomers may have more caretaking responsibilities in retirement than previous generations.

Given longer life expectancies, women are also more likely to provide caretaking for their spouses as they age (Rosenthal and Gladstone 1993). This was consistent with our participants' experiences, with gender surfacing as an important factor. In exploring reasons for early retirement, we found that 31 per cent of women and only 9 per cent of men identified caretaking duties as a reason for deciding to retire early. Caretaking responsibilities for male spouses in heterosexual relationships often fall on the wife, as women are more likely to live longer and experience widowhood than men (Rosenthal and Gladstone 1993). Women in Canada are also more likely than men to describe caretaking responsibilities as having a major impact on their daily lives (Angus Reid Institute 2019).

This included the care of grandchildren. Almost 59 per cent of the Class of '73 had grandchildren, and 60 per cent of those had between one and three grandchildren (Figure 6.6). On average, participants with grandchildren had three grandchildren. Only four participants had grandchildren who lived with them, and these grandchildren ranged from two to nineteen years old as of 2019. Of those with grandchildren, 94 per cent said they were a very important part of their lives, 4 per cent said they were somewhat important, and 1 per cent said they were not important.

- At the time of our interview, Lucy had been retired for eight and a half years. She described the broad reach of her caretaking duties – caring for individuals from several generations through sicknesses and transition periods, thankful that her retirement allowed her to continue this work. Lucy's caretaking duties were widespread in the

Figure 6.6: How Many Grandchildren do You Have?

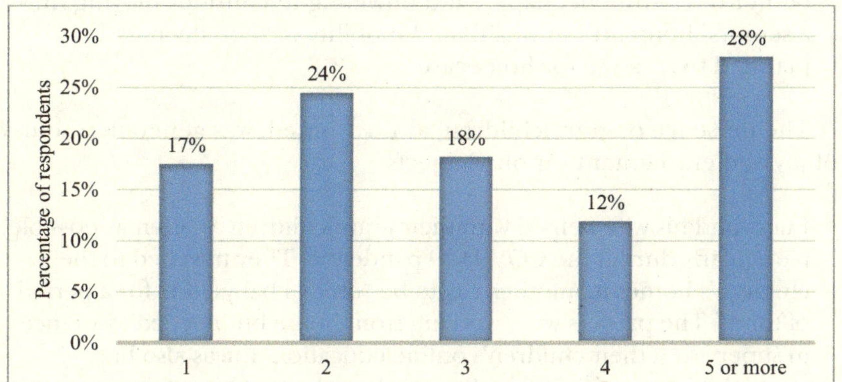

sense that she aided many family members, but she considered her grandchildren the "best part of our lives":

[When] I retired in 2012, I had one grandson, but between, my dad needed some cancer treatments, and I drove him to different places. My daughter-in-law needed cancer treatments. Then, my mother-in-law got cancer. Our daughter-in-law died in February 2015, and they had two little boys. So, my husband and I were going to [the city] to look after them two or three days a week. Well, my dad died [in] December 2014; my mother-in-law died in September 2014. So, there was a lot going on in that period. We were both glad to be retired because we looked after – we did a lot for the grandchildren; we did a lot for our parents.

- Esther, who retired because of her own health issues, suspected that her ailing father was subjected to elder abuse by the person who cared for him, and she and her brother "dealt with that for three or four years before he passed."
- Willow's caretaking duties for her permanently disabled son (discussed earlier) were extensive and ongoing.
- Ella's mother lived with her, and Ella described real challenges in caring for her. Her mother was in her nineties and experiencing dementia. As her condition deteriorated, when she was left on her own for part of a day she would forget to eat or that she was being picked up for an appointment. When Ella came home, "she'd be yakking at me because she had nobody to talk to all day. I know she was lonely." Ella retired sooner than she had planned to care for her mother.

- On the other hand, Eric's mother was fiercely independent, living on her own – mobile, happy, and unwilling to consider moving into a seniors' home. If her health and mobility were to decline, Eric planned to arrange for homecare.

The presence of grandchildren, as Lucy noted, was generally a source of joy and enrichment for our subjects.

- Lucas and his wife helped with their grandchildren as often as possible, particularly during the COVID-19 pandemic. They travelled to their children's homes in another city to be "official babysitters for a period of time." The parents were working from home but needed assistance in supervising their children's online education. Lucas also had grandchildren in the United States, whom he and his wife were unable to visit because of travel restrictions during COVID, though they were thankful that they could communicate with them technologically.
- Marco's son, daughter-in-law, and children lived with him and his wife during the COVID-19 pandemic. Notwithstanding the occasional challenges arising from such close living arrangements, Marco was "deeply attached" to his children and grandchildren and played an active role in the grandchildren's care and supervision.
- Connie, by contrast, was a "hands-off grandparent" because her daughter and husband were "super independent . . . Even when she had the baby, she didn't want me to come." However, COVID changed things. Her daughter needed assistance, and during the pandemic, Connie's granddaughter spent several days a week at her home.

Some interviewees had virtually no contact with their children and families and deeply lamented such estrangement.

- James, who divorced when his son was a teen, does not see his grandson. This was partly the result of the strained relationship he had with his son in his formative years: "We just never patched anything up really from his teen days, and then he wasn't much older than nineteen when he went out west."

Family bonds endured and were extended as the life course evolved in complex and uncertain times. Not only were children often dependent materially on their parents for longer periods than in the past, but COVID-19 was a major and unprecedented source of disruption in the lives of Canadian families. The health needs of our subjects' aging parents were accompanied by the uplifting presence of grandchildren who helped sustain and enrich family relationships.

Religion

As they navigated family and community life, to what degree did religion matter to members of the Class of '73? A 2019 Statistics Canada survey found that religiosity had declined in Canada over the years, though most Canadians (68 per cent) "reported having a religious affiliation, and over half (54 percent) said their religions were somewhat or very important to how they live their lives" (Cornelissen 2019, 2).

Our respondents appeared to follow national trends, though Class of '73 members constituted an older and less culturally diverse demographic than the sample surveyed by Statistics Canada. Did their attitudes towards religion change as they approached their retirement years? In the Phase 6 survey, 47 per cent of Class of '73 participants said that religion was very important or somewhat important, 19 per cent said it was neither important or unimportant, and 34 per cent said it was unimportant.

When we compared the same individuals in Phase 6 and Phase 7, we found that their interest in religion increased as they aged. In the Phase 7 survey, conducted in 2019, 62 per cent reported that religion was very important or somewhat important, 9 per cent said it was neither important or unimportant and 29 per cent said it was not important to them (Figure 6.7).

Religious commitments, then, were somewhat mixed. The decline in religious identification and practice was greater among younger than older people, and as the Class of '73 members demonstrated, religious identification revived, to some degree, by the time the Phase 7 survey was conducted. Lefebvre and Chakravarty (2010), among others (Kuepfer 2020; Sherkat 1988; Hwang et al. 2022), contend that even as formal religious rituals diminish, individuals pondering the meaning of life may still have a form of "latent spirituality" (Lefebvre and Chakravarty 2010, 38).

Figure 6.7: How Important is Religion to You?

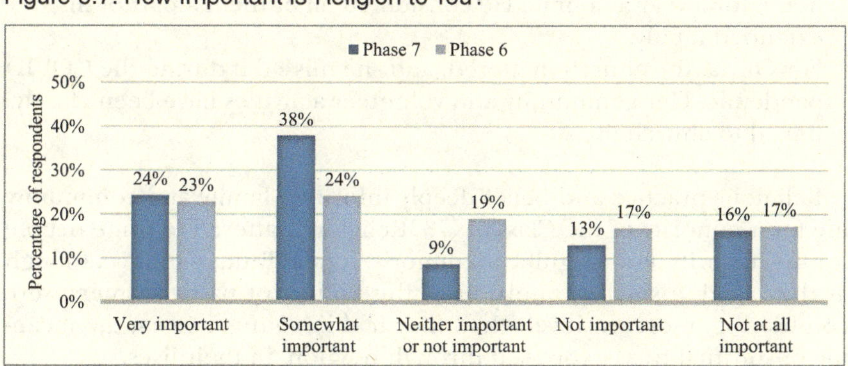

They might turn to organized religion in a "selective manner" (41), particularly with respect to life course rites of passage linked to such significant signposts as birth, marriage, and death, and their practices are likely to be associated with the religion of their childhood.

Phase 7 interviewees expressed a range of views, though, overall, few appeared to be very devout.

- Eric asserted quite bluntly, "I don't do religion."
- While Noah was "completely irreligious," he agreed with his wife that their children should attend Sunday school. She remained active on the "social service side of the church" – not the religious side.
- Similarly, Violet encouraged her children to attend church to embed in their values an understanding of religion and a community service ethic.
- While Lydia attended church in rural Ontario regularly as a child, her family no longer did so.
- Esther's father was an atheist, though her mother did believe in God. Her own family members were not churchgoers, though she believed in "something bigger than all of us, but I wouldn't give it a name."
- By contrast, shared religious values mattered immensely in Lucas's marriage. Raised in a Christian environment, where religious practice was confined to church attendance, he and his wife became deep believers and brought this faith into their home, where Bible study was undertaken daily. Religious commitment informed their volunteer work in Canada and abroad. Their three children made "independent" decisions to "follow in Christ's path" and now "have a lifestyle and value system that is like our own."
- Religious devotion inspired Joseph's initiative to create a mission for refugees in Uganda. Over the years, he and his wife have supported educational exchange opportunities for students from developing countries. They have hosted seven students who have lived in their home for a year at a time. He considered all of them a part of his extended family.
- For Olivia, the church mattered, and she missed it during the COVID pandemic. Her community and volunteer activities have been closely linked to church life.

Religious practice and belief deeply informed family and community life for a minority of the Class of '73. Religion mattered to some degree for the majority. For a significant minority it held little relevance, though as they aged, a small proportion of this cohort of baby boomers were considering, more positively than they had in younger years, the meaning of spirituality, as expressed through religion, in their lives.

Looking Back

Family mattered to the Class of '73. Our most recent survey showed that 75 per cent were very satisfied with family life and 21 per cent were somewhat satisfied (Figure 6.8). This compared to 54 per cent who were very satisfied with their work or careers (39 per cent being somewhat satisfied), and 54 per cent who were very satisfied with their education (with 36 per cent somewhat satisfied).

Broken down more finely with respect to values that provided the greatest satisfaction, family, relationship with spouses, and children surpassed all others (Figure 6.9). These results resemble those from

Figure 6.8: Satisfaction with Family Life

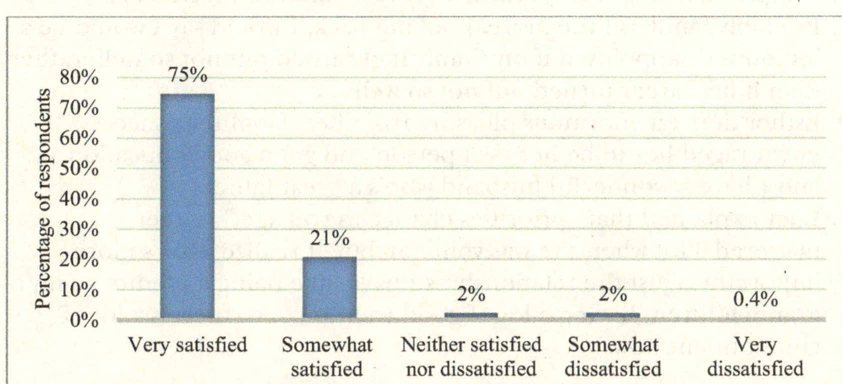

Figure 6.9: Value That Gives You the Most Satisfaction

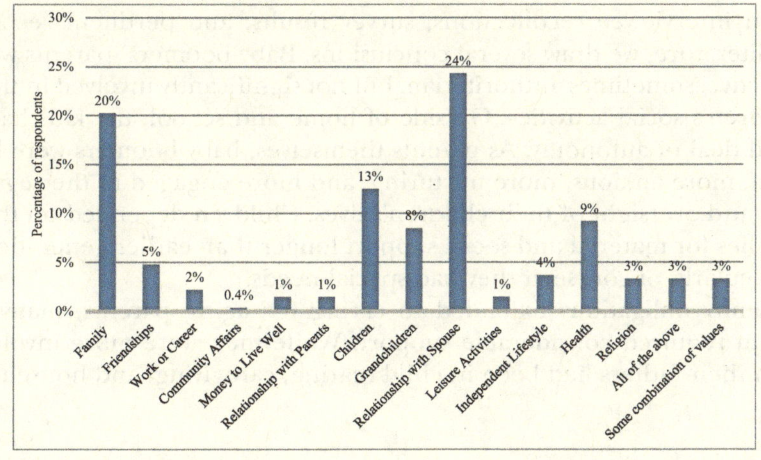

the 1995 Physical Activity Monitor, which explored Canadians' "overall life satisfaction." The study found that for those aged forty-five to sixty-four (mirroring at the lower end the age of Class of '73 participants), 91 per cent found home life to be very important to their well-being – in comparison with 69 per cent who found work to be very important to their well-being (Canadian Fitness and Lifestyle Research Institute 1997).

- Asked what brought the greatest satisfaction in life, Eric answered simply, "Family." There were some "rough times," he noted. "But my wife and I supported each other through that. We stuck to our values, and things worked out . . . It's all about family."
- Noah found it difficult to rank the satisfaction derived from family compared with work, "because they're so interconnected . . . Probably family a little more. Looking back, I would say I would be a lot more disappointed if my family had turned out not so well, rather than if my career turned out not so well."
- Esther derived enormous pleasure from her daughter's success: "I encouraged her to be her own person and get a good education . . . and I have a wonderful husband who's a great father."
- Lucy explained that "priorities change as you age." Career mattered a lot when she was younger, but "I realize what's more important is just the relationships I have, like being a mentor to my grandchildren, having a lot of good friends . . . so there's a lot of contentment now."

Conclusion

From interviewee recollections, survey results, and pertinent secondary literature, we draw several conclusions. Baby boomers' parents were directive, sometimes authoritarian, but not significantly involved in their children's social activities. Outside of home and school, the kids had a good deal of autonomy. As parents themselves, baby boomers were less strict, more anxious, more nurturing, and more engaged in the regulation and oversight of their children's lives. Children depended on their families for material and social support longer than earlier generations, particularly, of course, if they had special needs.

Family obligations extended to caring for aging parents, many of whom required considerable support. While men were more involved than their fathers had been in child-rearing, caregiving, and household tasks, women continued to carry more of the domestic responsibilities. Grandchildren were a deep source of fulfilment for our subjects. Religion mattered, and its importance grew as our study participants aged, but only a minority of the class appeared deeply devout.

Married, in common-law partnerships, or single, Class of '73 members constructed their family lives divergently, deriving profound satisfaction from the rewards that these intimate connections produced.

7 Moving On: The Class of '73's Later Life Experiences

In this chapter, we examine yet another important milestone in the lives of Class of '73 members – their transition to retirement. While baby boomers may think of retirement as an important life course stage, they are approaching it in new ways (Genoe, Liechty, and Marston 2018). Unlike earlier generations that emphasized a clear separation between work and retirement, baby boomers prioritize work-life balance – even after retirement (Kojola and Moen 2016; Sargent et al. 2013). This indicates that the journey to retirement and the retirement experience itself are distinct for this generation.

While Canadian research literature focuses on retirement planning and experiences, there is still a lack of understanding regarding the demographic and life experiences that influence retirement outcomes for baby boomers. This chapter aims to address this gap by reviewing relevant literature, analysing survey and interview data, and assessing the impact of demographic factors on the various paths taken by the Class of '73 participants.

We note at the outset that more than half the sample participants (all baby boomers) had retired in 2019. Among those who chose to retire, most had moderate incomes, expressed satisfaction with their careers, viewed their careers as important, faced few mobility issues, and valued financial stability. Additionally, there was little difference in the proportion of men and women who retired at this stage in their lives.

Other studies on baby boomers suggest three stages for retirement: pre-retirement, the initial transition, and mid-transition (Genoe, Liechty, and Marston 2018). These stages include the planning and conceptualizing of retirement, the first tastes of increased free time, and the eventual balance of free time with new, structured endeavours (Genoe, Liechty, and Marston 2018). As baby boomers navigate the unique economic circumstances of the twenty-first century and live longer than previous generations, they continue to pave their own path through these stages.

The Changing Landscape of Retirement in Canada

Research on retirement began during the late 1940s and early 1950s. However, given the significant changes in economic and employment conditions since that period, some scholars are sceptical about the relevance of such research to current issues. Changes that have transformed retirement in Canada include:

- An increase in nonstandard work since the 1990s
- The changing nature of work made increasingly unattractive because of a continuous increase in job demands (e.g., time pressure, work volume)
- The substantial increase of women in the labour force began in the late 1960s (in 1954, only 12.9 per cent of women aged fifty-five to sixty-four were in the labour force, and by 2006, their labour force participation had increased to 48.7 per cent [McDonald and Donahue 2011]).

Hazel (2018) employed data derived from the Labour Force Survey to determine respondents' main activity in the previous twelve months and found that, during the past two decades, the labour force participation rate for those aged sixty and older has nearly doubled from 14 per cent in 1997 to 26 per cent in 2017. The author also found that just over a quarter of older people who worked or wanted to work had a postsecondary education, compared with about 18 per cent of those who did not work and did not want to work. According to a US survey conducted in 2014, 80 per cent of semi-retirees indicated that they sought employment because they wanted to work. Moreover, the survey found that working after retirement is more common among workers with higher socio-economic status (Cray 2023).

Denton and Spencer (2009) reviewed the measures used by various studies of retirement in Canada and the United States between 1982 and 2007 and concluded that no agreed-upon or single measure dominates the research literature. Much of the current literature points to what people are *not* doing (e.g., being engaged in labour market activities). Therefore, an alternative strategy might be to place more emphasis on what people *are* doing – employing measures based on time-use surveys and addressing not only the number of hours spent working for pay but also hours engaged in productive household activities, such as caring for others (Denton and Spencer 2009).

Venne and Hannay (2017) focused on issues specific to the retirement of female baby boomers, highlighting demographic changes (e.g., increased labour force participation and lower fertility rates) that have contributed to women's changing roles in the workforce and society in general. In the past, marriage typically determined the retirement age for women, given that women tended to retire when their spouses, who were usually about two to three years older, retired. In analysing a random sample of older employees and retirees from a large Midwestern manufacturing organization, Talaga and Beehr (1995) found that the decision to retire often depends on the retirement status of one's spouse. However, with women's increased participation in the labour force, their retirement patterns have become increasingly complex and more disjointed from those of their spouses (Venne and Hannay 2017).

The intention or decision to retire hinges on several factors. Gettings and Anderson (2018) provided a concise summary that includes age (with older people being more likely than younger people to retire); health factors, where younger people may be forced to retire given specific health issues; work involvement, where the likelihood of fully retiring decreases as involvement with work increases; the very nature of the work performed, where workers in physically demanding jobs are forced to retire earlier; and job lock, where employees want to retire but perceive that, for any number of reasons, they cannot. Recent research has focused on the role of multiple midlife experiences in predicting retirement intentions and has demonstrated, for example, that job changes, becoming a parent later in life, and getting a late divorce all link to weaker intentions of retiring early.

While there are very few studies on how couples communicate their decision to retire, Ho and Raymo (2009) employed data from the first seven waves of the Health and Retirement Study (1992–2004) to examine the extent to which couples held joint retirement expectations and the role that couple-level agreement played in facilitating joint retirement. They found that wives' and husbands' expectations were equally significant predictors of a joint retirement. Couples who anticipated a joint retirement were more than three times as likely to retire together than those who did not, although couples in which only one spouse anticipated a joint retirement were just as likely to retire together as those in which both spouses anticipated doing so.

Retirement Planning and Financial Literacy

Considering the ongoing changes to the pension system and pension coverage, Canadians must plan for their retirement carefully. Between

1977 and 2013, the proportion of employed Canadians covered by Registered Pension Plans decreased from 46 per cent to 38 per cent, primarily because of a decline in defined benefit plan coverage (Uppal 2016). This means that private pension plans and savings will become an even more important element in securing an adequate retirement income and requires that Canadians become more knowledgeable about saving for retirement.

Uppal (2016) employed data from the 2009 and 2014 cycles of the Canadian Financial Capability Survey to analyse the changes in retirement planning, focusing on the relationship between financial literacy and retirement planning. They found that people's capacity to prepare for retirement, both in terms of knowing how to prepare and being prepared, went down between 2009 and 2014. In 2014, 78 per cent of twenty-five- to sixty-four-year-old labour market participants claimed to be prepared for retirement, compared to 81 per cent in 2009. In addition, the proportion of respondents who indicated they knew how *much* to save to maintain their desired standard of living in retirement went down from 46 per cent in 2009 to 45 per cent in 2016 (Uppal 2016).

Socio-economic characteristics were reflected in both the proportion of individuals who were financially preparing for retirement and those who knew how much to save. After controlling for various socio-economic characteristics, those with the highest financial literacy scores were 18 per cent more likely to be financially prepared for retirement and to know how much they needed to save than those with the lowest financial literacy scores.

Our earlier research revealed that despite historical forces impacting all study participants, Class of '73 members had diverse experiences with respect to growing up and fashioning life pathways (Anisef et al. 2000). When cohort members encountered a downturn in Ontario's economy in their mid-twenties and early thirties, a significant number experienced personal uncertainty in the form of unemployment, underemployment, job insecurity, and downward social mobility. Nevertheless, our research also revealed substantive variations in the experiences and perceptions of cohort members, illustrating the importance of including personal agency when examining (and understanding) how members adapt to the hurdles they encounter in their transition from adolescence to adulthood (Anisef et al. 2000).

Similarly, we anticipated that our analysis of retirement planning and experiences of the Class of '73 would show that the road to retirement is far from singular, varying by structural factors such as sex, socio-economic origins, and location, and by personal agency (e.g., interests, motivation, self-efficacy).

In 2019, the mean retirement age in Canada stood at 64.3 years. Public-sector workers had a slightly lower average age at 62.6 years, private-sector employees were at 64.4, and the self-employed worked until age 67.1 (Statistics Canada 2022d). Although mandatory retirement in Ontario had ended in 2006 (Sebastiano 2006), the retirement norm of sixty-five continues to dominate most policies and business practices. This benchmark was instituted in the 1930s – almost one hundred years ago, when the average life expectancy was sixty-two years (Mihaildis 2021).

At the time of the last interviews in 2019, cohort members were approximately sixty-four years old. Figure 7.1 shows the percentage of Class of '73 participants in Phase 7 who chose to retire from 1998 to 2020.

In the Phase 7 sample, 55 per cent of participants reported being completely retired, 15 per cent said they were partly retired, and 30 per cent said they were not retired at all. Retirement status also varied by type of employer (Figure 7.2), with 41 per cent of those who had worked in the private sector being completely retired, compared with 46 per cent of those in the public sector and 8 per cent of those who were self-employed.

Most participants (49 per cent) retired between 2015 and 2020, while 39 per cent retired between 2009 and 2014, 10 per cent between 2003 and 2008, and 2 per cent between 1998 and 2002. Assuming our participants were about sixty-four years old in 2019, many of them retired between the ages of sixty and sixty-six, but a substantial number (39 per cent) retired between the ages of fifty-four and fifty-nine.

Statistics Canada would deem *any* involvement in the labour market as not being retired. When we employ this definition, 55 percent of our

Figure 7.1: Year Officially Retired

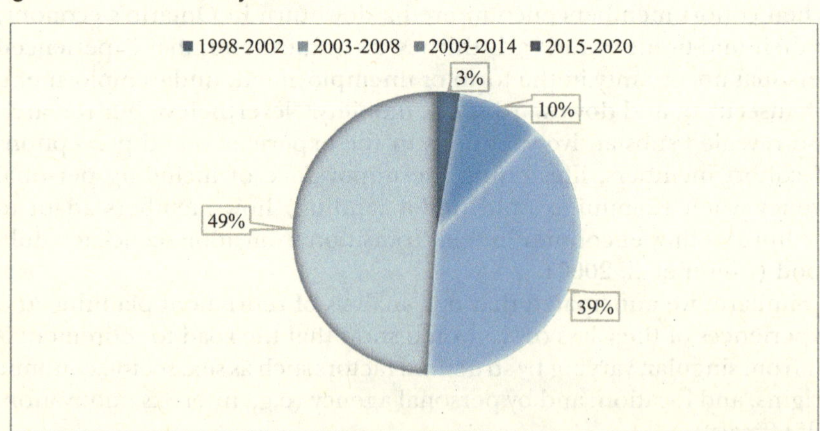

Figure 7.2: Job Sector and Retirement Status

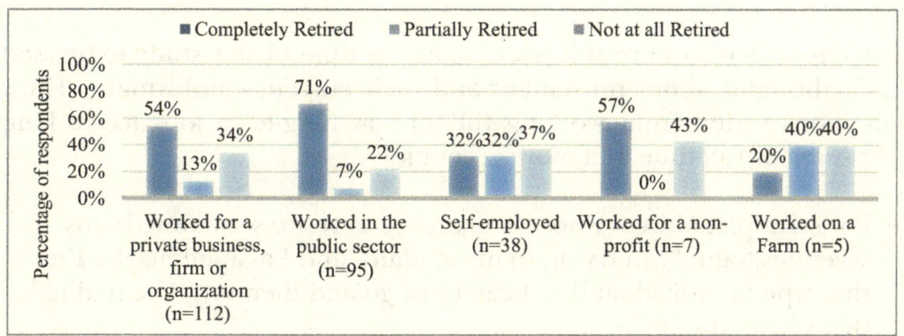

Figure 7.3: Retirement Status, by Gender

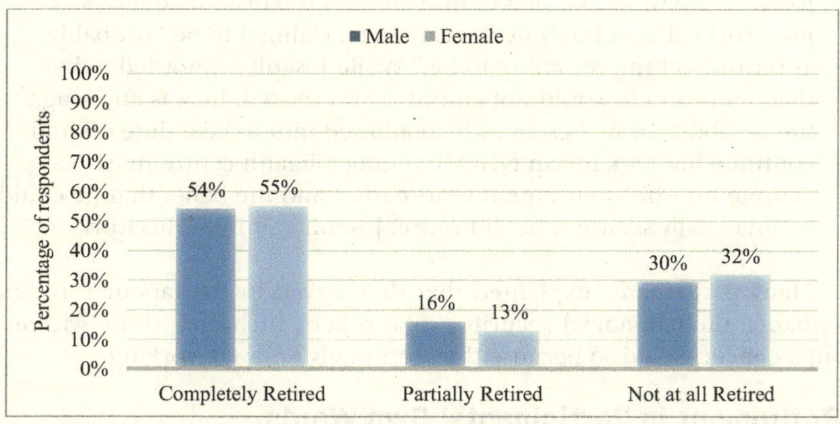

sample is retired, which is lower than the Canadian average for all seniors. Our study participants were 51 per cent male and 49 per cent female, and retirement status held true across gender identities, as shown in Figure 7.3.

While exact comparisons are difficult to find at a national level (and simply not possible at the provincial level), the 2016 Canadian census revealed that more than half of men (53.5 per cent) and 38.8 per cent of women aged sixty-five reported working full – or part-time (Statistics Canada 2017b). In our Phase 7 sample, around 45 per cent of both men and women reported that they were working full – or part-time. Thus, the uptake rate of retirement in Phase 7 appears less than the national average.

Employed Participants

Interviewees who were still working at the time of our study expressed their thoughts about retirement and their current employment. Their situations varied from working full-time at long-term jobs to working part-time or full-time in a more recent job.

- For example, Marco, who was planning to retire sometime in his seventies, said, "I'm trying to make plans, and I assume maybe I'm that type of individual that I can't just go and then say, 'I've had it, that's it,' and stop."

Other participants felt similarly about their connection to their work and keeping busy.

- Joseph, who worked much of his career in the insurance industry and now works almost full-time in real estate, claimed to be "probably as retired as I'm ever going to be." While Joseph acknowledged that many others would not consider him retired, he was enjoying the flexibility of real estate, which allowed him to take time off and continue his work for an NGO, building a health centre in Africa. Despite his wife's retirement years earlier and the belief that he could be financially secure if he did retire, Joseph continues his work.

Many participants explained that they stayed in the labour force to enhance their financial security, while others, including those without such concerns, did so because they genuinely enjoyed working.

Retirement in Participants' Own Words

The onset of retirement can prove complicated for someone who has highly regarded and enjoyed their career.

- Robert, a retired landscaper and park developer, described the period of adjustment that follows retirement:

When I retired, I lost my identity. [When I worked,] I'd walk into a room and there'd be a chair awaiting me. Everybody phoned me and called me for my advice and asked me for help. And I have retired, and you really do become like a nobody. Even the guys in the trucks don't wave at you anymore. So it takes a while to adjust to it. And you just must get busy. You just must get active and do all those things that you have never had time to do before. And I enjoy the moment because you know it's a great place to be in life.

- Samuel, who had been retired for less than a year at the time of his interview, was generally happy with his decision, but he thought that a part-time work arrangement could be beneficial:

The idea of still working would be good because when I got up in the morning, I had something to do, whereas right now I get up in the morning, I don't have to do anything for the most part. I think it's partly true that, if I was still working, it would be better in some circumstances, but on the other hand is you can't just say, well, I'm gone for the next two or three days. I couldn't work part-time.

Others had no regrets about leaving work.

- Hazel described her transition to retirement at age fifty-seven and finding ways to fill her time:

I always tell people, "When you first retire, the first two weeks are like you're on holiday." And then maybe the third week might feel, oh, you got lucky, you got a three-week holiday. And then, I'd start wanting to go back to work or find something. But no, it never happened. I got so busy with other things that I didn't miss it at all.

- Although she enjoyed her work, Violet chose to retire so that she could engage in all the activities she had always wanted to without the risk of declining health. In preparation for feeling blue and bored about retirement, Violet coined an acronym, EVE, to guide her:

It stands for exercise, volunteer, and education. When I was working and busy, I didn't have time, but I quite enjoyed going to the gym. I couldn't exercise as much as I wanted, but now that I'm retired, I have a more disciplined exercise regime.

Other participants chose to forgo the shift to retirement for the time being.

- Olivia, who was still employed, started a new job at sixty-four and planned to continue it for a while.

I think when I started the job at sixty-four, I thought I must give it a good few years. I didn't think it was fair to them, because it does take a while sometimes to get up to speed as to what happens in any organization. So, I thought I'd work at least to seventy. But, frankly, if I'm still able to work, I'd rather be working.

- Similarly, Marco, who was still employed as a busy accountant as he approached sixty-five, expressed concern about full-time retirement, even as he planned to reduce his weekly work hours:

> You know, I really haven't [retired], and it may be out of fear because I just don't know. I ask many of my clients, "Well, what do you do since you've been retired?" And, you know, you get varying people, different experiences, but it's – you know, it's amazing how so many people say – you know, I shouldn't say so many people. There's a good significant percentage that says it's the best thing they ever did, and a significant percentage say it's the worst thing you can do.

Regardless of retirement status, study participants most frequently reported spending their time watching TV or going on holiday and less frequently reported volunteering, working on educational pursuits, or caring for relatives and partners. While no notable differences between retirement status and time spent on various activities (volunteering, exercising, socializing, watching television, etc.) manifested, retirees described a range of activities that filled their time in their post-work lives. Some found new hobbies and passions.

- Ella, a retired administrative clerk, extolled the virtues of line dancing:

> If you had told me that after I retired, line dancing would be one of my favourite things to do, I would have thought you were crazy. Because I don't dance, like I do not dance. But these line dancing things, it's like, when people come at you, "Oh, you're so good at this," and you're like, wow, you've got to be kidding me.

- Sophia kept busy with her grandchildren and friends and learning musical instruments:

> I have two granddaughters now. One just came in October, but the other one is four now, and she has come occasionally to spend time with us, and that's nice. I also have dinner with friends. I also joined [a band]. I didn't even know how to play a musical instrument, and I always wanted to learn, and everybody else in my family plays. So, this band was started up.

Even those not yet retired had definite activity plans once their timetable became clear.

- Eric, who was still employed as a dentist at the time of the interview, stated that he was "going to play." He intended to engage in outdoor activities, such as hiking, mountain biking, and kayaking.

Overall, although retirement may have brought an initial adjustment period to participants' lives, it eventually meant more time for them to focus on family, try new skills, or pick up old hobbies. Lots of participants were happy to be able to experience life the way they wanted before their health or that of their friends and family members deteriorated. In all, participants' retirement experiences and planning seemed contingent on various factors, including finances, friends, and family.

Different Paths to Retirement Planning

As Figure 7.4 shows, when planning for early retirement participants most often indicated that they wanted to enjoy life while still young and fit (39 per cent). Some had poor health (37 per cent) or wanted to spend time with family (31 per cent). Figure 7.5 indicates that participants who planned for delayed retirement most often said that they could not afford to retire (70 per cent), that they liked their job (43 per cent), or that they were affected by the 2008 recession (27 per cent).

Figure 7.4: Reasons for Early Retirement

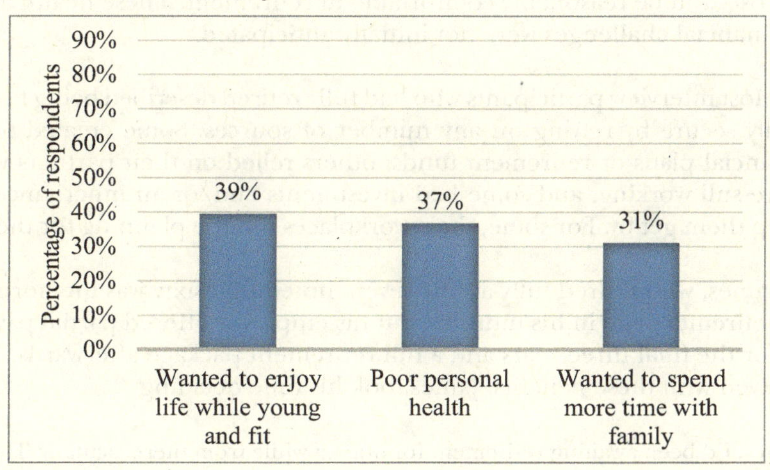

Figure 7.5: Reasons for Delayed Retirement

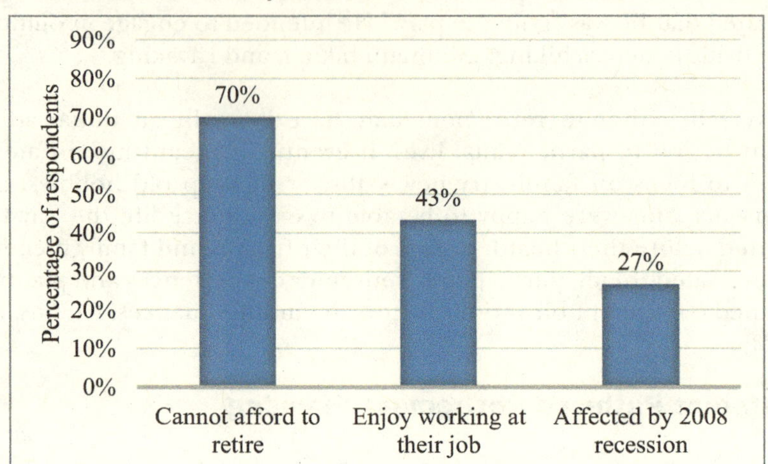

Those who took early retirement often had to do so for health-related issues.

- Serious health concerns forced both Hailey and her husband to leave work but also left them with reduced pensions and increasing medical bills. Through benefits, pension income, government support, and other funds, they could cover their medical-related costs and be reasonably comfortable in retirement. These health and financial challenges were not initially anticipated.

Most interview participants who had fully retired described being financially secure by relying on any number of sources. Some created solid financial plans or retirement funds, others relied on their partners who were still working, and some had investments and/or an inheritance to help them get by. For some, their workplaces did the planning for them.

- James, who retired fully at fifty-seven, noted that sixty was the normal retirement age in his industry, but his employer offered partial pay for the final three years and a full retirement package afterwards. Even with these benefits, James took his time deciding:

Yes. I'd been awaiting retirement for quite a while from there, actually. The work was getting so monotonous. But when they offered retirement, they gave me thirty days to think about it. And they said, here's a letter. We're offering you a buyout. They called it a grow-up. You have got thirty days to make up your mind. And I took right down to the last five minutes before they closed the office, and I handed my paper in.

- Similarly, Henry had a tough time deciding on future retirement plans. Unlike James, however, Henry was still employed full-time and had not planned sufficiently. He did not have a private pension plan, nor was he able to coordinate retirement planning with his common-law partner:

So, this made it difficult for me to plan, especially not seeing a plan. Again, it all depends on where you are in life and your whole situation, because you must take your partner in life into consideration too. Not to blame them for your shortcomings, but also you can say, "Well, if I were with somebody different, I could've gone and done this," where we would've done it together instead of me wanting to do it all alone.

- Like Henry, Samuel, now fully retired, considered his wife's situation. As Ho and Raymo (2009) explained, couples who anticipate joint retirement are more likely to retire jointly than couples where neither partner expects to retire jointly. Samuel also noted some of the most common reasons for retirement – such as financial security and wanting to enjoy life while still young and healthy:

My wife had retired about a year previous, so I wanted, while in good health, to take advantage of it, and I knew financially that once we'd crossed two major hurdles financially – one is the boys were no longer in the university, so I wasn't paying university bills, and [second] the house got paid for. So, suddenly, the cost of living had gone way down, or as one cousin said, it's like having a major pay raise suddenly.

Of those who had not retired at all, 33 per cent expected their living standards to decline somewhat or a lot when they retired, compared with 11 per cent of those who partially retired and 15 per cent of those who had completely retired. A myriad of factors and life events can cause financial or personal hardships and can then alter one's expected retirement timetable and influence one's retirement planning.

Future Retirement Plans

Of those study participants who were not yet retired at the time of our survey, 44 per cent planned to completely retire, 40 per cent planned to partially retire, 13 per cent had no plans to retire, and 4 per cent told us that they were not sure of their future.

Of those who were partly retired, 68 per cent planned on fully retiring sometime soon, whereas 27 per cent did not plan on fully retiring, and 5 per cent were unsure of their future. Of those study participants who were either partially or not at all retired, 61 per cent expected no change in their retirement plans, 26 per cent planned on taking early retirement, 11 per cent planned to delay their retirement, and 2 per cent were unsure if their plans would change in the future (Figure 7.6).

The average retirement age for Canadians in 2019 was 64.3 (Statistics Canada 2022d). Of the Class of '73 cohort, 32 per cent indicated that they would like to be completely or partly retired by age sixty-five, and 25 per cent believed that they could retire by that age. On average, these late boomers estimated they could retire by sixty-eight.

These numbers resemble the results of a 2009 study on baby boomers' retirement in Australia, which found that 30–50 per cent of boomers anticipated a decline in their standard of living once retired (Humpel et al. 2009). Financial circumstances and public policy can greatly affect how boomers plan and carry out their retirement (Humpel et al. 2009), and these effects can be amplified for boomer women, who may have more precarious employment histories and increased caregiving duties (Sawyer and James 2018).

The major distinction between those who were completely retired versus not at all retired relates to self-reported stress levels, with 71 per cent of those who were completely retired evaluating their stress levels as *not very stressful* or *not at all stressful* (Figure 7.7). By contrast, only 29 per cent

Figure 7.6: Retirement Plans of Those Partially Retired and Not at all Retired

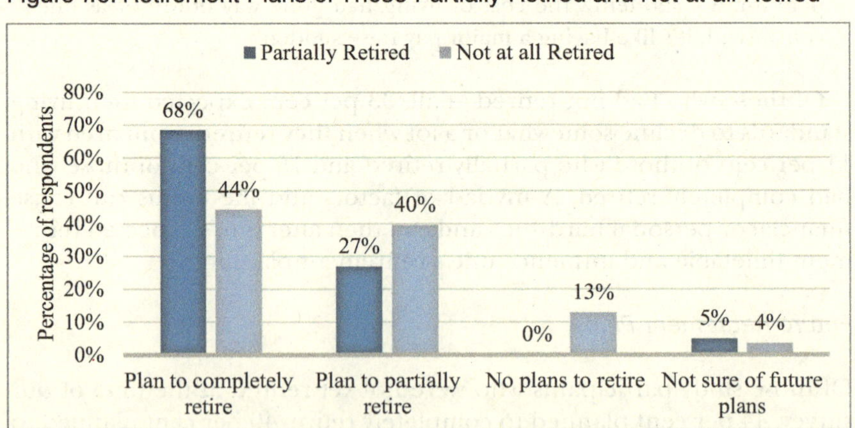

Figure 7.7: Stress Levels by Retirement Status

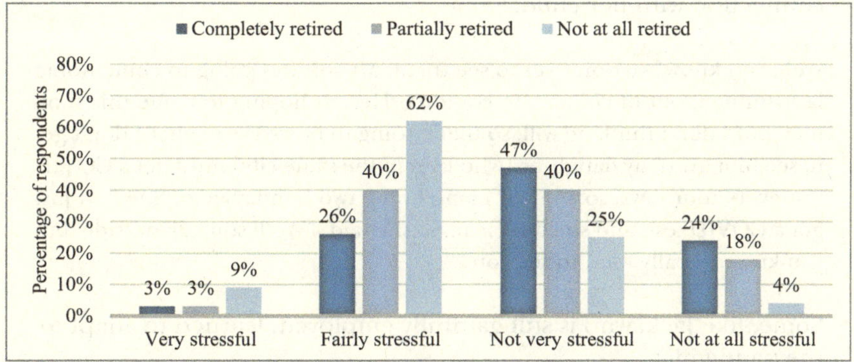

of the not-retired participants rated their stress levels as *not very stressful* or *not at all stressful*. However, happiness levels and both mental and physical health ratings were similar across all groups.

The Impact of COVID-19

More than three years after the COVID-19 pandemic began, its impact on Canadians (and others around the world) was clear. The most immediate threat to health correlated hugely with age. Thus, there was a one in twenty chance that people born at the start of the Second World War or earlier would contract the virus and die. The probability of dying for those at the lower end of the age spectrum was extremely low (Duffy 2021).

We asked all our study participants about the impact of COVID-19 on their lives and the lives of family members and friends. We learned that generally, while COVID-19 had more severe health consequences for participants' older parents, the pandemic's main impact for participants was felt in restrictions to everyday activities and relationships.

• Noah, now retired, said that the pandemic had a limited effect on his daily life:

We've been lucky in that we're already retired. So that eliminates many issues. You don't have to be anywhere; you don't have to go anywhere. There's no place you want to go, and you can't go in terms of work. It's restrictive, but we have always chosen to do our recreational leisure time activities outdoors anyway. So, it means you keep doing it.

- Hailey was concerned about the impact of COVID-19 on her connection with her children:

  Well, you know, we don't get to see them. My son was going to come home last summer, but of course, he couldn't. He was hoping to come this summer, but I don't think he will, so that's going to be two years that I don't get to see him. And my daughter [who lives in the same city] must get a COVID test every four days, so she did come home two Sundays ago. She had just got a COVID test, and she was clear. So she said, "We'll still talk outside, but you know, I really want to see you."

- Some, like Jack, who is still gainfully employed, learned to adapt to the pandemic:

  I learned how to be alone. So now it's not really affecting me except occasionally you go, "I have not been out for dinner in a while," or "I haven't been out to drink in a while." However, I have friends who call me. One nice thing is that in the business that I'm running, I get one or two or three phone calls a day, and people, we talk about different things, so that's nice. I have like an outlet. Now, they are strangers, but occasionally, you get someone with whom you can have an interesting conversation.

A few participants took the time to learn or try new things, such as knitting or cleaning out their houses.

- Emma described the effects of COVID-19 on her life in this way:

  We like to get together, share meals, barbecue, and so on. We're unable to do that now. We miss that and family functions. We like the theatre. We don't get to the theatre as much as we did when we were in the city, but we'll try to get to it as much as we can. We also like concerts, but we don't get to go.

Other participants did not feel as though their lives had been changed that much but acknowledged the impact that the loss of in-person social gatherings had on their children or grandchildren. They lamented the lack of family visitations and hoped for the return of some sense of normality to their daily lives.

- While Lucy did not think the pandemic had adversely affected her life, she expressed concern about its impact on her mother:

  Yeah. My mom lives in a retirement flat. She has Alzheimer's, but up until she got COVID in January, she didn't have any personal care workers; she could still manage her day and her personal care. She was in hospital, so

COVID really knocked her out. She's back physically to what she was. Cognitively, she'll never come back, but she remembers everything. But back to the way she was at Christmas time, like still watching her TV shows. She could still play bingo with the others, but lockdown's been hard on her. She got COVID through a staff member where she lived, but she's doing better. She's eighty-seven; my father-in-law's eighty-nine.

- Lucas, on the other hand, indicated that the pandemic had an adverse impact on his life:

Fortunately, my wife and I love spending time together, and we enjoy similar activities. And so, I've not been depressed. I may have had COVID back in the spring because I had all the symptoms for eight days, but I tested negative. But our friends have said, "Oh, you must have had it; the test just didn't pick it up." And it affected me and still affects me when I want to really exert myself. I'm quite physically active, you know. I did play a little hockey in the fall before they shut it down. Also, with COVID, I could no longer keep up with the guys. But I think I'm growing out of that; I think I'm pushing through that.

Despite the challenges of COVID-19, some participants pointed to the unexpected benefits that the pandemic produced. Participants acknowledged that it was easier to connect with others through Zoom, catch up with old friends, or attend social gatherings virtually.

- Joseph told us,

With the interruption of COVID, which takes away some of the normal activities that I'd be participating in, I would say that I'm probably more satisfied now than I was, even when I was working full-time . . . I don't have to commute to the city; I've got more control of my time.

- While acknowledging some of the adverse effects of the pandemic on his family, Marco also reflected on what he felt were positive aspects of COVID:

You know, so I hear that's it's been tough for everybody in varying degrees. And then you realize that we've spent so much time as a family together. It's amazing the bonding – you know, we're not running around frenetically trying to take in all eight or ten hours of the day but sitting. My son's sitting with my wife and doing some recipes.

Conclusion

This chapter has explored how the Class of '73 conceptualized, planned for, and experienced retirement. Just over half (55 per cent) of our participants were retired at approximately age sixty-four. This is consistent with the Canadian average retirement age of 64.3 in 2019. There were no significant gendered differences in retirement status, and the sample included an almost even distribution of male and female respondents.

Data released by Statistics Canada in September 2022 showed that as of August 2022, "a record-high of 307,000 Canadians had retired over the previous twelve months, up from 233,000 a year earlier" (Rubin 2022). While some of this significant increase can be attributed to the impact of the COVID-19 pandemic, other data from Statistics Canada indicate that this trend began before the pandemic.

Some participants described experiencing retirement as a permanent holiday. Others struggled to figure out how to spend their newly found free time. Their experiences in retirement largely included taking up a new physical activity or a new hobby. Many also described spending more time with family and friends and taking care of others. Those who were not yet retired foreshadowed the activities they would do with more free time, and those who were partially retired often described having found a satisfactory balance between work and life obligations. While some wished that their retirement could come sooner, others saw themselves continuing part-time work for the foreseeable future. As the Class of '73 moves towards and beyond average retirement age, it seems their retirement status varies based on elements of their life course, along with their personal desire regarding ongoing work.

These retirement trends resemble previous studies on baby boomers that show baby boomers' paths to retirement are increasingly flexible compared to previous generations, with more baby boomers slowly decreasing work hours or continuing part-time work longer (Kirsh 2021). Like other studies on baby boomers and retirement, our research also found fewer gendered differences in the pathways to retirement compared to previous generations, a likely result of changing gender roles and more equal participation of men and women in the workforce (Kirsh 2021).

In sum, Class of '73 experiences seem consistent with the previous limited research on Canadian retirees. They align with the multiple ways that retirement has been defined in legal and social spheres. Some participants were fully retired, some partially retired, some retired from one job to move on to another. Only 44 per cent of those not yet retired planned to completely retire in the future, demonstrating the assorted forms of retirement, including part-time work, that have emerged since mandatory retirement ended in 2006.

8 Are They Happy?

Many Class of '73 study participants noted that turning sixty marked an important milestone – one that prompted them to reflect and evaluate the various life course transitions and trajectories they had experienced as related to employment, family, and personal accomplishments. Two-thirds of our sample identified as either fully or partially retired in 2019, making their subjective evaluation of well-being or life satisfaction particularly interesting at this stage in life. While there is no consensus among researchers regarding how to measure happiness, most agree that assessing how happy, well, or satisfied people are with their life depends on multiple factors, including employment, relationships, physical and mental health, financial status, and the fulfilment of goals and desires (Becker and Trautmann 2022).

In this chapter, we aim to assess the subjective well-being of the Class of '73 through a combination of survey data and interview materials. We also reference in-depth interviews to explore regrets or unfulfilled opportunities expressed by select interviewees. First, however, we review the research related to subjective well-being and its relationship to life events and aging.

Researchers who work with the general concept of "subjective well-being" have examined related constructs – including happiness, stress, mental/physical health, and personal life satisfaction (Powdthavee et al. 2019). Other authors explore positive aging with a focus on satisfaction with life, intellectual efficacy, active engagement in life, lack of disability, and independent functioning, as well as a positive adaptation to the process of aging (Quadagno 2018). For almost a decade, Helliwell et al. have produced the *World Happiness Report,* which ranks countries according to respondents' "self-assessed life evaluations" (Helliwell et al. 2024, 14).

The research literature frequently equates well-being and health. One's overall health is reflected in one's subjective sense of well-being, which includes emotional and cognitive aspects as well as physical health. In fact, researchers bent on exploring the origins of happiness have identified mental health as the single most important predictor of happiness (Powdthavee et al. 2019). Well-being and health, in turn, are frequently measured in terms of general satisfaction with life (Chen et al. 2019).

We note, too, the non-linear relationship between age and happiness. A recent study explored the connection between various measures of subjective well-being (consisting of happiness and life satisfaction measures) and age in samples of individuals under seventy in 145 countries, controlling for education, marital, and labour force status, among others (Blanchflower 2021). A rigorous analysis of the country-level data revealed the relationship of age and well-being in all 145 countries as U-shaped, with the lowest level of subjective well-being occurring at an average age of about fifty. In other words, subjective well-being is higher at both younger and older ages and generally reaches a nadir or low point at midlife, when many of us are caught between responsibilities involving children, parents, and careers. (See also Erin Anderson 2024.)

When statistical controls are removed, the U-shaped relationship between age and happiness becomes far less pronounced. In other words, to understand whether a person is probably happier in his or her golden years, one must consider the fact that older people are more likely to experience ill health, lower income, and a greater probability of living alone (Duffy 2021). While our study of the Class of '73 does not permit us to test the U-shaped relationship between age and subjective well-being, we can describe the level of subjective well-being participants described in 2019, when they were sixty-four years old on average.

We used five survey questions to provide a portrait of the participants' subjective well-being:

1. Would you describe your life as very stressful, fairly stressful, not very stressful, or not at all stressful?
2. Thinking about your life in general, how happy are you with your life? Are you: very happy, somewhat happy, or not at all happy?
3. In the past few months, how healthy have you felt? Regarding your physical health, would you say you have felt very healthy, somewhat healthy, neither healthy nor unhealthy, somewhat unhealthy, or very unhealthy?
4. What about your mental health? Would you say you have felt very healthy, somewhat healthy, neither healthy nor unhealthy, somewhat unhealthy, or very unhealthy?

5. Thinking back to when you were in high school and the kinds
   of hopes you had then, how satisfied are you with the way things
   have turned out for you now in each of the following areas?
   ("Personal life" was one area listed, and participants were asked
   to circle one of five choices ranging from very satisfied to very
   dissatisfied.)

Well-Being

Most participants were very satisfied (68 per cent) or somewhat satisfied (28 per cent) with their personal life (Figure 8.1). No participant
indicated that they were very dissatisfied with their personal life. This
seems consistent with national self-reported data on life satisfaction;
in 2019, Canadians rated their life satisfaction at an average of 7.11,
with 10 being the best possible life for them (Ortiz-Ospina and Roser
2013).

This pattern continued when we explored participants' general levels
of happiness with their lives. Virtually all – 99 per cent of participants –
indicated they were very or somewhat happy with their current life
(Figure 8.2).

However, when asked about their current stress levels, participants varied in their responses, with 44 per cent rating their lives as either very or

Figure 8.1: Satisfaction with Personal Life

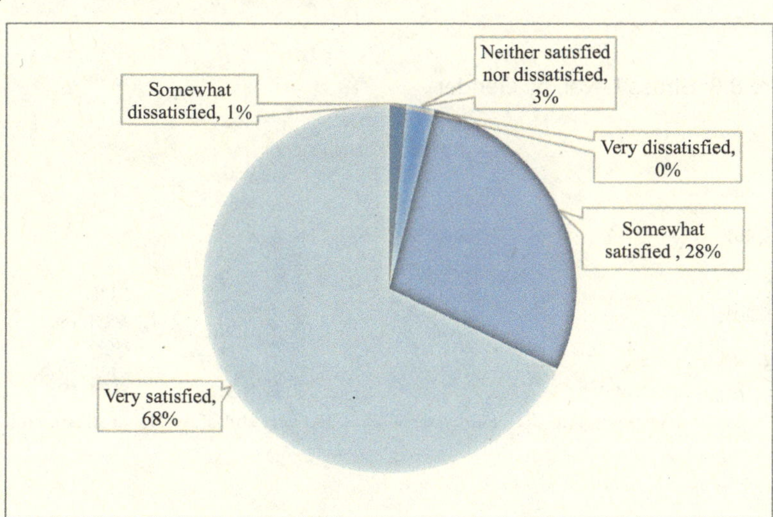

Figure 8.2: Generally, How Happy are You with Your Life?

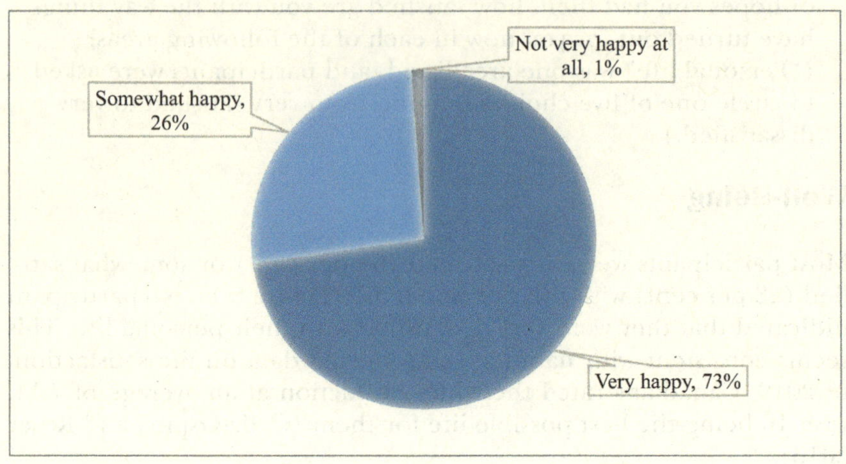

fairly stressful and 56 per cent reporting that their lives were not at all or not very stressful.

Unlike other variables, we found that self-reported stress levels varied according to gender. Consistent with national trends (Statistics Canada 2021b), women more frequently reported higher levels of life stress. Approximately half of the women rated their stress level as very or fairly stressful, compared with 38 per cent of men (Figure 8.3).

Figure 8.3: Stress Level, by Gender

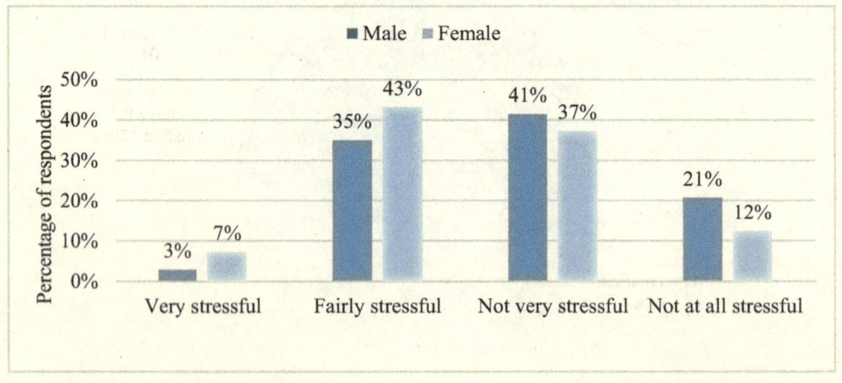

Health

We also asked study participants about how physically and mentally healthy they had felt over the past several months. Most described their health in positive terms. In fact, 85 per cent rated their physical health as very or somewhat healthy (Figure 8.4), and 96 per cent rated their mental health as very or somewhat healthy (Figure 8.5).

Figure 8.4: In the Past Several Months, How Physically Healthy Have You Felt?

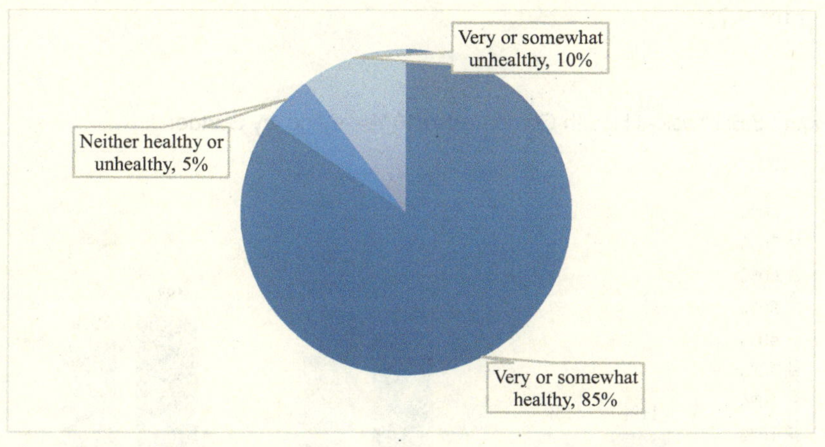

Figure 8.5: In the Past Several Months, How Mentally Healthy Have You Felt?

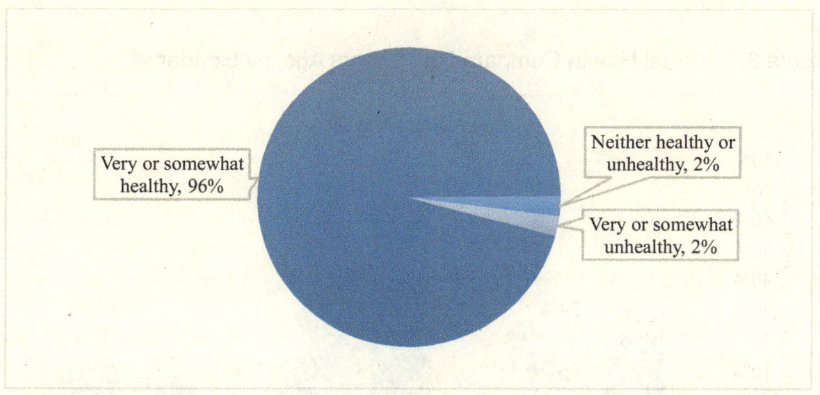

When asked to compare their current health to that of ten years earlier, 46 per cent noted their physical health was about the same, with 43 per cent saying it was worse now. With respect to their mental health, by contrast, while most participants (65 per cent) felt that their mental health was about the same now as compared to ten years ago, 23 per cent thought it was better now, and only 12 per cent reported that it was worse.

Once again, we observed deviations along gender lines – a greater proportion of males (48 per cent) self-reported that they felt physically worse in 2019 than the previous ten years, while a smaller proportion of males (8 per cent) than females (15 per cent) indicated that they felt mentally worse in 2019 than they had ten years earlier (Figure 8.6 and Figure 8.7).

Figure 8.6: Physical Health Compared to 10 Years Ago, by Gender

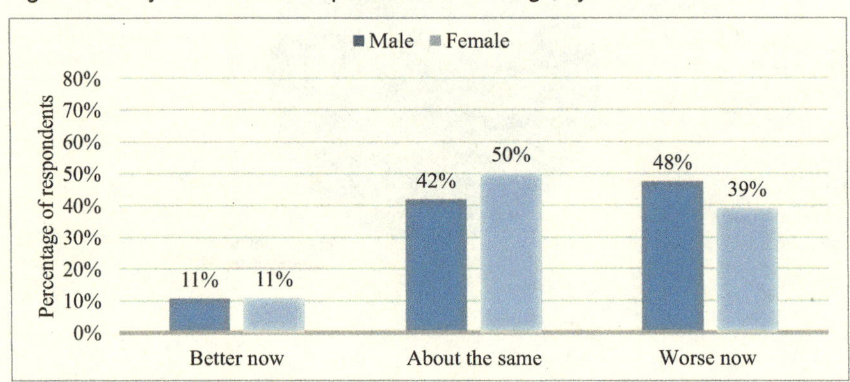

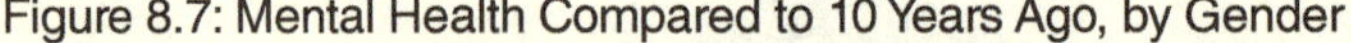

Figure 8.7: Mental Health Compared to 10 Years Ago, by Gender

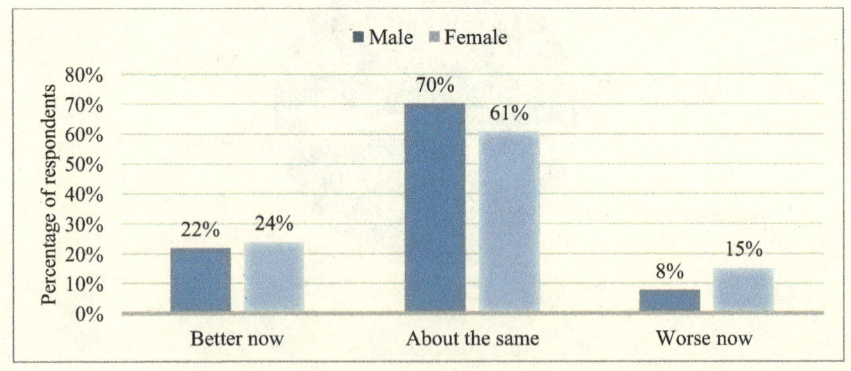

Despite some participants describing a diminishment of their physical health, only 28 per cent considered themselves limited in their physical activities. These results track those of Badley et al. (2015), who analysed Canada's longitudinal National Population Health Survey 1994–2012 and found baby boomers' health as they age to be consistent with that of previous generations. On average, baby boomers rated their health in the good–very good range, with only slight reductions in their health ratings from 1994–5 to 2010–11.

While our survey findings generally paint a healthy picture of Class of '73 participants, in terms of both physical and mental health, the interviews we conducted after the survey portion of the study was completed in 2019 provided a broader perspective on their health.

- Some, like Hazel, described their good health as "just the normal aches and pains of someone who just turned sixty-five."
- Sophia, when asked about her physical health, stated, "Yeah, I'd say so generally. People say I look younger than I am. I just try to keep busy. I think I've been in pretty good health."

Others provided lists of current illnesses or medical problems that ran within the family.

- When Oliver, who had worked in a bank, was queried about his health, he had this to say:

You know it's funny, I take after my mum; my mum passed away in 2012. She was eighty-seven. I'm sixty-five, going to be sixty-six; people take me for about age fifty. I have a full head of hair; I don't have any grey hair. I'm not real overweight, I bicycle and walk. I take after my mum's side. It was my dad's side that had all the heart problems.

- Violet addressed the issue of future health by retiring earlier rather than later, to make the most of her time and experience everything she wanted. Although somewhat fearful of contracting Alzheimer's since it runs in her family, Violet told us,

I'm very lucky, I keep physically active and no health problems. I'm sixty-four so, I don't know, maybe it's coming. A reason why I also wanted to retire was I'm healthy. I don't want to work until sixty-seven and sixty-eight and finally retire, and then you're not well enough to travel or hike or do other activities that you'd like to do. That was one of my motivating factors to retire because I still have my health, and even though I love my job and I could see I could keep on going and be quite happy, I just thought enough was enough already.

Some study participants, while reporting they were in good health, nonetheless had issues.

- James, who had worked in the automotive industry, told us,

  I wrenched my back, and I had that injury from years ago. And I just had an MRI done here about three years ago, and I found that I had a displaced disk basically. And the two vertebrae are offset, and I've got a pinch in the nerve canal, so I lost the use of one leg for a little while. And it's come back, though; I can walk and everything; I had a little bit of a limp, but it's come back.

- Similarly, Henry, who had worked for many years as a labourer, had this to say:

  Yes, not bad, you know, like, seriously, when I look around, and I really feel guilty when I look at my brothers and sisters. I have not done too badly. And about four years ago, I had not quite a heart attack – one of my arteries was like 90 percent plugged, and they had to put a stent into me. And yeah, I'll admit it: this winter, I put a few pounds on; I'm off because I broke the 200 mark; I'm 207, you know, so I work on that. But I've had one hernia, two hernia operations, and that again comes. I'm a small man, but I take on big challenges, and sometimes it's not a smart thing to do.

- Emma, after telling us that her health was not bad, added the following comment:

  I had a couple of curious health issues, and I didn't know what they were, but it's under control now. I had lupus, so I didn't know what that was all about. And then I had kidney issues, which caused a scare, like, "Oh my gosh, I'm going on dialysis." But it worked – we have that under control, so other than that, it's pretty good.

Some study participants reported that they had experienced more serious health issues over the years.

- Samuel told us,

  I mean I had a bout with cancer – non-Hodgkin's lymphoma – eight years ago, and that's all clear. You know, I did my treatment for five years, and then they stop doing the treatment five years after you do your chemo. Other than that, probably the blood pressure is a little higher than it must be, and you eat more, eat healthier. Well, part of it is because now we've got the time to prepare healthy food.

- Willow, while asserting that her health was good, admitted to experiencing a certain amount of stress given her husband's situation:

Well, I would say my husband's health has been okay. He had gone through different things. He had gone through a bout of anxiety – I think he's probably always had it, but it's taken different forms. It first surfaced when he lost his brother in 2010. And I think we had a rough year in 2010 as well. There were several deaths and many upsets that year. So, we lost three very close people; one being his brother, one of our best nurses, and his grandmother were all lost within a three-to-four-month timeframe.

Few spoke directly about their mental health throughout their lives.

- Charlotte described her depression after a split from her husband: "I got very depressed, and it took me two years to get out of that. And I was on meds and seeing somebody. Mental health is health, and you know that's what happened to me then."

Despite participants describing various health issues and most describing their health as worse or the same as in 2010, they also described their health over the previous few months as very or somewhat healthy. In their current lives, participants also described themselves as being happy and content with life.

Regrets

During the interviews, participants were asked to reflect on their lives since we first contacted them in 1973, when they were in Grade 12. We asked them to identify any regrets or unfulfilled hopes and aspirations until this point in their lives. Roese and Summerville (2005) provide a meta-analysis of findings related to people's biggest regrets in life, seeking to examine common major regrets and the domains in which they occur (e.g., career vs. romance, school vs. children). Overall, their analysis shows that people's biggest regrets arise from their perceptions of missed opportunities, which had potential prospects for change, growth, and renewal.

- This was consistent with Jack's experience:

You're always going to regret the opportunities you don't take, but you will rarely regret the ones you do, because with the ones you do, at least you know the way it turned out. You never go, "What if? What if? What if?" So,

I've had many other opportunities I did not take that I wish I had, but in the scheme of things, I did pretty well.

In a meta-analysis of older adults in the United States, Roese and Summerville (2005) found six biggest life regrets that fell into the following life domains (in descending order of frequency): education, career, romance, parenting, self-improvement, and leisure. When we examined the responses we received concerning this question, we found:

- Approximately one-third indicated they had no tangible regrets
- About one-third expressed regret about not pursuing a postsecondary education or not pursuing an alternative field of study
- One woman and two LGBTQ individuals expressed regrets about not having children
- One woman expressed regret about not having the opportunity to travel more
- Another woman wished that today's information and technology had been available to her in making career choices.

Regrets Around Postsecondary Education and Field of Study

- Sophia, a librarian, did not like the idea of having regrets concerning the choices she made in her life:

But if I did do something, I probably would have got my teaching degree. I don't think I would have picked that over getting a master's in library science. I would have had less time with my kids if I had a career like that. I liked the fact that my husband had a big career, and I had some work, but I could be at home and manage the house.

- Similarly, Willow, who worked as an administrative assistant at a power company and later at a publishing firm, indicated that if she could turn back the clock, she would have enrolled in college.
- Although not sure what she would have done with a postsecondary education, Sophia indicated that there were other possibilities:

I would probably have, but I just don't know where I would have fallen. I may have gone into something with animals because I've always been a big animal lover, so something like a veterinary assistant was a possibility. Maybe teaching again. You know, you go to college, and you take something, and you think, "Oh, I see something better."

- Hailey, who drove a school bus and worked as a school custodian, also expressed regret about not pursuing a postsecondary education:

   I assume the only thing I regret is that I didn't further my education. I wish I had because when I graduated Grade 12, I always wanted to be a kindergarten teacher. At that time, all you needed was Grade 12, and then you went into teachers' college, and I regret that I didn't go back to North Bay to do that.

- Lucas, who worked for thirty-five years in human resources and became a vice-president in that field, would have liked to have enrolled in a teachers' college as an alternative pathway:

   At the time, it was very tough to enter a teachers' college. And [my career] turned out great. So, I don't want to say I regret [not applying to teachers' college], but I did have some classmates who pursued it and entered [programs] within a year or two. But at the time, I thought it was difficult. So, I didn't pursue my dream.

- James, after completing high school, took on a tool-and-die apprenticeship and wound up working for a large automobile manufacturer. He told us that:

   I'd often thought that I would have liked to have gone to university and done something different. I'm happy with the way life turned out. I wonder sometimes, if I'd taken courses to be a doctor or a lawyer, if that would have worked out for me. I was never that sort of person. But the way I see doctors and lawyers today – especially lawyers – it's like, wow, I wouldn't mind some of that.

Regrets About Career Choices

Several men raised doubts about their career choices.

- Marco, who went into accounting, recalled,

   I had two sorts of roads back then. I was thinking of either engineering or accounting, and I often wondered, "Would that have been more satisfying?" I mean, it's all obviously water under the bridge, but that's something that really intrigued me, and it was very close. I only went into accounting because, at that time, there were more jobs. Essentially, I was thinking of engineering but thought I'd got to get a job.

- Joseph, who worked in various computer-related areas in a data centre and insurance company before becoming a real estate broker, had this to say about his career choices:

I'm not disappointed. On various occasions, I might have been better off had I pursued another area of interest. I thought of potentially going into law, but we can't look back and regret that decision. I've no complaints.

- Olivia regretted not obtaining her professional credentials earlier in her career. She also lamented the fact that her mother did not live to see her graduate.

I think if I really had one regret, it would be that I should have gone back to school before I did to get my accounting designation instead of working for a while. You know, instead of waiting until I was forty to go back to school. I would have probably done it a lot earlier. And, I guess, one regret that I had was that my mother passed away before I got my CGA – she had always been quite a big supporter of me going back to school. So that was hard – on graduation day not to have her there.

Generally, those Class of '73 members with regrets wished they had obtained further education to widen their career opportunities or try new things. They wondered what opportunities might have arisen had they obtained a post-secondary education or followed a different a career path. While generally satisfied with the paths they had chosen, wistfully they pondered, "What if?"

Regrets About Not Having Children

- Jack, a successful businessperson with a background in engineering and data analysis, expressed regret over not having children, noting the barriers that existed for aspiring gay parents when he was younger. "Now, gay people can do it, through IVF, etc." But he's not sure people in their sixties should have children:

My next-door neighbour is going to be seventy, and his kid will be only nine years old. It's not the best time to be there as a dad because you could get ill when you get older and not as active. That is a regret, but it's a regret I didn't really have much control over.

- Theodore, also gay, was asked whether he and his partner had regrets over not having children. He responded,

That I didn't. In a way, I mean, I think I would have been a good dad. But how can you make such a huge decision if your partner really isn't interested? So, you just live with it.

- Charlotte, an actor, also reflected on her life without children and wondered if they would have been the right choice for her:

  So, yes, no children. That is a regret on my part. But simultaneously, I don't know if I would have been such a great mom . . . I don't know if I'd have the effort to put into it. I mean that's why we didn't do it when we were in our twenties – because we were concentrating on our different careers.

Other Regrets

- In reflecting on the what-ifs of his life, Henry said,

  Oh yeah. I should have listened to an old farmer who I knew very well and not got married at such a young age. And that would've changed a lot. Not that I regret, you know . . . you'd always go to that place where, oh yeah, well if you didn't get married, you wouldn't have the kids you've got, and blah, blah, blah. But you know, if I had been in a different place . . . I would've had the balls to pursue my dreams, my dreams of going out into the world and doing what I wanted to.

Like Henry, other participants wondered about the roads not taken – the possibilities that might have opened had they taken a different path in life.

No Tangible Regrets

- Olive, who obtained a Bachelor of Commerce degree and subsequently a chartered accountant's degree, expressed satisfaction with the way her life had turned out and had few regrets. She told us,

  I had my health; I had no financial worries. I have three healthy, university-educated, gainfully employed children. I've got some great friends.

- Lucy, who had trained as a dental hygienist, also felt that her life had been full:

  I think as you get older, your priorities change. My hope was to have a career and a family, and I could do that. But we don't have a cottage or a boat. We're lucky enough to go on holiday, but I realize what's more important is just the relationships that I have. I'm a mentor to my grandchildren, and I have several good friends to hang out with. I'm very pleased with how life has turned out.

- Robert, who had Graves' disease as a child and worked at a series of diverse jobs during his life (e.g., making tin cans, cooking/camp attendant, turf management on a golf course, and manager for parks and cemeteries), voiced few complaints. He summarized his life as follows:

I was just so fortunate that I had some opportunities at the right time. And sometimes failing, if you fail forward, it's not so bad. And if you learn from those failures, you're a better person for it at the end of the day. So, I don't beat myself up too much with some of my past failures. As for regrets, well, I've just been so fortunate . . . But no, I can't really say I've got any regrets.

Those participants with few or no regrets reflected on the positive aspects of their lives. Some noted the presence of strong social support networks (family and friends); others described their good luck and fortune, while others expressed an overall sense of satisfaction with the way their lives turned out.

Conclusion

During the COVID-19 pandemic, both retired and non-retired study participants sought strategies for adjusting to the loss of in-person social connections and finding new ways to spend their time. Despite the pandemic, participants generally described themselves as being physically and mentally healthy. They also described high levels of life satisfaction and happiness, regardless of retirement and health status.

However, our analysis did reveal important sex differences, with women more likely to self-report higher levels of life stress than men. Moreover, when women were asked to compare their mental health across a ten-year period (ending in 2019), they indicated that they felt mentally worse.

These findings generally echo those found in a national survey conducted by Statistics Canada in 2021 entitled The Canadian Social Survey – COVID-19 and Well-being (CSS-CW). The study gathered data on Canadians and their personal experiences during the COVID-19 pandemic; the collection period coincided with pandemic closures and physical distancing measures across most provinces. Findings from the CSS-CW indicated that one-quarter of Canadians experienced high levels of stress during this period. When asked about the amount of stress experienced in their lifetimes, women (27 per cent) were more likely to self-report that they felt quite a bit or extremely stressed most days, compared with 23 per cent of men (Statistics Canada 2021b). These findings were found to be consistent with trends observed in 2013 and 2014 in Canada, before the pandemic.

The results are largely consistent with those of the *World Happiness Report*, which found that of 143 countries ranked over the period 2021–22, Canada stood fifteenth. Notably, its ranking slipped from eleventh over the period 2017–19, likely reflecting some growing stressors in Canadians' daily lives (Helliwell et al. 2020, 23, 2024, 15).

While interviewed study participants reflected on numerous life regrets, including the absence of children, varying career pathways, or lost opportunities, the majority described themselves as content with how their lives had played out.

9 Conclusions

This book tells the story of a generation over the course of five decades. We have tracked the life course of Ontarians who were in Grade 12 in 1973 and were at this most recent "check-in," either retired, moving towards retirement, or intending to keep working for the foreseeable future. With the group in their early to mid-sixties, we've reported on their educational paths, work and family lives, and perspectives on the past, present, and future. Our examination of individual lives in the context of significant – even dramatic – social and economic changes offer unique insights into the baby-boom cohort, along with the times in which its members grew up and matured.

We used life course theory, a model we introduced in *Opportunity and Uncertainty: Life Course Experiences of the Class of '73* (Anisef et al. 2000), to help conceptualize and explain these developments. We argued that the dynamic between two central forces shapes lifespans profoundly – the surrounding social environment and the personal agency one exercises daily. As individuals, we have little or no control over phenomena such as class structure, regional disparities, gender and racial hierarchies, technological change, economic conditions, pandemics, and retirement policies. Governments and corporations determine the overall allocation of material resources, which form society's opportunity structures.

Nevertheless, individuals are far from powerless. Youth choose specific educational and occupational paths, based on their interests and personalities, with or without family support, and they do so within the context of larger social structures and forces. For example, even if a young couple's income is modest, their decision to purchase a home may have long-term consequences for their standard of living. Depending on market dynamics (such as current mortgage interest rates and house prices), they may accumulate unsustainable debt, causing them to struggle or secure valuable equity, allowing them to successfully navigate uncertain economic times. If one has a say in the matter, the timing of one's departure from the workforce will affect one's sunset years. Structure, agency, and historical context are all addressed in life course theory, as are the dynamic ways in which they interact.

Participants in our study are from the baby boomer generation, comprising people born between 1946 and the mid-1960s. This group lived through the unique social, political, and economic contexts of the post–Second World War era, and we have followed their lives over a period of nearly fifty years. In Canada, their worlds featured rapid technological change, rising levels of consumption, and increasing population, all of which created a distinct opportunity for varying pathways through aging and the life course (Phillipson et al. 2008; Ranson 2022). Because of its size, the baby boom generation has had and continues to have an enormous effect on social systems such as healthcare, social security, retirement practices, and housing markets (Ranson 2022). It presents as an intriguing cohort to study and track, particularly through a life course perspective.

Education

What have we learned about the Class of '73 cohort based on our mixed-methods approach (detailed in Chapter 1)? They emerged from an extraordinarily expanded educational system that saw rising high school graduation rates and higher levels of postsecondary participation, particularly among women, than in the recent past. Young people had high educational and occupational aspirations, and with parental encouragement, students perceived extended schooling as a critical determinant of future occupational and material success. The new community college system in Ontario (established in 1965) provided an alternative, and increasingly popular, training pathway, particularly for women and for those interested in shorter-term schooling that focused on job skills rather than academic postsecondary education. Indeed, both our survey and interviews revealed the appeal community colleges held for young women seeking careers as early childhood educators, dental hygienists, laboratory technicians, and the like.

Notwithstanding public policies that expanded educational opportunities, social class distinctions persisted and, in some ways, were reinforced by the school system. Just as now, students from lower socio-economic backgrounds were less likely to attend university than their more affluent peers and more likely to enter the workforce directly after high school or enrol in community college. Those with more highly educated parents who promoted university education, either directly or indirectly, were more likely to follow in their parents' academic footsteps.

However, these patterns do not represent everyone's experience – statistics, by their very nature, report on averages and not exceptional cases. We learned from our interviews that some students from low-income families, including recent immigrants, made it to higher education, and once there, their social class origins lost significance as a predictor of their future occupations or incomes. Those who grew up in rural Ontario proved more likely to enter and remain in the middle class if they attended university.

By contrast, subgroup analysis of the survey revealed that some individuals from affluent backgrounds did not pursue or complete university for a variety of reasons – other interests, personal relationships, or health concerns may have influenced their life paths. We also acknowledge that our study did not reach those who were unable or unwilling to be surveyed or interviewed or those who dropped out before graduating from high school; those histories remain unknown. Even if our participants' overall trajectories were predicted accurately, their individual stories varied greatly because of their social origins, and we attempted to capture both specific and general experiences in recounting their decades-long journeys.

We note further that our participants' children had high educational attainment – the majority completed university or college, a probable sign that occupational success depends more on high levels of formal education now than when the Class of '73 graduated from high school. Despite this high level of achievement for the children of the Class of '73, evidence continues to reveal that parental education plays a role in how well one's children perform academically. This is especially true when it comes to perpetuating educational disadvantage. In our interview sample, for example, *all* children who had not pursued postsecondary education had Class of '73 parents who also had no credentials beyond high school.

Employment

We also observed discernible patterns of employment within the cohort. Our participants witnessed and contributed to significant changes in the way work was managed and conducted. Since the 1980s, computerization, robotics, and corporate restructuring have had an impact on almost everyone's life. Rather than engaging in formal educational programs (though some individuals did so), our participants largely learned on the job or enrolled in short courses to upgrade their skills. New technology transformed the workplace, from the factory floor to the hospital lab to the accounting office, and the Class of '73 was demographically at the forefront of this shift. They adapted – some more easily than others – and while they encountered a steep learning curve at times, they appeared to manage the occupational disruption caused by new technology.

The turbulent economy, which had seen waves of growth and retraction since the 1970s, potentially raised more concerns. The impact of economic uncertainty fell harder on some industries than others. The decline of manufacturing was especially noticeable in Ontario, as was the significant growth of the service sector, which employed most of the working population by the turn of the millennium. The economic downturn in 2008–9 was almost unprecedented, but because Class of '73 members were veteran employees with seniority at the time, they were less affected by this disruption than young people in the early stages of their careers.

The permanent entry of women into the labour force in the late twentieth and early twenty-first centuries held enormous importance for this cohort. It reflected the removal of many barriers to traditionally male-dominated professions and vocations. Unlike previous generations, women with unconventional interests could potentially follow them, and those with high occupational aspirations could potentially realize them. Extended maternity and parental leave allowed more Canadian mothers to take time off while retaining their jobs. The shifting policy landscape was now influencing life paths and personal choices. The transformation, however, was not complete. Individually, women might still face gender bias on the job, and they remain likely to earn less than men in similar positions. Furthermore – whether by choice, socialization, or a combination of the two – women and men continued to dominate specific occupation workforces (e.g., nurses vs. auto mechanics).

Shifting Cultural Landscape

We also learned that changes were afoot in the workplace and community regarding the experiences of racialized populations seeking to overcome cultural and institutional barriers that had long impeded their full participation in society. Canada's commitment to nondiscrimination in the workplace and other institutions was enshrined in the highest law of the land with section 15 of the Charter of Rights and Freedoms, which came into force in 1985, along with provincial human rights laws.

Immigrants were increasingly nonwhite, and multiculturalism emerged as a distinguishing feature of Canada's self-definition. Offices, factories, schools, and hospitals became more diverse over time, particularly in larger urban areas. Individually, members of racialized groups – a distinct minority in our study, given the early 1970s demographics –

reported relatively little overt discrimination, but they and their white peers increasingly recognized tensions around race relations as organizations grappled with traditional attitudes amid changing demographics.

LGBTQ2S cohort members mostly concealed their sexual orientation as they entered the workplace, fearing intolerance or ostracization from coworkers and even family members. They became more open towards the end of their careers, sensing greater public acceptance of different sexual orientations, though they remained wary and unconvinced that full equality of treatment had been achieved. This conflict, like that of racial minorities, was ongoing and unresolved.

As baby boomers reached adulthood, religious values and practices shifted as well. Many Canadians identified with a religious community, but they valued and practised religion less than their parents' generation. Though a small percentage of the population manifested as deeply religious, Canadians experienced more secular times in the 1970s. Nonetheless, as our participants grew older, their interest in religion revived to some degree. Religious organizations, in addition to meeting spiritual needs, may have provided a sense of community and social connection during the retirement years.

Households, Families, and Child-Rearing

Change also appeared within the household and family, as gender roles shifted without undergoing drastic change. Unmarried couples cohabited more than ever before, and the law caught up with this reality by recognizing common-law spouses' legal rights. Men's and women's ages at marriage rose, while birth rates fell as couples chose to have fewer children than previous generations. Men did more housework than in the past, but women continued to do most household tasks, a pattern that persisted long after their children had left the family home. Women were also more likely than men to adjust their work schedules to accommodate childcare and other domestic demands.

Baby boomers adopted a variety of child-rearing styles, but certain patterns distinguished their approaches from those of their parents. Boomers were less authoritarian and more directive than their parents. To put it another way, the Class of '73 generation experienced more discipline but also more autonomy in their social lives as children than their own offspring. This shift resulted from parents' desire to help their children cultivate their interests, achieve their goals, and avoid perceived dangers as they grew up. Following legal reforms in the late 1960s, divorce rates increased, causing additional stress in some families, particularly those led by single mothers. In the latter half of the twentieth century, the Western world appeared to have become more child-centred. Such broad generalizations come with risks, but both survey data and interviews tended to support these conclusions.

The baby boomers' children differed from previous generations in another way: they typically lived at home until well into their twenties. Since the 1990s, the rising cost of housing and unevenness in the labour market have hampered the efforts of young people, even well-educated ones, to attain financial self-sufficiency. Furthermore, the children of more than 40 per cent of our study's participants left the family home (possibly to attend university) and later returned to live with their parents for a period.

Approaching Retirement

Even as they cared for their children, our subjects felt increasingly obligated to care for their aging parents, who were living longer than ever. Women were more likely than men to be responsible for parental support and far more likely to cite such concerns as a reason for retiring. At the same time, our participants sought to assist with grandchildren whenever possible, with female spouses again playing a larger role than males. Overall, grandchildren brought the Class of '73 grandparents joy, fulfilment, and family bonding.

Along with caring for elders and engaging with grandchildren – though lower birth rates have reduced the number of grandchildren across Canada (Statistics Canada 2019) – retirees filled their days pursuing current pastimes or cultivating new interests, exercising, gathering with friends, travelling, and connecting with family more frequently. At the same time, some people felt challenged without the daily routines that full-time employment provided, especially if they had not developed other interests.

Many of our participants planned to continue working or transition into full retirement gradually. Like other Canadians looking for a better work-life balance, they turned to part-time work because they valued the structure (and the work) that such a schedule provided, along with the increased freedom to pursue other interests. As researchers discovered, people from this generation desired a more positive retirement experience than simply "not working." In an era when compulsory retirement has significantly diminished, they increasingly seek a workable transition rather than a sharp adjustment to retirement years. As baby boomers navigate the unique economic circumstances of the twenty-first century and live longer than previous generations, they continue to forge their own path through these stages.

For the Class of '73, the transition to retirement was smoothest for those who had planned and had sufficient resources (pension and/or savings) to live comfortably. Those who were forced to leave their jobs earlier than expected because of stress, conflict, or illness tended to struggle more with this life course transition. Single adults might be particularly affected by the loss of work-based social relationships.

Though none of our interviewees considered themselves poor (in fact, the Class of '73 was, on average, significantly better off than other Canadians of similar ages), those retirees who were poor would have faced enormous challenges (Statistics Canada 2022c). More than 60 per cent of our subjects who had not yet retired believed their standard of living would not change after retirement, while slightly more than 30 per cent expected their standard of living to decline somewhat or significantly.

Financial circumstances and public policy can have a significant impact on how boomers plan and carry out their retirement (Humpel et al. 2009). These effects may be exacerbated for boomer women who have more precarious employment histories and increased caregiving responsibilities (Sawyer and James 2018). Canadian public policy, which provided the Canada Pension Plan and Old Age Security along with the Guaranteed Income Supplement for the poorest, helped mitigate the poverty rate for those over sixty-five. At 4.7 per cent, this rate was significantly lower than for younger Canadians and lower than in most other OECD countries, though single women of all ages remained especially vulnerable to poverty (Employment and Social Development Canada 2022; Statistics Canada 2022c).

COVID-19

We took advantage of the opportunity in face-to-face interviews to question our subjects about the impact of the pandemic on their lives, as neither retirees nor anyone else had planned for the outbreak of COVID-19. The sessions took place in the autumn and winter of 2020–1, six months to a year after the World Health Organization's declaration of a worldwide pandemic. The interviews were all conducted through Zoom, a by-product of working and social life under COVID. Rather than visiting subjects in their homes, as we had done in earlier stages of the project, we easily conversed with them online, reaching people all over Canada.

As we've mentioned throughout the book, our participants were dealing with COVID-19 in various ways, some better than others. Most were unable to see loved ones or saw them only infrequently, which caused stress and regret. Those who had visited their elderly parents regularly were particularly concerned. Interviewees who did not have partners felt especially isolated; one participant told us that our conversation was the longest human interaction they had had in a year.

Most experienced periods of boredom, and instead of engaging in social activities, they sought to stay active and fit by walking on a regular basis. Some expressed occasional frustration when children lived in the family home, especially when space was limited. Those who remained employed learned, like many people worldwide, to do their jobs online, with some feeling relieved to eliminate their daily commute. Those we spoke with appeared to be in good health, though those suffering from the pandemic or other illnesses were unlikely to be available for interviews. To summarize, the pandemic disturbed but did not appear to have harmed their lives.

Life Satisfaction

Indeed, our subjects experienced considerable satisfaction with their personal lives, with 96 per cent indicating they were satisfied or very satisfied. In a related question, nearly all participants claimed to be happy or very happy with their current lives. Nonetheless, 44 per cent (more women than men) reported some level of current stress, and roughly one-third of our interviewees expressed regret about certain aspects of their lives since Grade 12. The most common disappointment among this group was their failure to pursue postsecondary education or to pursue a different postsecondary path.

Class of '73 members fared well mentally compared to ten years earlier, but many more people, particularly men, felt less healthy than in the previous decade. Our respondents, who had lived through an era of enormous change, much uncertainty, and periodic turmoil, had nonetheless reached an age of contentment, enriched by family and aided by unique educational and occupational opportunities that had arisen in the late twentieth and early twenty-first centuries.

Closing Remarks

Overall, the Class of '73 study's Phase 7 findings show evidence of structured individualization (Rudd and Evans 1998) or bounded agency (Evans 2002), both of which are key concepts in the life course perspective we use throughout the book. Class of '73 members' experiences are structured and limited in the sense that social advantages and disadvantages are passed down through generations. We discovered that Class of '73 participants' parents' educational level played a significant role in their own educational attainment, which in turn affected their occupational paths and transitions into retirement. We also saw how the children of Class of '73 participants benefited from or were limited by their parents' education.

Nonetheless, we found significant evidence of social mobility (particularly upward social mobility) and heard in interviews that study participants felt a significant amount of control and agency over their lives. The respondents discussed several key life elements – choosing to attend university when no one else in their family had, responding to occupational opportunities, taking risks in changing jobs or becoming self-employed, challenging gender norms and conventions, and deciding to continue working or retire – as agentic rather than structurally determined.

Longitudinal studies have been a cornerstone of social science research in many countries, providing valuable insights into human development and societal changes over extended periods (Bengtson 1975; Bengtson and Roberts 1991; Clausen 1993; Elder 1974, 1998; Hauser, Sheridan, and Warren 2000; Marmot and Shipley 1996). While the United States, Australia, and the United Kingdom have established histories of conducting such studies, Canada has lagged in this area (Robson, 2021). However, the Class of '73 project in Canada shares several commonalities with these international longitudinal studies while also possessing unique characteristics.

These studies typically share key features, including long-term follow-up spanning decades, a focus on transitions and trajectories examining how early life experiences influence later outcomes and an emphasis on the historical context that recognizes the impact of social change on individual lives. Despite these similarities, important differences exist among the studies. Each had a unique focus within the life course perspective, such as the Wisconsin Longitudinal Study's (WLS) emphasis on educational and occupational attainment, the Whitehall Studies' emphasis on social determinants of health (Marmot and Shipley 1996), or Bengtson's concentration on intergenerational relationships. Data collection and analysis methods varied, with some studies relying more on quantitative data and others incorporating qualitative elements. Researchers also made distinct theoretical contributions to the life course perspective, such as Elder's emphasis on timing in life events, the WLS's empirical evidence of stratification, and Bengtson's focus on intergenerational solidarity. Additionally, the geographic focus differed, ranging from national studies to more regionally or provincially centred projects.

Common findings across these longitudinal studies have provided invaluable insights into human development, social mobility, and the long-term effects of early life experiences. Family socio-economic status and parental education levels have been identified as strong predictors of children's educational outcomes, while early academic performance in adolescence directly predicts adult educational attainment. Higher educational attainment has been consistently linked to better occupational outcomes, including more stable and higher-paying jobs. Several studies reveal persistent gender differences in domestic responsibilities, despite increased educational and occupational attainment for women, who often face greater challenges in balancing career and family obligations (Clausen 1993). Furthermore, educational and occupational attainment have been found to strongly predict financial security in retirement (Bengtson and Roberts 1991; Elder 1998). Through these findings, longitudinal studies have contributed significantly to our understanding of individual and societal changes over time, shaping our knowledge of human development and social dynamics.

Our study tells the story of a baby boomer generation through nearly half a century of data collection – an unparalleled span in Canadian data collection history. We believe our findings highlight the importance of such longitudinal analysis. The data gathered illustrate the complex ways that earlier life conditions (such as socio-economic status or parental background) influence young people's trajectories and shape their life course. Even with significant attrition over time, this project has unearthed social processes that would be impossible to capture in one-time cross-sectional surveys or even a short-term longitudinal study.

Appendix 1: Methodological Background to the Study of the Class of '73

The study of the Class of '73 began in 1972 when university enrolments were still growing but applications for admissions declined. At the same time, trend data led to increasingly inaccurate enrolment projections. To address this, the Ontario Ministry of Colleges and Universities (MCU) sought to monitor high school students' attitudes and behaviours regarding their educational plans as a projection tool. The MCU approached Paul Anisef to conduct this study. With assistance from the Institute for Social Research (ISR) at York University, researchers surveyed Ontario Grade 12 students in the spring of 1973. They selected ninety-nine high schools representing four types of communities across Ontario and secured participation from ninety-seven schools. ISR staff administered survey questionnaires in one or two Grade 12 classrooms per school, collecting 2,555 usable responses for what became Phase 1 of the project. This study did not include those students who had left school before Grade 12, estimated at 20–30 per cent of the Class of '73.

The MCU aimed to determine whether behavioural trends could be predicted based on intentions, sponsoring two follow-up studies. In Phase 2, conducted in November 1973, researchers performed a telephone survey to learn about respondents' activities and plans for fall 1974. This phase, which achieved an 84.4 per cent response rate from 2,156 participants, revealed that many former students had entered the workforce or started attending community colleges. Phase 3 followed in October and November 1974, eighteen months after the initial survey. This phase compared respondents' earlier career aspirations with their actual outcomes and recorded responses from 2,163 participants, maintaining an 84.7 per cent response rate.

During the 1970s, some public groups expressed concerns about oversaturating the job market with highly trained young adults amid slower economic growth. Critics also questioned the value of postsecondary education in job preparation. The limited information available on the education-labour market connection prompted further research, leading to a third follow-up study.

In the fall of 1977, Paul Anisef and colleagues Anton H. Turrittin and Gottfried Paasche proposed extending the study into a longitudinal project. Nearly five years had passed since Phase 1, allowing researchers to explore links between education and employment outcomes. The team noted that Canadian longitudinal studies of youth rarely extended beyond short follow-ups. By beginning the study while participants were still in Grade 12, the Class of '73 study set itself apart from similar Canadian panel research of the era.

The study also aimed to investigate the effects of factors like gender, socio-economic status, and urban/rural origins on access to postsecondary education. By applying a social stratification perspective, the team sought to deepen social science research on how societal institutions shape individual life chances. They hoped Phase 4 would provide empirical findings to test competing sociological perspectives, such as functional and conflict paradigms.

During Phase 4, researchers maintained their commitment to a survey approach, which had proven effective in earlier phases for generating generalizable findings. Recognizing the limitations of surveys in capturing individual perspectives, they added qualitative methods. The team conducted unstructured interviews with a subgroup of one hundred participants from the Toronto area, selecting a smaller group for in-depth interviews.

Researchers began designing the main follow-up survey in the summer of 1978. They sent a one-page questionnaire to parents to update participants' contact information and gather preliminary details about their education, employment, and marital status. With financial support from the MCU, the team traced subjects, distributed questionnaires, and processed responses. They contacted participants with a newsletter summarizing findings from earlier phases, ultimately obtaining responses from 1,522 individuals (59.6 per cent of the Phase 1 sample).

Researchers published their findings in "Is the Die Cast?" in 1980. This report and related papers and articles sparked discussions within the social science and policy communities, sustaining interest in the longitudinal project. The findings illuminated educational and occupational pathways, analysed through lenses such as gender, socio-economic status, and region of origin.

Phase 5, conducted in the summers of 1987 and 1988, involved brief telephone interviews to update contact information and gather new data.

Now joined by Fredrick D. Ashbury, the study team secured responses from 1,129 participants, or 44.2 per cent of the original sample.

Between 1989 and 1991, the team analysed data from Phase 5 and developed a broader conceptual framework for Phase 6. They decided to use a life course perspective, which considers transitions to adulthood as non-linear processes. By 1992, additional researchers had joined the team, including Paul Axelrod, a social historian; Carl E. James, a sociologist with the Faculty of Education; Zeng Lin, a doctoral candidate in sociology – all at York University – and Etta Baichman-Anisef, a master's student at the Ontario Institute for Studies in Education.

Supported by a research grant from the Social Science and Humanities Research Council (SSHRC), the team traced participants and developed a research design for Phase 6. They contacted respondents in January 1994 with a newsletter and summary of Class of '73 events, receiving positive responses from 160 individuals for interviews. Focus group interviews involving forty-four participants across Toronto, London, and Ottawa supplemented the survey. Researchers pretested the questionnaire and sent it to participants in January 1995, receiving 788 responses (30.8 per cent of the original sample).

While longitudinal studies often lose participants over time, the team evaluated the representativeness of Phase 6 respondents using gender, socio-economic status, and regional variables. The evaluation confirmed that the sample remained representative, though rural respondents and participants with low socio-economic status outside Metro Toronto were slightly overrepresented. For a detailed discussion of the methodology used in Phase 7 of the study, see chapter 1. During Phase 7, Professor Wolfgang Lehmann of the Department of Sociology at Western University joined the research team. In addition, two PhD students, Erica Thomson from the Department of Sociology at McMaster University and Erika McDonald from the Department of Sociology at York University joined the team.

Readers may contact the authors for further details on the methodology and research findings.

Source: This appendix is adapted from Anisef et al. (2000, 3–8).

Appendix 2: Sample Attrition over the Seven Phases of the Class of '73 Study

Longitudinal studies, such as the Class of '73, often experience sample attrition or participant loss over time. This phenomenon has been previously examined in our publications (Anisef et al. 2000; Robson et al. 2020) and in appendices of earlier reports from the Class of '73, including those from Phase 3 (Anisef 1975) and Phase 4 (Anisef, Paasche, and Turrittin 1980). In this appendix, we further investigate sample attrition with the inclusion of data from Phase 7.

In Phase 7, the sample retains 11 per cent of the original cohort from 1973, indicating a 64.5 per cent attrition rate from Phase 6. Since Phase 6 in 1995, only two cohort members have been confirmed deceased. We undertook extensive efforts to contact all other known cohort members, a process detailed both in the main text and extensively in Robson et al. (2020). Given the extended period and the unique nature of our study, assessing whether a 35.5 per cent retention rate after twenty-two years of non-contact is high or low is challenging. Nevertheless, our sample has remained relatively representative across the respective phases.

Table A1 illustrates the attrition of our sample from survey to survey concerning key variables. Table A2 presents the distribution of selected background characteristics across each survey phase. Notably, Table A1 shows that nearly all participants were retained during the early phases, from Phase 1 and Phase 2 in 1973 to Phase 3 in 1974. As expected, attrition increased as the intervals between phases lengthened. Although the final Phase 7 survey retained only 11 per cent of the original sample, it remains somewhat representative of the initial cohort in Phase 1 in most respects.

Table A2 examines this representativeness, showing that the gender ratio of respondents remained consistent throughout all phases, achieving near gender parity. Phase 7 retained slightly more members from rural areas compared to those from Metro Toronto or other cities in Ontario, though the difference is not substantial (~8 per cent vs. ~11 per cent and ~14 per cent, respectively) compared to Phase 1. However, regional representation is relatively similar between Phase 6 and Phase 7. Table A1 indicates that a higher percentage of participants from rural areas were retained across the later phases. Retention across socio-economic status (SES) was similar for all categories, with the highest retention from low SES and the lowest from medium-low SES. The retention difference between SES categories was less than five per cent, indicating similar representation between Phase 1 and Phase 7. This is supported by Table A2, where SES representation from Phase 1 to Phase 7 remains within 6 per cent of the original survey.

The most significant disparities in representativeness were found in educational attainment, with more respondents in Phase 7 having obtained university degrees or college diplomas compared to earlier phases. This shift reflects a broader societal trend of increased educational attainment over time and is not significant enough to raise concerns about attrition bias in our sample. Furthermore, this increase aligns with the Class of '73's educational orientation (Anisef et al. 2000).

Significant efforts were made to contact members of the Class of '73 after a gap of over twenty years between Phase 6 and Phase 7. However, limited funding and the absence of government databases made this search particularly challenging (Robson et al. 2020). The lack of comparable long-term studies in Canada complicates the assessment of our attrition rates. Previous findings indicate that similar international longitudinal studies with higher retention rates often benefited from access to government databases and more frequent participant follow-ups (Anisef et al. 2000). Consequently, evaluating the overall success of our attrition is challenging, leading us to compare our phases internally to ensure general representativeness and to examine retention rates across key variables as shown in Table A1.

Table A1. Sample Attrition over Seven Phases of the Class of '73

Variable			1973 Phase 1	1973 Phase 2	1974 Phase 3	1979 Phase 4	1987/88 Phase 5	1995 Phase 6	2019 Phase 7
	Cases		2,555	2,156	2,163	1,522	1,129	788	280
	% of original cases		100.0%	84.4	84.7	59.6	44.2	30.8	11.0
	% of previous survey		100.0%	84.4	100.3	70.4	74.2	69.8	35.5
Region in 1973	Metro Toronto	n=535	100.0%	89.3	85.4	52.0	37.6	23.6	7.9
	Other cities	n=1182	100.0%	85.7	83.8	60.2	43.1	28.3	10.6
	Rural areas	n=838	100.0%	79.4	85.4	63.5	49.4	37.9	13.5
Socio-economic status 1973	High	n=582	100.0%	90.9	87.1	64.1	46.6	32.3	10.8
	Medium high	n=538	100.0%	88.7	86.7	61.5	47.2	34.8	11.9
	Medium low	n=626	100.0%	81.5	83.1	56.7	41.1	28.1	8.8
	Low	n=666	100.0%	79.4	84.2	59.5	44.4	29.9	13.1
	Missing cases SES		143	111	109	67	46	28	11
Socio-economic status 1973HIGH SES	Metro Toronto	n=167	100.0%	92.8	89.8	63.5	41.3	31.1	12.0
	Other cities	n=300	100.0%	92.0	86.0	63.7	46.0	30.0	10.0
	Rural areas	n=115	100.0%	85.2	86.1	66.1	55.7	40.0	11.3
Socio-economic status 1973 LOW SES	Metro Toronto	n=89	100.0%	94.4	92.1	47.2	33.7	11.2	2.2
	Other cities	n=259	100.0%	81.1	81.9	58.3	41.7	27.0	15.8
	Rural areas	n=318	100.0%	73.9	84.0	63.8	49.7	37.4	13.8
Educational attainment 1979	High school only	n=571				100.0%		48.9	17.7
	Some college/university	n=219				100.0%		43.8	16.0
	College diploma	n=293				100.0%		56.7	22.2
	University degree	n=439				100.0%		54.0	18.0

*Based on educational attainment in 1979

Table A2. Background Variable Distribution over Seven Phases of the Class of '73

Variable		1973 Phase 1	1973 Phase 2	1974 Phase 3	1979 Phase 4	1987/88 Phase 5	1995 Phase 6	2019 Phase 7
Gender	Cases	2,551	2,156	2,163	1,522	1,129	781	280
	Males	48.9%	48.7%	48.7%	48.0%	47.8%	48.3%	50.7%
	Females	51.1	51.3	51.3	52.0	52.2	51.7	49.3
Region in 1973	Cases	2,555	2,156	2,163	1,522	1,124	778	280
	Metro Toronto	20.9%	22.2%	21.1%	18.3%	17.9%	16.2%	15.0%
	Other cities	46.3	47.0	45.8	46.8	45.3	42.9	44.6
	Rural areas	32.8	30.1	33.1	35.0	36.8	40.9	40.4
Socio-economic status in 1973	Cases	2,412	2,045	2,054	1,445	1,078	750	269
	High	24.1%	25.9%	24.7%	25.6%	25.1%	25.1%	23.4%
	Medium high	22.3	23.3	22.7	22.8	23.6	24.9	23.8
	Medium low	26.0	24.9	25.3	24.4	23.8	23.5	20.5
	Low	27.6	25.9	27.3	27.2	27.5	26.5	32.3
Educational attainment	Cases				1,522		778*	279
	High school only				37.5%		35.9%	25.1%
	Some college/university				14.4		12.3	9.3
	College diploma				19.3		21.3	29.7
	University degree				28.8		30.5	35.8

References

Abada, T., F. Hou, and B. Ram. 2009. "Ethnic Differences in Educational Attainment Among the Children of Canadian Immigrants." *Canadian Journal of Sociology* 34 (1): 1–28. https://doi.org/10.29173/cjs1651.

Ahmed, W. 13 November 2019. "Measuring Ontario's Urban-Rural Divide." Ontario 360 Policy Papers. https://on360.ca/policy-papers/measuring-ontarios-urban-rural-divide/.

Anderson, E. 3 August 2024. "School of Joy." *Globe and Mail.* www.theglobeandmail.com/canada/article-can-happiness-be-taught-academics-who-hope-to-answer-that-have-found/.

Andres, L. 2015. *A Retrospective Analysis of the Sequence of Life Course Events Over 22 Years.* Vancouver: BC Council on Admissions and Transfer. https://files.eric.ed.gov/fulltext/ED553997.pdf.

Andres, L., W. Lauterbach, J. Jongbloed, and H. Hümme. 2021. "Gender, Education, and Labour Market Participation Across the Life Course: A Canada/Germany Comparison." *International Journal of Lifelong Education* 40 (2): 170–89. https://doi.org/10.1080/02601370.2021.1924302.

Angus Reid Institute. 12 August 2019. "Caregiving in Canada: As Population Ages, One-in-Four Canadians Over 30 Are Looking After Loved Ones." http://angusreid.org/wp-content/uploads/2019/08/2019.08.12_Caregiving.pdf.

Anisef, P., P. Axelrod, E. Baichman-Anisef, C.E. James, and A.H. Turrittin. 2000. *Opportunity and Uncertainty: Life Course Experiences of the Class of '73.* Toronto: University of Toronto Press. https://doi.org/10.3138/9781442678101.

Anisef, P., J.G. Paasche, and A.H. Turrittin. 1980. *Is the Die Cast? Educational Achievements and Work Destinations of Ontario Youth. A Six Year Follow-Up of the Critical Juncture High School Students.* Toronto: Ontario Ministry of Colleges and Universities.

Anisef, P. (1975). The critical juncture: Realization of the educational and career intentions of grade 12 students in Ontario. Ministry of Colleges and Universities, Ontario.

Axelrod, P. 1982. *Scholars and Dollars: Politics, Economics and the Universities of Ontario, 1945–1980.* Toronto: University of Toronto Press. https://doi .org/10.3138/9781442679603

Badley, E.M., M. Canewares, A.V. Perruccio, S. Hogg-Johnson, and M.A. Gignac. 2015. "Benefits Gained, Benefits Lost: Comparing Baby Boomers to Other Generations in a Longitudinal Cohort Study of Self-Rated Health." *Milbank Quarterly* 93 (1): 40–72. https://doi.org/10.1111/1468-0009.12105.

Baker, M. 1989. *Canadian Youth in a Changing World.* Ottawa: Library of Parliament, Research Branch, Political and Social Affairs Division.

Balakrishnan, T.R., E. Lapierre-Adamczyk, and K.K. Kroki. 1993. *Family and Childbearing in Canada: A Demographic Analysis.* Toronto: University of Toronto Press.

Beaujot, R., and D. Kerr. 2007. "Emerging Youth Transitions Patterns in Canada: Opportunities and Risks." *PSC Discussion Papers Series* 21 (5): article 1. https://ir.lib.uwo.ca/cgi/viewcontent.cgi?article=1016&context=pscpapers.

Becker, C.K., and S.T. Trautmann. 2022. "Does Happiness Increase in Old Age? Longitudinal Evidence from 20 European Countries." *Journal of Happiness Studies* 23: 3625–54. https://doi.org/10.1007/s10902-022-00569-4.

Bengtson, V.L. 1975. "Generation and Family Effects in Value Socialization." *American Sociological Review* 40 (3): 358–71. https://doi.org/10.2307 /2094463

Bengtson, V.L., and R.E.L. Roberts. 1991. "Intergenerational Solidarity in Aging Families: An Example of Formal Theory Construction." *Journal of Marriage and the Family* 53 (4): 856–70. https://doi.org/10.2307/352993

Berger, J., and A. Motte. November 2007. "Mind the Access Gap: Breaking Down the Barriers to Postsecondary Education." *Policy Options.* http://irpp .org/wp-content/uploads/assets/po/ontario-2007-dalton-mcguinty/berger .pdf.

Bernstein, B. 1977. "Social Class, Language, and Socialisation." In *Power and Ideology in Education*, edited by J. Karabel and A.H. Halsey, 473–86. Oxford: Oxford University Press.

Bianchi, S.M., J.P. Robinson, and M.A. Milkie. 2006. *Changing Rhythms of American Family Life.* New York: Russell Sage Foundation.

Blanchflower, D.G. 2021. "Is Happiness U-Shaped Everywhere? Age and Subjective Well-Being in 145 Countries." *Journal of Population Economics* 34: 575–624. https://doi.org/10.1007/s00148-020-00797-z.

Bonikowska, A., and G. Schellenberg. 2013. *An Overview of the Working Lives of Older Baby Boomers.* Ottawa: Statistics Canada. https://www150.statcan .gc.ca/n1/en/pub/11f0019m/11f0019m2013352-eng.pdf?st=qeB7D_Q-.

Bourdieu, P. 1977 [1972]. *Outline of a Theory of Practice.* Translated by R. Nice. Cambridge: Cambridge University Press.

– 1990 [1980]. *The Logic of Practice.* Translated by R. Nice. Cambridge: Polity Press.

Bourdieu, P., and J.C. Passeron. 1977 [1970]. *Reproduction in Education, Society and Culture.* Translated by R. Nice. London: Sage.

Bourdieu, P., and L.J. Wacquant. 1992. *An Invitation to Reflexive Sociology.* Chicago: University of Chicago Press.

Bowlby, G. February 2007. "Defining Retirement." *Perspectives on Labour and Income* 8 (2). Ottawa: Statistics Canada. https://www150.statcan.gc.ca/n1/pub/75-001-x/10207/9584-eng.htm.

Boyd, M., and M. Vickers. 2000. "100 Years of Immigration in Canada." *Canadian Social Trends* 58 (Autumn): 2–13. Ottawa: Statistics Canada (Cat. No. 11-008). https://boydmon.artsci.utoronto.ca/wp-content/uploads/2020/11/2000_Boyd_Vickers_100yrs_Imm-2.pdf.

Brown, P. 2013. "Education, Opportunity and the Prospects for Social Mobility." *British Journal of Sociology of Education* 34 (5–6): 678–700. https://doi.org/10.1080/01425692.2013.816036.

Burke, J.B., and J.E. Stets. 2022. *Identity Theory: Revised and Expanded.* Oxford University Press. https://doi.org/10.1093/oso/9780197617182.001.0001

Campbell, J., and L. Gilmore. 2007. "Intergenerational Continuities and Discontinuities in Parenting Styles." *Australian Journal of Psychology* 59 (3): 140–50. https://doi.org/10.1080/00049530701449471.

Campbell, M. 30 August 2016. "Forget Teen Pregnancy: Older Moms Are the New Normal." *Maclean's.* www.macleans.ca/society/health/forget-teen-pregnancies-older-moms-new-normal/.

Canadian Council on Learning. 2006. *Canadian Postsecondary Education: A Positive Record – An Uncertain Future.* Ottawa: Canadian Council on Learning. https://files.eric.ed.gov/fulltext/ED525257.pdf.

– 2009. *Postsecondary Education in Canada: Meeting Our Needs? 2008–2009.* Ottawa: Canadian Council on Learning. https://eric.ed.gov/?id=ED525254.

Canadian Dental Association. 2022. "The Economic Realities of Practice." www.cda-adc.ca/en/services/internationallytrained/economic/.

Canadian Education Statistics Council. December 2010. *Education Indicators in Canada: Report of the Pan-Canadian Education Indicators Program.* Ottawa: Statistics Canada. www.statcan.gc.ca/pub/81-582-x/81-582-x2010004-eng.htm.

Canadian Fitness and Lifestyle Research Institute. June 1997. *Progress in Prevention: "Life Satisfaction.".* Ottawa: Canadian Fitness and Lifestyle Research Institute.

Chatoor, K., E. MacKay, and L. Hudak. 2019. *Parental Education and Postsecondary Attainment: Does the Apple Fall Far from the Tree?* Toronto:

Higher Education Quality Council of Ontario. https://heqco.ca/pub
/parental-education-and-postsecondary-attainment-does-the-apple-fall-far
-from-the-tree/.

Chen, L.-Y., E. Oparina, N. Powdthavee, and S. Srisuma. 2019. "Have
Econometric Analyses of Happiness Data Been Futile? A Simple Truth
About Happiness Scales." IZA Institute of Labour Economics Discussion
Paper no. 12152. https://doi.org/10.2139/ssrn.3390139.

Chetty, R., D. Grusky, M. Hell, N. Hendren, R. Manduca, and J. Narang. 2017.
"The Fading American Dream: Trends in Absolute Income Mobility Since
1940." *Science* 356 (6336): 398–406. https://doi.org/10.1126/science
.aal4617.

Chiu, J. 9 November 2020. "Why Canada's Media Industry Is in More Danger
Than You Think – and What We Can Do to Save It." *Toronto Star*. www.
thestar.com/business/2020/11/09/why-canadas-media-industry-is-in-more
-danger-than-you-think-and-what-we-can-do-to-save-it.html.

Clausen, J.A.1993. *American Lives: Looking Back at the Children of the Great
Depression.* New York: Free Press.

Clément, D. 2009. *Canada's Rights Revolution: Social Movements and Social
Change, 1937–1982.* Vancouver: University of British Columbia Press.

– 2016. *Human Rights in Canada: A History.* Waterloo, ON: Wilfrid Laurier
University Press. https://doi.org/10.51644/9781771121644

Cornelissen, L. 28 October 2019. *Religiosity in Canada and Its Evolution from
1985 to 2019.* Cat. no. 75-006-X. Ottawa: Statistics Canada. https://www150
.statcan.gc.ca/n1/en/catalogue/75-006-X202100100010.

Cornell, B. 30 October 1973. "Woman Engineers Get Good Jobs." *Toronto Star*,
E3.

Cornwall, M., and D.L. Thomas. 1990. "Family Religion and Personal
Communities: Examples from Mormonism." *Marriage and Family Review* 15
(1–2): 229–52. https://doi.org/10.1300/J002v15n01_11.

Cray, K. 31 May 2023. "Semi-Retirees Know the Key to Work-Life Balance." *The
Atlantic.* www.theatlantic.com/family/archive/2023/05/semi-retirement
-jobs-meaning-popularity/674234/.

Curtis, B., D.W. Livingstone, and H. Smaller. 1992. *Stacking the Deck: The
Streaming of Working-Class Kids in Ontario Schools.* Toronto: Our Schools/Our
Selves.

Daly, M. 2020. "Generations, Age and Life Course: Towards an Integral Social
Policy Framework of Analysis." *Contemporary Social Science* 15 (3): 291–301.
https://doi.org/10.1080/21582041.2018.1455107.

Denton, F.T., A.L. Robb, and B.G. Spencer. 1981. *Unemployment and Labour
Force Behaviour of Young People: Evidence from Canada and Ontario.* Toronto:
Ontario Economic Council/University of Toronto Press. https://doi
.org/10.3138/9781442653719

Denton, F.T., and B.G. Spencer. 2009. "What Is Retirement? A Review and Assessment of Alternative Concepts and Measures." *Canadian Journal on Aging* 28 (1): 63–76. https://doi.org/10.1017/S0714980809090047.

Di Matteo, L. 2015. *An Analysis of Public and Private Sector Employment Trends in Canada, 1990–2013.* Vancouver: Fraser Institute. www.fraserinstitute.org /sites/default/files/analysis-of-public-and-private-sector-employment -trends-in-canada.pdf.

Doyle Driedger, S. 25 July 2004. "Maclean's Poll '02: Parents Say Kids OK." *Canadian Encyclopedia.* Republished from "What Parents Don't Know (or Won't Admit)." *Maclean's,* 30 September 2002. www.thecanadianencyclopedia .ca/en/article/macleans-poll-02-parents-say-kids-ok.

Duffy, B. 2021. *The Generation Myth: Why When You're Born Matters Less Than You Think.* New York: Basic Books.

Eichler, M., A.-M. Pedersen, and A. McIntosh. 14 January 2021. "Same-Sex Marriage in Canada." *Canadian Encyclopedia.* www. thecanadianencyclopedia.ca/en/article/same-sex-marriage-in-canada.

Elder, G.H., Jr. 1974. *Children of the Great Depression: Social Change in Life Experience.* University of Chicago Press.

– 1978. "Family History and the Life Course." In *Transitions: The Family and the Life Course in Historical Perspective,* edited by T.K. Hareven, 17–64. New York: Academic Press. https://doi.org/10.1016/B978-0-12-325150-3.50008-8

– 1998. "The Life Course as Developmental Theory." *Child Development* 69 (1): 1–12. https://doi.org/10.1111/j.1467-8624.1998.tb06128.x.

Employment and Social Development Canada. 23 March 2022. "Canada's Poverty Rate Decreased Significantly in 2020." *News Release.* www.canada .ca/en/employment-social-development/news/2022/03/canadas-poverty -rate-decreased-significantly-in-2020-federal-emergency-and-recovery -benefits-mitigated-the-pandemics-economic-impact.html.

Erwin, L., and D. MacLennan. 1994. "Introduction: Historical Backgrounds and Critical Perspectives." In *Sociology Education in Canada: Critical Perspectives on Theory, Research and Practice,* edited by L. Erwin and D. MacLennan, 1–25. Mississauga, ON: Copp Clark Longman.

Evans, K. 2002. "Taking Control of Their Lives? Agency in Young Adult Transitions in England and the New Germany." *Journal of Youth Studies* 5 (3): 245–69. https://doi.org/10.1080/1367626022000005965.

Fass, P.S. 2016. *The End of American Childhood: A History of Parenting from Life on the Frontier to the Managed Child.* Princeton, NJ: Princeton University Press. https://doi.org/10.1515/9781400880430

Fast, J., N. Keating, J. Eales, C. Kim, and Y. Lee. 2020. "Trajectories of Family Care Over the Life Course: Evidence from Canada." *Ageing and Society* 41 (5): 1145–62. https://doi.org/10.1017/S0144686X19001806.

Ferguson, J.S. 2016. *Women and Education: Qualifications, Skills and Technology.* Ottawa: Statistics Canada. https://www150.statcan.gc.ca/n1/pub/89 -503-x/2015001/article/14640-eng.htm

Fingerman, K., and M. Dolman-MacNab. 2013. "The Baby Boomers and Their Parents: Cohort Influences and Intergenerational Ties." In *The Baby Boomers Grow Up: Contemporary Perspectives on Midlife,* edited by S. Krauss Whitbourne and S.L. Willis, 237–59. New York: Routledge. https://doi .org/10.4324/9781315820958-14

Finnie, R., E. Lascelles, and A. Sweetman. 2005. *Who Goes? The Direct and Indirect Effects of Family Background on Access to Postsecondary Education.* Ottawa: Statistics Canada. https://www150.statcan.gc.ca/n1/en/catalogue /11F0019M2005237.

Fisher, D. 1999. "Canada: Influences on the Educational Systems, Twentieth -Century Developments, the Place of Education in the Society." https:// education.stateuniversity.com/pages/1811/Canada.html.

Foot, R., E. Yarhi, and A. McIntosh. 2 March 2020. "Canadian Charter of Rights and Freedoms." *Canadian Encyclopedia.* www.thecanadianencyclopedia.ca/en/article/ canadian-charter-of-rights-and-freedoms.

Frank, K., Y. Zhe, and M. Frenette. 27 January 2021. *The Changing Nature of Work in Canada Amid Recent Advances in Automation Technology.* Ottawa: Statistics Canada, Economic and Social Reports. https://www150 .statcan.gc.ca/n1/en/pub/36-28-0001/2021001/article/00004-eng .pdf?st=97kM_Fv3.

Genoe, M.R., T. Liechty, and H.R. Marston. 2018. "Retirement Transitions Among Baby Boomers: Findings from an Online Qualitative Study." *Canadian Journal on Aging* 37 (4): 450–63. https://doi.org/10.1017 /S0714980818000314.

Gettings, P.E., and L.B. Anderson. 2018. "Applying a Life Course Perspective to Retirement: A Literature Review and Research Agenda for Communication Scholars." *Annals of the International Communication Association* 42 (3): 224–41. https://doi.org/10.1080/23808985.2018.1497453.

Gidney, R. 1999. *From Hope to Harris: The Reshaping of Ontario's Schools.* Toronto: University of Toronto Press. https://doi.org/10.3138/9781442675087

Goldthorpe, J.H. 1996. "Class Analysis and the Reorientation of Class Theory: The Case of Persisting Differentials in Educational Attainment."*British Journal of Sociology of Education* 47 (3): 481–505. https://doi.org/10.2307 /591365.

– 2003. "The Myth of Education-Based Meritocracy: Why the Theory Isn't Working." *New Economy* 10 (4): 189–93. https://doi.org/10.1046/j.1468-0041 .2003.00324.x.

Gower, D. 1996. "Canada's Unemployment Mosaic in the 1990s." *Statistics Canada Perspectives on Labour and Incomes*, Spring. Cat. no. 75-001-XPE. https://www150.statcan.gc.ca/n1/en/pub/75-001-x/1996001/article/2524 -eng.pdf?st=CqipxW6T.

Green, L. 2010. *Understanding the Life Course: Sociological and Psychological Perspectives*. Malden, MA: Polity Press.

Haque, E. 2018. "Language, Race and the Impossibility of Multiculturalism." In *Race and Racialization: Essential Readings*, edited by T. Das Gupta, C.E. James, R. Maaka, G.-E. Galabuzi, and C. Andersen, 259–74. Toronto: Canadian Scholars' Press.

Hauser, R.M., J.T. Sheridan, and J.R. Warren. 2000. "Socioeconomic Achievements of Siblings in the Life Course: New Findings from the Wisconsin Longitudinal Study." *Research on Aging* 21 (2): 338–78. https:// doi.org/10.1177/0164027599212008.

Hazel, M. 2018. *Reasons for Working at 60 and Beyond*. Ottawa: Statistics Canada. https://www150.statcan.gc.ca/n1/pub/71-222-x/71-222-x2018003-eng.htm.

Heinz, W.R. 1991. "Status Passages, Social Risks and the Life Course: A Conceptual Framework." In *Theoretical Advances in Life Course Research*, edited by W.R. Heinz, 51–65. Weinheim: Deutscher Studien Verlag.

– 1995. "Status Passages as Micro-Macro Linkages in Life Course." In *Society and Biography: Interrelationships between Social Structure, Institutions and the Life Course*, edited by A. Weimann and W.R. Heinz, 51–66. Weinheim: Deutscher Stuiden Verlag.

Helliwell, J.F., R. Layard, J.D. Sachs, J.E. De Neve, L.B. Aknin, H. Haifang, and S. Wang. eds. 2020. *World Happiness Report 2020*. New York: Sustainable Development Solutions Network.

Helliwell, J.F., R. Layard, J.D. Sachs, J.E. De Neve, L.B. Aknin, and S. Wang. eds. 2024. *World Happiness Report 2024*. Oxford: University of Oxford, Well Being Research Centre.

Hirshhorn, R., and Hirshhorn Consulting Inc. 2015. *Impacts of Structural Changes in the Canadian Economy*. Ottawa: Industry Canada. https://ised -isde.canada.ca/site/economic-analysis-statistics/en/economic-research /research-papers/impacts-structural-changes-canadian-economy /impacts-structural-changes-canadian-economy.

Ho, J.H., and J.M. Raymo. 2009. "Expectations and Realization of Joint Retirement among Dual-Worker Couples." *Research on Aging* 31 (2): 153–79. https://doi.org/10.1177/0164027508328308.

Human Resources Development Canada. 2003. *A New Generation of Canadian Families: Raising Young Children: A New Look at Data from National Surveys*. Ottawa: Human Resources Development Canada; Winnipeg: Healthy Child Manitoba. https://publications.gc.ca/site/eng/256744/publication.html

194 References

Humpel, N., K. O'Loughlin, Y. Wells, and H. Kendig. 2009. "Ageing Baby
Boomers in Australia: Evidence Informing Actions for Better Retirement."
Australian Journal of Social Issues 44 (4): 399–415. https://doi
.org/10.1002/j.1839-4655.2009.tb00155.x.

Hwang, W., X. Zhang, M.T. Brown, S.A. Vasilenko, and M. Silverstein. 2022.
"Religious Transitions Among Baby Boomers from Young Adulthood to
Later Life: Association with Psychological Well-Being Over 45 Years." *The
International Journal of Aging and Human Development* 94 (1): 23–40. https://
doi.org/10.1177/00914150211029892.

James, C.E. 2010. *Seeing Ourselves: Exploring Race, Ethnicity and Culture.* 4th ed.
Toronto: Thompson Educational Publishing.

– 2021. *Colour Matters: Essays on the Experiences, Education, and Pursuits of Black
Youth.* Toronto: University of Toronto Press. https://doi.org/10.3138
/9781487538781

James, C.E., and L.E. Taylor. 2023. *First-Generation Student Experiences in Higher
Education: Counterstories.* New York: Routledge. https://doi.org/10.4324
/9781003090281

Janovicek, N. 2015. "Oral History and Ethical Practice After TPCS2." In *The
Canadian Oral History Reader,* edited by K.R. Llewellyn, A. Freund, and N.
Reilly (2015, 73–97. Kingston: McGill-Queen's University Press. https://doi
.org/10.1515/9780773583528-005

Jeon, S.-H., L. Huju, and Y. Ostrovsky. 16 December 2019. *Measuring the Gig
Economy in Canada Using Administrative Data.* Analytical Studies Branch
Research Paper Series. Ottawa: Statistics Canada. https://www150.statcan.
gc.ca/n1/pub/11f0019m/11f0019m2019025-eng.htm.

Kirsh, B. 2021. "Gender and Generation: Focus on Women Baby Boomers'
Approaches to Retirement." In *Gender and Generations: Continuity and
Change,* edited by V. Demos and M.T. Segal, 95–113. Advances in Gender
Research 30. Bingley: Emerald Publishing. https://doi.org/10.1108
/S1529-212620210000030005.

Kojola, E., and P. Moen. 2016. "No More Lock-Step Retirement: Boomers'
Shifting Meanings of Work and Retirement." *Journal of Aging Studies* 36 (1):
59–70. https://doi.org/10.1016/j.jaging.2015.12.003.

Krahn, H. 2022. "Social Class, Post-Secondary Education, and Occupational
Outcomes." In *Social Inequality in Canada: Dimensions of Disadvantage,* edited
by M.M.H. Hwang, E. Grabb, and J.G. Reitz, 88–101. 7th ed. Toronto:
Oxford University Press.

Krahn, H., and G.R.S. Barron. 2016. "Intergenerational Transfers of
Advantage: Parents' Education and Children's Educational and
Employment Outcomes in Alberta." In *Education and Society: Canadian
Perspectives,* edited by W. Lehmann, 36–50. Toronto: Oxford University
Press.

Krahn, H., A. Howard, and N. Galambos. 2015. "Exploring or Floundering?: The Meaning of Employment and Educational Fluctuations in Emerging Adulthood." *Youth & Society* 47 (2): 245–66. https://doi.org/10.1177 /0044118X12459061.

Krahn, H., and A. Taylor. 2005. "Resilient Teenagers: Explaining the High Educational Aspirations of Visible Minority Youth in Canada." *Journal of International Migration and Integration* 6 (3): 405–34. https://doi. org/10.1007/s12134-005-1020-7.

Kuepfer, J.A. 2020. "Boomers & Aging: Seeking & Recognizing Spiritual Resources." *Journal of Religion, Spirituality & Aging* 32 (3): 224–46. https:// doi.org/10.1080/15528030.2019.1608491.

Kwan, C.C. 2000. "Restructuring in the Canadian Economy: A Survey of Firms." *Bank of Canada Review* (Summer), 15–26. www.bankofcanada.ca /wp-content/uploads/2010/06/r004-eb.pdf.

Lareau, A. 2003. *Unequal Childhoods: Class, Race and Family Life.* Berkeley: University of California Press. https://doi.org/10.1525/9780520949904

Lefebvre, S., and K.G. Chakravarty. 2010. "Youth, Spirituality, and Religion in Canada and Quebec." *Annual Review of the Sociology of Religion* 1: 29–63. https://doi.org/10.1163/ej.9789004187900.i-488.11.

Légaré, J., and A. Cossette. 2012. "Comparing the Economic Well-Being of Baby Boomers aand Their Parents in Quebec and Ontario." In *The Family, the Market or the State? Intergenerational Support Under Pressure in Ageing Societies,* edited by G. De Santis, 83–97. Berlin: Springer. https://doi .org/10.1007/978-94-007-4339-7_4.

Lehmann, W. 2007. *Choosing to Labour? School-Work Transitions and Social Class.* Montreal: McGill-Queen's University Press.

– 2014. "Habitus Transformation and Hidden Injuries: Successful Working -Class University Students." *Sociology of Education* 87 (1): 1–15. https://doi .org/10.1177/0038040713498777.

– 2016. "Sociology of Education in Canada: History, Theory, and Research." In *Education and Society: Canadian Perspectives,* edited by W. Lehmann, 4–19. Toronto: Oxford University Press.

– 2023. "Mobility and Stability: Post-Graduate Employment Experiences of Working-Class Students." *Journal of Education and Work* 36 (1): 79–93. https://doi.org/10.1080/13639080.2022.2128188.

Llewellyn, K.R., A. Freund, and N. Reilly. eds. 2015. *The Canadian Oral History Reader.* Montreal: McGill-Queen's University Press. https://doi.org 10.1515/9780773583528.

Maclean's. 1975. "Getting on with the Seventies." January 21.

Mandell, N., and B. Sweet. 2005. "Exploring Limits to Parents' Involvement in Homework." In *Preparing for Postsecondary Education: New Roles for Governments and Families,* edited by R. Sweet and P. Anisef,

249–72. Montreal: McGill-Queen's University Press. https://doi.org 10.1515/9780773573178-013

Marmot, M.G., and M.J. Shipley. 1996. "Do Socioeconomic Differences in Mortality Persist After Retirement? 25-Year Follow-Up of Civil Servants from the First Whitehall Study." *BMJ*, 313 (7066): 1177–80. https://doi .org/10.1136/bmj.313.7066.1177.

McDonald, L., and P. Donahue. 2011. "Retirement Lost?" *Canadian Journal on Aging* 30 (3): 401–22. https://doi.org/10.1017/S0714980811000298.

Mihaildis, A. 26 December 2021. "Re-envisioning Aging in Canada." *Toronto Star.* www.thestar.com/opinion/contributors/2021/12/26/re-envisioning- aging-in-canada.html.

Mitchell, B.A., and E.M. Gee. 1996. "Young Adults Returning Home: Implications for Social Policy. In *Youth in Transition: Perspectives on Research and Policy*, edited by B. Galaway and J. Hudson, 61–71. Toronto: Thompson Educational Publishing.

Mitchell, P.J. 2010. *Canada's Shrinking Families: Why Families and Getting Smaller and What to Do About It.* Ottawa: Institute of Marriage and Family Canada. www.imfcanada.org/archive/139/canadas-shrinking-families.

Moffatt, M. 2021. *The Big Shift: Changes in Canadian Manufacturing Employment, 2003–2018.* Ottawa: Smart Prosperity Institute. https://fsc-ccf.ca /wp-content/uploads/2021/05/The_Big_Shift_Executive_Summary-EN.pdf.

Moffatt, M., A. Couthino, and J. McNally. 2021. *Made in Ontario: A Provincial Manufacturing Strategy.* Ottawa: Smart Prosperity Institute. https://on360. ca/wp-content/uploads/2021/06/ON360_MadeInOntario_v4.pdf.

Morissette, R. 30 November 2018. *Changing Characteristics of Canadian Jobs, 1981–2018.* Economic Insights no. 086. Cat. no. 11-626-X. Ottawa: Statistics Canada. https://www150.statcan.gc.ca/n1/en/pub/11-626-x/11-626 -x2018086-eng.pdf?st=quqcs_so.

Mortimer, J.T., and J. Staff. 2022. "Agency and Subjective Health from Early Adulthood to Mid-Life: Evidence from the Prospective Youth Development Study." *Discover Social Science and Health* 2: article 2. https:// doi.org/10.1007/s44155-022-00006-0.

Ontario Human Rights Commission. 2001. *Human Rights in Ontario.* Toronto: Ontario Human Rights Commission. www.ohrc.on.ca/en.

Ortiz-Ospina, E., and M. Roser. 14 May 2013. *Happiness and Life Satisfaction.* Oxford: Our World in Data. https://ourworldindata.org /happiness-and-life-satisfaction#citation.

Owram, D. 1997. *Born at the Right Time: A History of the Baby Boom Generation.* Toronto: University of Toronto Press. https://doi.org/10.3138/9781442657106

Pearce, L.D. 2015. "Religion and Youth." In *International Encyclopedia of the Social & Behavioral Sciences*, edited by J.D. Wright, 298–306. 2nd ed. https:// doi.org/10.1016/B978-0-08-097086-8.84031-3.

Penning, M.J., and Z. Wu. 2015. "Caregiver Stress and Mental Health: Impact of Caregiving Relationship and Gender." *The Gerontologist* 56 (6): 1102–13. https://doi.org/10.1093/geront/gnv038.

Pepe, A.A. 19 April 2011. "The Evolution of Technology for the Accounting Profession." *CPA Practice Advisor.* www.cpapracticeadvisor.com/2011/04/19 /the-evolution-of-technology-for-the-accounting-profession/1159/.

Peters, V. 2004. "Working and Training: First Results of the 2003 Adult Education and Training Survey." Statistics Canada Education, Skills and Learning Research Paper No. 015. Cat. no. 81-595-MIE2004015. https:// www150.statcan.gc.ca/n1/pub/81-595-m/81-595-m2004015-eng.pdf.

Pew Research Center. 6 October 2016. *The State of American Jobs: How the Shifting Economic Landscape Is Reshaping Work and Society and Affecting the Way People Think About the Skills and Training They Need to Get Ahead.* Washington, DC: Pew Research Center. www.pewresearch.org/social-trends /2016/10/06/the-state-of-american-jobs/.

Phillipson, C., R. Leach, A. Money, and S. Biggs. 2008. "Social and Cultural Constructions of Ageing: The Case of the Baby Boomers." *Sociological Research Online* 13 (3): 1–14. https://doi.org/10.5153/sro.1695.

Porter, J. 1965. *The Vertical Mosaic: An Analysis of Social Class and Power in Canada.* Toronto: University of Toronto Press. https://doi.org 10.3138 /9781442683044

Porter, J., M. Porter, and B.R. Blishen. 1982. *Stations and Callings: Making It Through the School System.* Toronto: Methuen.

Powdthavee, N., A.C. Plagnol, P. Frijters, and A.E. Clark. 2019. "Who Got the Brexit Blues? The Effect of Brexit on Subjective Wellbeing in the UK." *Economica* 86 (343): 471–94. https://doi.org/10.1111/ecca.12304.

Power, S., T. Edwards, G. Whitty, and V. Wigfall. 2003. *Education and the Middle Class.* Maidenhead: Open University Press.

Prentice, A., P. Bourne, G.C. Brandt, and B. Light. 1988. *Canadian Women: A History.* Toronto: Harcourt Brace Jovanovich.

Quadagno, J. 2018. *Aging and the Life Course: An Introduction to Social Gerontology.* 7th ed. New York: McGraw Hill.

Quinn, E.K., A. Harper, E. Rydz, P.M. Smith, M.W. Koehoorn, and C.E. Peters. 2021. "Men and Women at Work in Canada, 1991–2016." *Labour and Industry* 30 (2): 401–12. https://doi.org/10.1080/10301763.2021.1872841.

Ranson, G. 2022. *Front-Wave Boomers: Growing (Very) Old, Staying Connected, and Reimagining Aging.* Vancouver: On Point Press. https://doi.org 10.59962 /9780774890519

Rea, K.J. 1985. *The Prosperous Years: The Economic History of Ontario, 1939–1975.* Toronto: University of Toronto Press.

Reay, D., G. Crozier, and D. James. 2011. *White Middle-Class Identities and Urban Schooling.* London: Palgrave Macmillan.

Rist, R.C. 1977. "On Understanding to Processes of Schooling: The Contributions of Labeling Theory." In *Power and Ideology in Education*, edited by J. Karabel and A.H. Halsey, 292–305. New York: Oxford University Press.

Robson, K. 2021. "An Essay on the Challenges of Doing Education Research in Canada." *Journal of Applied Social Science* 15 (2): 183–96. https://doi.org/10.1177/19367244211003471

Robson, K., P. Anisef, D. Northrup, and A. Grearson, A. 2020. "Panel Recovery After 22 Years: How We Reactivated a 45-Year Cohort Study in Canada." *Longitudinal and Life Course Studies* 12 (1): 1–13. https://doi.org/10.1332/175795920X16009650086121.

Roese, N.J., and A. Summerville. 2005. "What We Regret Most . . . and Why." *Personality and Social Psychology Bulletin* 31 (9): 1273–85. https://doi.org/10.1177/0146167205274693.

Rosenthal, C.J., and J. Gladstone. 1993. "Family Relationships and Support in Later Life." *Journal of Canadian Studies* 28 (1): 122–38. https://doi.org/10.3138/jcs.28.1.122.

Royal Commission on Bilingualism and Biculturalism. 1967–70. Report. 6 vols. Ottawa: Queen's Printer.

Rubin, J. 13 September 2022. "New Data Shows 50% Jump in Retirements – a Trend That's Making the Labour Shortage Even Worse." *Toronto Star.* www.thestar.com/business/2022/09/13/a-record-number-of-canadians-retired-in-the-last-year-and-its-not-likely-to-stop-any-time-soon.html.

Rudd, P., and K. Evans. 1998. "Structure and Agency in Youth Transitions: Student Experiences of Vocational Further Education." *Journal of Youth Studies* 1 (1): 39–62. https://doi.org/10.1080/13676261.1998.10592994.

Sargent, L.D., M.D. Lee, B. Martin, and J. Zikic. 2013. "Reinventing Retirement: New Pathways, New Arrangements, New Meanings." *Human Relations* 66 (1): 3–21. https://doi.org/10.1177/0018726712465658.

Sawyer, A.M., and S. James. 2018. "Are Baby Boomer Women Redefining Retirement?" *Sociology Compass* 12 (10): article e12625. https://doi.org/10.1111/soc4.12625.

Sebastiano, C. 8 December 2006. "End Nears for Mandatory Retirement in Ontario." *Benefits Canada News.* www.benefitscanada.com/news/bencan/end-nears-for-mandatory-retirement-in-ontario/.

Settersten, R.A., Jr., G.H. Elder, Jr., and L.D. Pearce. 2021. *Living on the Edge: An American Generation's Journey Through the Twentieth Century.* Chicago: University of Chicago Press.

Sherkat, D.E. 1988. "Counterculture or Continuity? Competing Influences on Baby Boomers' Religious Orientations and Participation." *Social Forces* 76 (3): 1087–114. https://doi.org/10.2307/3005704.

Smith, M. 2005. *A Civil Society? Collective Actors in Canadian Political Life.* Peterborough, ON: Broadview Press. https://utppublishing.com/doi/book/10.3138/9781487593667

Stamp, R. 1982. *The Schools of Ontario, 1876–1976*. Toronto: University of Toronto Press. https://doi.org/10.3138/9781487575427

Statistics Canada. 1978. *Historical Compendium of Education Statistics, from Confederation to 1975*. Ottawa: Government of Canada.

– 2012. *Fifty Years of Families in Canada, 1961–2011*. Cat. No. 98-312-X2011003. Ottawa: Minister of Industry. https://www12.statcan.gc.ca/census -recensement/2011/as-sa/98-312-x/98-312-x2011003_1-eng.pdf.

– 2015. "Divorce Rates, by Year of Marriage [Data Table]." Table 39-10-0028-01. https://www150.statcan.gc.ca/t1/tbl1/en/tv.action?pid=3910002801.

– 29 June 2016. "150 Years of Immigration in Canada." https://www150. statcan.gc.ca/n1/pub/11-630-x/11-630-x2016006-eng.htm.

– 2017a. *Education Highlight Tables, 2016 Census*. Ottawa: Statistics Canada. https://www12.statcan.gc.ca/census-recensement/2016/dp-pd/hlt-fst /edu-sco/Table.cfm?Lang=E&T=11&Geo=00&SP=1&view=2&age=6&sex=1.

– 29 November 2017b. "Working Seniors in Canada." *Census in Brief*. https:// www12.statcan.gc.ca/census-recensement/2016/as-sa/98-200 -x/2016027/98-200-x2016027-eng.cfm.

– 29 November 2017c. *Working Seniors in Canada: Census of Population, 2016*. (98-200-X2016027) [Data Set]. Ottawa: Statistics Canada. https://www12. statcan.gc.ca/census-recensement/2016/as-sa/98-200-x/2016027/98-200 -x2016027-eng.pdf.

– 25 October 2017d. "Housing in Canada: Key Results from the 2016 Census." *The Daily*. https://www150.statcan.gc.ca/n1/daily-quotidien/171025 /dq171025c-eng.htm#:~:text=Homeownership%20is%20strongly%20 related%20to,population%20aged%2065%20and%20over.

– 7 February 2019. "Family Matters: Grandparents in Canada." *The Daily*. https:// www150.statcan.gc.ca/n1/daily-quotidien/190207/dq190207a-eng.htm.

– 2020. "Retirement Age by Class of Worker, Annual [Data Table]." Table 14-10-0060-01. https://doi.org/10.25318/1410006001-eng.

– 23 March 2021a. "Canadian Income Survey, 2019." *The Daily*. https:// www150.statcan.gc.ca/n1/daily-quotidien/210323/dq210323a-eng.htm.

– 24 September 2021b. "Canadian Social Survey: Covid-19 and Well-Being." *The Daily*. https://www150.statcan.gc.ca/n1/daily-quotidien/210924 /dq210924a-eng.htm.

– 9 September 2022a. "Canada's Large Urban Centres Continue to Grow and Spread." *The Daily*. https://www150.statcan.gc.ca/n1/daily -quotidien/220209/dq220209b-eng.htm.

– 26 October 2022b. "The Canadian Census: A Rich Portrait of the Country's Religious and Ethnocultural Diversity." *The Daily*. https://www150.statcan. gc.ca/n1/daily-quotidien/221026/dq221026b-eng.htm.

– 9 November 2022c. *Disaggregated Trends in Poverty from the 2021 Census of Population*. Ottawa: Statistics Canada. https://www12.statcan.gc.ca/census- recensement/2021/as-sa/98-200-X/2021009/98-200-X2021009-eng.cfm.

– 2022d. "Retirement Age by Class of Worker, Annual [Data Table]." Table 14-10-0060-01. https://doi.org/10.25318/1410006001-eng.

Stearns, P.N. 2003. *Anxious Parents: A History of Modern Childrearing in America.* New York: New York University Press. https://doi.org/10.18574 /nyu/9780814786987.001.0001

Talaga, J.A., and T.A. Beehr. 1995. "Are there Gender Differences in Predicting Retirement Decisions?" *Journal of Applied Psychology* 80 (1): 16–28. https://doi.org/10.1037/0021-9010.80.1.16.

Taylor, A., and H. Krahn. 2013. "Living Through Our Children: Exploring the Education and Career "Choices" of Racialized Immigrant Youth in Canada." *Journal of Youth Studies* 16 (8): 1000–21. https://doi.org/10.1080/1 3676261.2013.772575.

Tiessen, K. 14 March 2014. *Seismic Shift: Ontario's Changing Labour Market.* Ottawa: Canadian Centre for Policy Alternatives. https://policyalternatives. ca/publications/reports/seismic-shift.

Toronto Star. 11 August 1973. "Toronto's Male-Dominated Bay Street Is Meeting Its Match."

Trifan, T.A., H. Stattin, and L. Tilton-Weaver. 2014. "Have Authoritarian Parenting Practices and Roles Changed in the Last 50 Years?" *Journal of Marriage and Family* 76 (4): 744–61. https://doi.org/10.1111/jomf.12124.

Twenge, J.M. 2023. *Generations: The Real Differences between Gen Z, Millennials, Gen X, Boomers, and Silents – and What They Mean for America's Future.* New York: Simon and Schuster.

Turcotte, M. 2011. *Intergenerational Education Mobility: University Completion in Relation to Parents' Education Level.* Statistics Canada. https://www150 .statcan.gc.ca/n1/pub/11-008-x/2011002/article/11536-eng.htm.

Uppal, S. 28 March 2016. *Insights on Canadian Society: Financial Literacy and Retirement Planning.* Ottawa: Statistics Canada. https://www150.statcan. gc.ca/n1/pub/75-006-x/2016001/article/14360-eng.htm.

Venne, R.A., and M. Hannay. 2017. "Demographics, the Third Age and Partial Retirement: Policy Proposals to Accommodate the Changing Picture of Female Retirement in Canada." *Journal of Women & Aging* 29 (6): 475–93. https://doi.org/10.1080/08952841.2017.1377541.

Wayland, S.V. 1997. "Immigration, Multiculturalism and National Identity in Canada." *International Journal on Group Rights* 5: 33–58.

Yosso, T. 2005. "Whose Culture Has Capital? A Critical Race Theory Discussion of Community Cultural Wealth." *Race, Ethnicity and Education* 8 (1): 69–91. https://doi.org/10.1080/1361332052000341006.

Zeman, K., and M. Frenette. 2021. "Youth and Education in Canada." In *Portrait of Youth in Canada: Data Report,* Chapter 3. Ottawa: Statistics Canada. https:// www150.statcan.gc.ca/n1/pub/42-28-0001/2021001/article/00003-eng.htm.

Index

Note: Page numbers in *italics* indicate figures or tables.